ROBESPIERRE

Robespierre

THE MAN WHO DIVIDES
US THE MOST

Marcel Gauchet

Translated by Malcolm DeBevoise

With a foreword by David A. Bell and Hugo Drochon

PRINCETON UNIVERSITY PRESS

PRINCETON & OXFORD

First published in French under the title *Robespierre: L'homme qui nous divise le plus* by Marcel Gauchet © Editions Gallimard, 2018

English translation and foreword copyright © 2022 by Princeton University Press

Published by Princeton University Press
41 William Street, Princeton, New Jersey 08540
99 Banbury Road, Oxford OX2 6JX

press.princeton.edu

First paperback printing, 2024
Paper ISBN 978-0-691-23496-0

The Library of Congress has cataloged the cloth edition as follows:

Names: Gauchet, Marcel, author. | DeBevoise, M. B., translator.
Title: Robespierre : the man who divides us the most / Marcel Gauchet ;
    translated by Malcolm DeBevoise.
Other titles: Robespierre. French
Description: Princeton : Princeton University Press, [2022] | "First published in
    French under the title Robespierre: L'homme qui nous divise le plus
    by Marcel Gauchet © Editions Gallimard, 2018." | Includes bibliographical
    references and index.
Identifiers: LCCN 2021048892 (print) | LCCN 2021048893 (ebook) |
    ISBN 9780691212944 (hardback) | ISBN 9780691234953 (ebook)
Subjects: LCSH: Robespierre, Maximilien, 1758–1794—Public opinion. |
    Revolutionaries—France—Biography. | France—Politics and government—
    1789–1799. | BISAC: HISTORY / Europe / France | PHILOSOPHY / Political
Classification: LCC DC146.R6 G3813 2022 (print) | LCC DC146.R6 (ebook) |
    DDC 944.04/092 [B]—dc23/eng/20211012
LC record available at https://lccn.loc.gov/2021048892
LC ebook record available at https://lccn.loc.gov/2021048893

British Library Cataloging-in-Publication Data is available

Editorial: Ben Tate and Josh Drake
Production Editorial: Nathan Carr and Natalie Baan
Jacket/CoverDesign: Pamela L. Schnitter
Production: Danielle Amatucci
Publicity: Carmen Jimenez and Alyssa Sanford
Copyeditor: Natalie Jones

Jacket/Cover image: Maximillien de Robespierre (1758–1794), 1792.
Heritage Image Partnership Ltd / Alamy Stock Photo

This book has been composed in Miller

Printed and bound by CPI Group (UK) Ltd, Croydon, CR0 4YY

CONTENTS

CONTENTS

FOREWORD BY DAVID A. BELL AND HUGO DROCHON

THE ENGRAVING, stark and horrible, shows a forest of guillotines. In the foreground, a man wearing a plumed hat and a tricolor sash, his feet trampling the French constitutions of 1791 and 1793, is dropping the blade on a helpless victim. Behind him stands a funerary monument inscribed with the words "Here lies all of France." The caption reads: "Robespierre, guillotining the executioner after having had all the French guillotined."[1]

This is still the image that much of the world has of Maximilien Robespierre (1758–1794): a bloodthirsty monster, the mastermind of the French Revolutionary "Reign of Terror." Yet Robespierre also has his admirers, who praise him as a true egalitarian and a precursor of socialism and continue to push to have a street named after him in Paris.[2] Few if any figures from the eighteenth century are still capable of provoking as intense an emotional response as this remarkably unemotional man. As Marcel Gauchet puts it in the title of this book, Robespierre is "the man who divides us the most."

Gauchet, who has generated his own share of division in his long career as one of France's leading intellectuals, has not written a biography of Robespierre. The book has nothing on the man's childhood, nor indeed on any of his life before its last five years, during the French Revolution. There is nothing on his private life, nor on his relationships, personal or political, with others. There is no "setting of the scene." Neither is the book a pure study of Robespierre's ideas, or an attempt to relate his thought to the things he read, although there are a few invocations of Rousseau, whom he worshipped. And this is not a traditional work of scholarship. There are no footnotes, no original archival research, no explicit engagement with the historiography. Instead Gauchet bases his interpretation almost solely on Robespierre's speeches, which, as he indicates, are easily found in his *Complete Works*.

The book then, as Gauchet states in his preface, is rather an interpretative essay, and one that operates on three distinct levels. Most obviously, it provides a new and challenging interpretation of Robespierre's thought

---

1. Robespierre guillotinant le boureau après avoir fait guillot.r. tous les Français : cy gyt toute la France : [estampe], https://exhibits.stanford.edu/frenchrevolution/catalog /tno47jn388o.

2. See for instance https://www.facebook.com/groups/351361054945737.

and action—especially in regard to human rights—between 1789 and 1794. It also uses Robespierre as a lens through which to understand the French Revolution more broadly. Finally, it uses Robespierre and the French Revolution together to ponder the great problem of how modern society freed itself, in Gauchet's words, "from immemorial submission to divine authority," and established "the idea of power legitimately created and exercised by human beings," with state sovereignty and individual liberty existing in harmony. For Gauchet, Robespierre is a tragic figure because he hoped to lay the foundations of the rights-respecting liberal-democratic order which we now venerate but could not escape from a fatally inappropriate vision of the people for whose rights he was fighting, and, instead of harmony, generated horror. He stands in one sense as an inspiration, but in another as a warning.

In this introduction, we will first provide our own brief sketch of Robespierre, for readers who may not have the familiarity that Gauchet could assume on the part of his French audience. We will then discuss Gauchet himself, and his prominent place in French intellectual life, and conclude with a consideration of the book and its significance.

***

Maximilien Robespierre lived the first five-sixths of his life without giving any indication that he would play a significant role in world history. An ambitious scholarship boy from the northern French town of Arras, he trained as a lawyer, and by his thirtieth birthday seemed destined for a future as a lonely pillar of his local bar association. Fussy, physically unimpressive, sexually repressed but intelligent and hardworking, he had a moderate reputation for taking on "enlightened" cases.[3]

Then, in 1789, France's Old Regime collapsed amid fiscal crisis and political paralysis. An ancient representative body called the Estates General transformed itself into a National Assembly and pledged to write a new constitution, amid considerable popular violence, including the storming of the Bastille in Paris. After decreeing the abolition of key forms of "feudal" privilege, the Assembly issued the Declaration of the Rights of Man and of the Citizen and moved forward with many other ambitious reforms. The French Revolution had begun.

3. There have been numerous biographies of Robespierre. Two of the best and most recent are Peter McPhee, *Robespierre: A Revolutionary Life* (New Haven, CT: Yale University Press, 2012) and Hervé Leuwers, *Robespierre* (Paris: Fayard, 2014). See also the essay by Jean-Clément Martin, *Robespierre: La fabrication d'un monstre* (Paris: Perrin, 2016).

As one of the twelve hundred members of the Assembly, Robespierre did not initially make much of an impression. But his passionate, closely argued speeches gradually gained him notice, as did his leading role in the political society that came to be known as the Jacobins. He argued that France should abolish the death penalty, renounce aggressive warfare, grant the right to vote to all adult men, and transform the monarchy into nothing but the passive agent of the national will. He lived simply, in rooms rented from a carpenter, and preached the virtues of austerity. His admirers named him "the Incorruptible."

For three years, between 1789 and 1792, Robespierre remained in this position of opposition, which led him (and many others) to what Gauchet considers a phantasmagorical exaggeration of the evil intentions of the people he opposed. At the same time, Robespierre became the focus of numerous attacks. Although even his allies warned him against "making a spectacle of yourself," he did constantly draw attention to himself, in a very Rousseauian form of moral exhibitionism. Indeed, as early as the spring of 1792 he was accused of aspiring to dictatorship.

As the Revolution turned more radical, his influence grew, and he increasingly cast himself as a champion of "the people" against counterrevolutionary conspirators. After popular militants overthrew King Louis XVI in August of 1792, leading to the proclamation of France's First Republic, he was elected to a new governing body, the National Convention. There, as part of a faction known as the Mountain, he led the fight for the king's execution, and for the implementation of ambitious and innovative new social programs, allying himself with the urban militants known as the *sans-culottes*. In the spring of 1793, armed sans-culottes forced the Convention to purge a rival faction, the so-called Girondins, after which Robespierre emerged as the most important and most visible political figure in France. He was no longer in opposition; he was in government.

Throughout 1793 and early 1794 the French Revolution struggled to survive, as its forces fought both a broad European military coalition and domestic rebels. The Convention's twelve-man Committee of Public Safety, which Robespierre joined in July 1793, functioned as something close to a collective dictatorship, directing military efforts and ruthlessly suppressing dissent. Thousands of alleged counterrevolutionaries were put to death, both after hasty trials and in massacres following the defeat of rebel forces. In a series of brilliant speeches and legislative reports, Robespierre defended the need for extraordinary government action and for the use of terror against the Revolution's enemies. He also sought to unite the French in utopian celebration of a deist "Supreme Being."

By the spring and early summer of 1794 the Committee's efforts had defeated the threats to the Revolution, but the repression only accelerated. Leading radicals turned on each other, and Robespierre succeeded in purging more rivals from the Convention, sending both his oldest friend Camille Desmoulins and the great orator Georges Danton to their deaths. The Revolution was devouring its own. On July 26—8 Thermidor by the new Revolutionary calendar—Robespierre gave a long, rambling speech that seemed to threaten yet more colleagues. The next day, a group of them denounced him, and, in a dramatic confrontation, the Convention as a whole turned against him and voted his arrest. His allies in the Paris Commune (the municipal government) rescued him and desperately tried to mobilize the sans-culottes, but the Convention moved more decisively. On 10 Thermidor, in the company of his closest ally and greatest admirer, the young Louis-Antoine Saint-Just, Robespierre went to the guillotine.

The men who overthrew him, known as the Thermidorians, had themselves participated enthusiastically in the repression, but now, to justify their action, they brought it to an end and placed all the blame for it on Robespierre's severed head. They denounced him as a bloodthirsty monster and claimed he had presided over a "system of terror" (they also coined two words with an impressive future: "terrorism" and "terrorist"). It was the beginning of the black legend that continues to dominate the popular image of the man, especially outside of France.[4]

Robespierre's reputation has changed over time. In nineteenth-century France, historians tended to refight the Revolution more than to analyze it. But even those most inclined to celebrate the events of 1789–1794, including the great Jules Michelet, generally took their distance from Robespierre. In the early twentieth century, though, he found an eloquent champion in the Communist historian Albert Mathiez, who praised Robespierre as an idealistic, sincerely egalitarian statesman driven (much like Joseph Stalin) to harsh but necessary measures because of the extraordinary dangers the Revolution faced from its enemies.[5] Throughout much of the century, the leading historians connected to the Sorbonne's Institute for the History of the French Revolution, and the pointedly named Society for Robespierrist Studies, defended versions of this thesis. Today, some historians belonging to this tradition argue that the repressive measures of 1793–94 reflected the

4. On this subject, see Martin, *Robespierre*, and Bronislaw Baczko, *Comment sortir de la Terreur: Thermidor et la Révolution* (Paris: Gallimard, 1989).

5. See notably the posthumous material collected in Albert Mathiez et al., *Études sur Robespierre, 1758–1794* (Paris: Messidor, 1988).

actions of a weak central government desperately trying to prevent broader eruptions of popular bloodshed.[6]

In the 1970s, however, the influential ex-Communist historian and intellectual François Furet developed a very different interpretation of the French Revolution. For Furet, the forces that radicalized the Revolution, and drove it toward terror, were not the external ones of counterrevolutionary opposition. Rather, a pathological internal dynamic rooted in an inability to conceive of sovereign power as divisible, and therefore to treat political opposition as anything but treason and conspiracy, pushed the revolutionaries into a deadly spiral of accelerating violent competition. Robespierre, for Furet, represented the absolute distillation of this internal dynamic. "What makes Robespierre an immortal figure," he wrote, "is not that he reigned over the Revolution for a few months, but that through him the Revolution spoke its purest and most tragic discourse."[7]

Furet's writings provoked vitriolic debate, especially during the Revolution's bicentennial celebrations in the 1980s.[8] Since then, the temperature of academic debate in French Revolutionary studies has dropped, in part because Furet, who died in 1997, had relatively few doctoral students who might have continued to develop his line of thought. But the broader late twentieth-century discussions in which he played a critical role continue to shape French intellectual life today, and in particular the work of influential writers such as Pierre Rosanvallon, Pierre Manent, Pierre Nora—and also the man whose work has focused most intently on the French Revolution: Marcel Gauchet.

In 1977 Furet was appointed President of the École des Hautes Études en Sciences Sociales (EHESS), the most prestigious research institute and graduate school in the social sciences in France. He immediately set up an informal politics discussion group, which was to be formalized in 1984 as the Institut Raymond Aron. The title honored the postwar French political theorist best known for his critique of the Marxism of Parisian

6. See notably Jean-Clément Martin, *Violence et révolution: Essai sur la naissance d'un mythe national* (Paris: Perrin, 2009); Sophie Wahnich, *La Liberté ou la Mort: Essai sur la Terreur et le terrorisme* (Paris: Éditions de la Fabrique, 2003).

7. François Furet, *Penser la Révolution française* (Paris: Gallimard, 1978), 87. This work of Furet's represents an important evolution beyond the study he cowrote with Denis Richet, *La Révolution* (Paris: Hachette, 1965).

8. See Steven Laurence Kaplan, *Adieu 89* (Paris: Fayard, 1993).

intellectuals in his 1955 book *The Opium of the Intellectuals*—leading to an infamous spat with his former friend Jean-Paul Sartre.[9] The *Centre Raymond Aron*, as it came to be known, continues to this day, going through a number of different titles. Furet was not only a preeminent historian of the French Revolution; he was also an able institution builder.

At its peak from the late 1970s to the early 2000s, the Centre brought together some of the leading French thinkers of the day—not least Furet himself—including the liberal-conservative Manent, the *"deuxième gauche"* theorist Rosanvallon (who was its director from 1992 to 2005), the antitotalitarian thinker Claude Lefort, and the historian of representative government Bernard Manin.[10] Although united in its opposition to the ambient French Marxism, the group remained a diverse one which above all shared, in Rosanvallon's words, an "ethos of discussion."[11] The Centre is widely credited for having revived democratic thinking in France, and having been at the forefront of the renewal of the French liberal tradition, notably through engagement with the work of Montesquieu, Condorcet, Constant, Guizot, and Tocqueville.[12]

Another member was Gauchet. Lefort introduced Gauchet to Furet, and Furet invited him to join the early discussion group that prefigured the Centre. Furet's impact on Gauchet's life was significant. He introduced him to his brother-in-law Nora, the hugely influential publisher who became famous for his work on French identity and memory.[13] In 1980 Nora asked Gauchet to become the editor of a new journal he was launching, *Le Débat*, which, until it ceased appearing in 2020, was one of France's leading intellectual periodicals. In 1989, with the support of Nora and Furet, Gauchet also joined the EHESS, and became a formal member of the Centre. Furet had a significant impact on Gauchet's thought, especially in the way he saw the French Revolution above all as a struggle over the meaning and application of egalitarian and democratic ideals.[14]

9. Raymond Aron, *The Opium of the Intellectuals* (Abingdon: Routledge, 2017).

10. Pierre Manent, *An Intellectual History of Liberalism* (Princeton, NJ: Princeton University Press, 1994); Pierre Rosanvallon, *The New Social Question: Rethinking the Welfare State* (Princeton, NJ: Princeton University Press, 2000); Claude Lefort, *Democracy and Political Theory* (Cambridge: Polity, 1991); Bernard Manin, *The Principles of Representative Government* (Cambridge: Cambridge University Press, 2010).

11. Pierre Rosanvallon, "Sur quelques chemins de traverse de la pensée du politique en France," *Raisons politiques* 1, no. 1 (2001): 49–62.

12. See Hugo Drochon, "Raymond Aron's 'Machiavellian' Liberalism," *Journal of the History of Ideas* 80, no. 4 (2019): 621–42.

13. Pierre Nora, ed., *Rethinking France* (Chicago: University of Chicago Press, 2001–2010).

14. See Furet, *Penser la Révolution*, and François Furet, *Revolutionary France: 1770–1880* (Oxford: Blackwell, 1992).

Lefort was the other significant influence. Close to the phenomenologist Maurice Merleau-Ponty, Lefort developed a theory of democracy that was to inform Gauchet's thinking. This was the idea of democracy as an "empty space": that after the beheading of the king the political body could no longer be incarnated, and that the desire to do so is a tyrannical—or indeed potentially totalitarian—one. Democracy is the recognition of the division of the social body and the institutionalization of conflict between its different parts, with the seat of power, now a mere collection of instruments, only being held temporarily by opposing groups that must make way for one another when their time is up. In this formulation democracy is characterized by its indeterminacy, with the concomitant ever-present desire—and threat—of wanting to fill that gap, to close the uncertainty, whether it is by a political leader (Führer, Duce) or (vanguard) party.[15]

Gauchet, who came from a provincial, Gaullist, Catholic working-class background—he grew up in rural Normandy—first prepared for a career as a secondary school teacher, but thanks to Lefort's influence while both were at the University of Caen, he decided to pursue an academic career. In many ways Gauchet represents a dying breed of students who were able to achieve social mobility through the meritocratic structures of what the French Third Republic had dubbed the *école républicaine*: the secular schools that the state had freed from religious control.

As a young man Gauchet had been a left-wing activist, joining demonstrations against the war in Algeria and the student protests of May 68. He seemed drawn toward anarchist and spontaneous movements, and already during his time at Caen had started to distance himself from the reigning Marxism. Since then, his direction of travel has no doubt been rightward, but the extent of it is hard to measure precisely. The accusation of being a "neo-reactionary" by fellow historian Daniel Lindenberg in 2002 went too far, but Gauchet has been known to offer conservative views on individualism, immigration, and Islam.[16] Certainly "liberalism," one of the principal themes of the Centre Raymond Aron, is positioned to the center-right in France, with its emphasis on political pluralism and the free market. Compared to his colleagues in French academia, still dominated by the left, Gauchet certainly seems more conservative—and his appointment to the EHESS caused an uproar there. Yet he has expressed ambiguous views, for example, on Macron's presidency, seemingly welcoming it at first but since taking a more critical stance, and reacting strongly against the accusation

15. Claude Lefort, "The Question of Democracy," in *Democracy and Political Theory* (Cambridge: Polity, 1991), 9–20.

16. Daniel Lindenberg, *Le Rappel à l'ordre: Enquête sur les nouveaux réactionnaires* (Paris: Seuil, 2002).

of being solely a satrap to power. Gauchet has insisted he has always been and will remain a socialist, and the conclusion of his *Robespierre* will be the occasion to review where he stands politically today.

Over the course of his career Gauchet has authored a number of important works. His first, published by Gallimard in 1980, was written with his then partner Gladys Swain and translated by Princeton University Press in 2012 as *Madness and Democracy: The Modern Psychiatric Universe*.[17] In it Gauchet and Swain attacked Foucault's indictment of modern psychiatry as wanting to "lock the mad away," arguing instead that the asylum originally embodied the revolutionary—if dashed—hopes of curing the insane by saving the glimmer of sanity left in them. A subsequent book, single-authored this time, brought him to national and international attention. Again published by Gallimard in 1985, it was translated into English, with a foreword by Charles Taylor, by Princeton University Press in 1997 as *The Disenchantment of the World*.[18] There Gauchet developed the ambitious thesis, perhaps linked to his own personal trajectory, of Christianity as the religion of the end or "exit" of religion: because Christianity, unlike other monotheistic creeds, recognizes a space for secular power—"render unto Caesar the things that are Caesar's, and unto God the things that are God's"—over time this allows humans to start running their own affairs, instead of following the dictates of an increasingly powerful, but also distant, God. This does not mean that religious belief has disappeared, but rather that religion, somewhat as in Nietzsche's thesis of the "death of God," no longer structures and legitimizes social and political life.

More recently Gauchet has written a four-volume history of democracy, from the French Revolution to today, under the broad title *The Advent of Democracy*.[19] Throughout the four volumes he developed the distinction between what is known in French as *le politique* and *la politique*, a distinction that is difficult to render in English but that might be captured, respectively, by the difference between the foundational principles of political regimes and what might be more readily described as politics as such, namely the types of policies pursued by different rulers, and the power plays that occur between them.

There is a historical dimension to this distinction too: previous monarchical societies were organized, in theory, according to the "divine right of

17. Marcel Gauchet and Gladys Swain, *Madness and Democracy: The Modern Psychiatric Universe*, trans. Catherine Porter (Princeton, NJ: Princeton University Press, 2012).

18. Marcel Gauchet, *The Disenchantment of the World: A Political History of Religion*, trans. Oscar Burge (Princeton, NJ: Princeton University Press, 1997).

19. Marcel Gauchet, *L'avènement de la démocratie* (Paris: Gallimard, 2007–2017).

kings," with transcendental laws imposed from outside and above—namely from God—and with society organized along hierarchical, familial, tradition and holistic lines, where everyone knew their place in the global order of things. In a word: the Old Regime. After the French Revolution this "heteronomous" society was replaced by an "autonomous" one, in which the fundamental law is drawn immanently from society itself, natural right and equality are recognized, representation and political parties in the political system are accepted, and the individual takes precedence over the whole. Herein lies the distinction between *le* and *la politique*. Yet, "heteronomy" does not entirely disappear in the face of rising "autonomy": there remains the need to maintain the original unity and principles upon which society itself is based, to offer a representation of the social order acting in common. Indeed, the process of increasing autonomy and individualization generates a kind of forgetfulness about its own preconditions: modern citizens come to view their freedom as an unconditioned fact about themselves, rather than as the product of a particular societal-political configuration grounded in the modern state, and that "fact" can be expanded to the point at which it threatens the very existence of the polity and the social fabric that emancipated the individual in the first place. For Gauchet, the hyper-individualism, globalization, and expansion of commercial activity since the 1970s and the advent of "neo-liberalism" has only exacerbated this tendency, and an echo of these views can be heard in his *Robespierre*.[20]

Already in 1980, which proved to be a decisive year in his life (first book with Swain, meeting with Furet and Nora, and editorship of *Le Débat*), Gauchet penned what become a famous article entitled "Les droits de l'homme ne sont pas une politique" ("Human Rights are not a politics"), in which he sketched out some of these ideas.[21] The immediate context was the desire of a part of the Parisian intelligentsia to show their support for Eastern European dissidents protesting communism. Given Marxism's rejection of human rights, these intellectuals thought the defense of human rights was the best way to aid them in their struggle. Although Gauchet wholeheartedly agreed with the defense of individual rights, he warned that although human rights might provide the legitimate basis for a new regime, it offers no indication for how the relation between state and individual should be organized, and Gauchet condemned these thinkers (Foucault, Derrida, and others) for failing to formulate one. Here

20. Many thanks to Gregory Conti and William Selinger for helping to formulate this passage.

21. Marcel Gauchet, "Les droits de l'homme ne sont pas une politique," *Le Débat* 3, no. 3 (1980): 3–21.

already we see the difference between *le politique* (human rights) and *la politique* (the need to construct a world together). In 1989 Gauchet would write a book directly on the seventeen articles of the French Declaration of the Rights of Man and of the Citizen of 26 August 1789.[22] Many of these themes have also found their way into his *Robespierre*, making it an ideal gateway into his thought.

⟨⸺⟩

As we have already indicated, *Robespierre* is not a conventional biography. Unlike the historian Peter McPhee, whose recent study of Robespierre's life places considerable emphasis on his pre-revolutionary experiences of social inequality, Gauchet states bluntly that such research is "futile . . . the events of 1789 made [Robespierre] another man, as though he had undergone a conversion." Gauchet also eschews any attempt to probe Robespierre's psychology, calling it something that "will forever remain impenetrable to us." For Gauchet, the Robespierre of 1789–94 was entirely shaped by the Revolution. "It was his destiny to grasp the motive forces of the Revolution better than anyone else, to make himself its spokesman and to reveal its meaning, as it were, to the actors themselves." The perspective is strikingly similar to Furet's.

Like Furet, Gauchet also sees the Revolution as having been driven forward by an essentially internal, political dynamic. The accelerating radicalization of 1789–93, and the systematic repression of 1793–94 both had their origin in the political stances adopted by the revolutionary movement as a whole in its early days. They proceeded neither from the need to rein in a wild, violent popular movement (summed up in Danton's famous apothegm, "let us be terrible to spare the people from being so"), nor from the need for emergency measures in the face of an existential threat.[23] Gauchet speaks of Robespierre's "delusional overestimation of the strength of opposition to the Revolution." Although his book does not come with a scholarly apparatus, he has clearly read and digested recent scholarship on the Revolution by the heirs of Mathiez and of the Sorbonne tradition (including especially the works of Jean-Clément Martin and Hervé

22. Marcel Gauchet, *La Révolution des droits de l'homme* (Paris: Gallimard, 1989). See also Marcel Gauchet, *La Révolution des pouvoirs: La souveraineté, le peuple et la représentation (1789–1799)* (Paris: Gallimard, 1995).

23. Cited in Dan Edelstein, *The Terror of Natural Right: Republicanism, the Cult of Nature, and the French Revolution* (Chicago: University of Chicago Press, 2009), 135.

Leuwers), but still disagrees fundamentally with their approach to the subject.[24]

Furet, however, saw the Revolution's radicalization as essentially pathological: a ruthless competition for power driven by the impossible ambition of setting an absolute sovereign people in place of the absolute monarch (Lefort's concept of the "empty space" left by the king had an influence here). Furet glimpsed in this pathology "the matrix of totalitarianism," and his horror at the crimes of Stalinism colored his interpretation of the earlier revolution and leeched away his sympathy.[25]

Gauchet, by contrast, in keeping with his professed socialism, has far more sympathy for the revolutionaries and the ends they pursued. As he writes: "The truth is that the ends were just and the means were horrifying." His Robespierre is more genuinely tragic than Furet's because—despite the man's ruthlessness, his self-aggrandizement, and his creeping paranoia—his ideal was a grand one.

How does a people rule itself, as opposed to submitting to a divinely anointed authority? This, according to Gauchet, was the fundamental question the French Revolution tried to answer. And Robespierre, he argues here, was the first to see with absolute clarity the principles upon which a democratic society could be based, namely the rights of man, that would replace the previous divine right of kings. This emphasis on human rights distinguishes Gauchet's reading of the French Revolution from both Furet's or indeed Lefort's. But if the rights of man answer the question of how to formulate *le politique*, they do not indicate how *la politique* should be conducted, namely what type of society should be built on those principles.

During the early stages of the Revolution, from the calling of the Estates General in 1789 through to August 1792, when he was in opposition to the king and to the then-dominant moderates, Robespierre used the rights of man to criticize the failings of the Revolution, in something of the same way Parisian intellectuals, according to Gauchet, used human rights to criticize the Eastern bloc after World War II. But as the Revolution continued, Robespierre had to formulate a positive vision of how society should be organized. Here, according to Gauchet, Robespierre failed, much as the French intellectuals of the twentieth century would also fail. He conjured up a fictive idea of "the people" who "always desire what is good" (even if "they do not always perceive what is good"), and

---

24. See references above.
25. Furet, *Penser la Révolution française*, 232.

insisted, even as he forged a tactical alliance with the sans-culottes, that
the problem of self-government could be solved by letting "the people"
rule, initially without any real sense of how they would actually do so. In
doing so, incidentally, he helped to reclaim the concept of "democracy,"
which most eighteenth-century thinkers had tended to identify with chaos
and mob rule.[26] Meanwhile, he proved utterly incapable of accepting the
idea that *la politique* might require the balancing of competing interests,
values, and perspectives. Instead, he dismissed all points of view different
from his own as counterrevolutionary, the product of plots and conspiracies that needed to be exposed and purged from the body politic.

It was during his year as the most influential figure in French government—July 1793 to July 1794—that what Gauchet calls Robespierre's
"absolutism of power in the name of principles" had the most tragic and
devastating effects. During this year, Robespierre wrote his most brilliant,
his most eloquent, and his most chilling speeches and reports, justifying inhumane repression in the cause of founding a humane state. "If
the mainspring of popular government in a time of peace is virtue, in a
time of revolution it is at once *virtue and terror*: virtue, without which
terror is fatal; terror, without which virtue is powerless." In this period,
Robespierre rejected the sans-culotte ideal of direct democracy but still
proved utterly unable to comprehend how a representative democracy
might function in practice. Every challenge that the Revolution faced in
this year of blood and fire simply reinforced his conviction that counterrevolutionary conspiracy lurked everywhere, even among his own
colleagues in the Convention, and that the Revolution's priority was to
eliminate its enemies, wherever they might be found. "Robespierre had
run up against the futility of his own vision," Gauchet writes. "This is
what brought about his downfall."

Could the Revolution have played out differently, with the Terror
avoided? Unlike Furet, who saw the road to Terror set as early as the spring
of 1789, Gauchet hints that this was possible. For him, the crucial moment
came with the execution of the king. From the onset of the Revolution
Robespierre had only envisaged limiting the role of the king, namely as the
passive agent of the nation's will, but after the fall of the monarchy in 1792
he came to see the death of the king as the only way to break with the old
regime and institute a new one on the basis of human rights. By executing

26. See Joanna Innes and Mark Philp, eds., *Re-imagining Democracy in the Age of
Revolutions America, France, Britain, Ireland 1750–1850* (Oxford: Oxford University Press,
2013).

the king, the French lost the chance to reconcile the state power that the monarchy incarnated with the new form of legitimacy associated with democracy and the rights of man. England, Gauchet argues in his conclusion, had been able to accomplish its own revolution in a more gradual and peaceful way, as its democratic demands had been able to graft themselves onto a constitutional monarchy that was able to accompany it. In France, in contrast, the Revolution was able to establish itself as legitimate but, in struggling to recreate the state on the basis of pure principle, veered into terror. Later, Gauchet adds, Napoleon found himself in the opposite situation: possessing the full power of the state but lacking democratic legitimation. The Tocquevillian theme is unmissable: although the king was dead, the power of the state that the monarchy had built up continued under the new regime. The task was to combine it with the new democratic legitimacy.[27] Eventually the two would in fact coincide: Gauchet explicitly says that the dual legacies of the French Revolution—democracy and potentially terroristic state power—have been reconciled, but he remains vague on when this reconciliation first took place and how.

For Furet the answer was during the Third Republic, which is why he closed his final book on the Revolution in 1880. For him that is when the French Revolution formally "ended," although the debates surrounding it continued. Robespierre himself had a plan to "end" the French Revolution, according to Gauchet, and his was to do so through a secular religious movement: the new cult of the Supreme Being. For Gauchet, however, this plan was bound to fail, because it brought back the religious aspect of the ancien régime that human rights had now replaced. Christianity in Gauchet's thought, after all, has functioned as the religion of the "end of religion," from which humankind would take control of its own destiny. But just because Robespierre could not bring the Revolution to a close did not mean that it had to end, as Burke evocatively put it, with nothing but "the gallows" to be seen at "the end of every vista."[28] This was a failure that Robespierre himself not only embodied, but was also instrumental in bringing about: it is the position he incarnated, of being unable to separate out le from la politique, that led to terror. Other options were—and remain—available.

In Gauchet's rendering Robespierre comes across as something of a populist figure, not in the demagogical sense but in combining the

27. Alexis de Tocqueville, *The Ancien Régime and the French Revolution* (Cambridge: Cambridge University Press, 2011).

28. Edmund Burke, *Revolutionary Writings: Reflections on the Revolution in France and the First Letter on a Regicide Peace* (Cambridge: Cambridge University Press, 2014), 79.

supposed "will of the people" with his person: Robespierre is described as the "*moi-peuple*"—"I, the People" in translation—which isn't without recalling a recent study.[29] In doing so Robespierre, in Gauchet's theory, claims to stand in that "empty space" left by the king when he took his fateful steps up to the guillotine.

The question remains whether the account Gauchet has offered us is one of France in particular or whether this is the story of modern democracy *tout court*. In his conclusion, Gauchet warns against a return of wanting to collapse *la politique* into *le politique*, as both Robespierre and the 1980s Parisian intellectuals did with human rights. He has left the exact nature of his target deliberately hard to pinpoint, but recently members of the Centre Raymond Aron have been known to come out against what they describe—drawing from Tocqueville—as the "extremes" of democracy: what we might recognize as contemporary "liberal identity politics."[30] Gauchet echoes this critique when he writes that "the Revolution of the Rights of Man has begun again in a certain sense, albeit in a different manner, no longer with a view to instituting a new political and social order, but with a view to indefinitely perfecting the workings of the existing order." He adds darkly that this development has a "destabilizing potential whose consequences are liable to be every bit as grave as those of the first eruption."

Whether this warning should be heeded or not we will leave to the reader to decide. What is certain is that the challenges the French Revolution raised—Who speaks in the name of the people? What role should religion play in democracy? How are we to articulate the relationship between the state and the individual?—are as urgent now as they were for Robespierre over two hundred years ago. Hopefully the task of figuring out how a people should rule itself will continue to occupy us for two hundred years more. In that quest Marcel Gauchet remains an invaluable guide.

29. Nadia Urbinati, *Me the People: How Populism Transforms Democracy* (Cambridge, MA: Harvard University Press, 2019).

30. Michael Scott Christofferson, "'The Best Help I Could Find to Understand our Present': François Furet's Antirevolutionary Reading of Tocqueville's *Democracy in America*," in *In Search of the Liberal Moment: Democracy, Anti-totalitarianism, and Intellectual Politics in France since 1950*, edited by Stephen Sawyer and Iain Stewart (New York: Palgrave Macmillan, 2016), 85–109.

THIS BOOK WAS WRITTEN from a quite particular point of view that I must briefly describe. Otherwise my approach to the subject, and the style I have adopted, are bound to come as a surprise to the reader.

Gallimard asked me to contribute a volume to its series devoted to those persons who "made France"—who fashioned its political and cultural physiognomy. No one will deny that Robespierre is one of them. But one thing separates him from all the others: whereas for some Robespierre represents what is best in the history of France, for others he represents the very worst.

It is in this perspective that the present work was conceived. My aim is not to produce yet another biographical portrait, even if obviously I cannot help but inquire into the sources of the man's behavior. I have not tried to write a comprehensive treatise that claims to cast new light on Robespierre's life and his work. I have tried instead to give a fresh interpretation of his revolutionary career and its legacy. I have sought to understand what, in the course of five years, from 1789 to 1794, determined the main features of the revolutionary experience, forever engraved in the memories of the French people, and which continue to act upon them still today—with diametrically opposed effects.

The fact that this undertaking involved a particular reading of the French Revolution is what persuaded me to accept the invitation of my friend Ran Halévi, the commissioning editor at Gallimard. I had already given considerable thought to Robespierre a number of years ago, on two occasions: first in *La révolution des droits de l'homme* (1989), and then in *La révolution des pouvoirs* (1995). My research prompted me to ponder the singular place Robespierre occupies in French history and enabled me to form some idea of how far the course of his revolutionary career, from ascent to downfall, summed up the fundamental features of an exceptional political experiment. I seized the opportunity now offered to me to try to get to the bottom of the matter by subjecting my earlier intuitions to more careful examination and developing their implications as fully as possible. The picture that emerged, both of the man and of the Revolution itself, seems to me to illuminate the nature of the lasting divisions that they have aroused.

My inquiry relies principally on Robespierre's own writings and speeches. All references are to the *Œuvres complètes de Maximilien Robespierre*, published in ten volumes by the Société des études robespierristes between 1910 and 1967, to which an eleventh volume of supplementary material was added in 2007. The dates given in the text will make it clear, I trust, where a given reference is to be found. Quotations from Saint-Just, numerous in the last part of the book, are taken from the edition of his *Œuvres complètes* edited by Miguel Abensour and Anne Kupiec and published by Gallimard in 2004. The debates of the several assemblies are cited, as is customary, with reference to the transcripts published contemporaneously by *Le Moniteur Universel* and later by the *Archives parlementaires.*

ROBESPIERRE

The Incorruptible
and the Tyrant

ROBESPIERRE IS THE NAME of the contradiction that continues to characterize the attitude of the French to their Revolution. A hero to some, reviled by others, Robespierre embodies at once the Revolution's promise, still alive today, and the bloody impasse to which it led. That the ambivalent legacy of this foundational moment should be summed up in one man is the distinctive feature of the French political tradition: that which forms the basis of its common understandings is at the same time what gives rise to its most profound divisions.

To be sure, the nature of these divisions has greatly changed over the course of the last two centuries, and Robespierre's image with it. His reputation has been the hostage and, symbolically, the stake of the successive battles through which the principles of 1789 came to be applied; royalists pitted against republicans to begin with, then moderate republicans against progressive republicans, and, after that, socialists against republicans. At first, Robespierre symbolized the monstrosity of the revolutionary movement in the eyes of the upholders of the ancien régime; the party of the Revolution, for its part, made him the prophetic emblem of its struggle for republican liberty. Once the Republic had been established, for better or for worse, divisions within the revolutionary movement itself were given new life, setting Feuillants against Jacobins, Girondins against Montagnards, Dantonists against Robespierrists. Many years later, with the Bolshevik Revolution and the formation of a worldwide Communist movement, Robespierre came to be seen as the herald, both execrated and exalted, of social revolution.

All these disputes now belong to the past. The last defenders of throne and altar have been routed by the forces of a republic whose legitimacy is accepted by virtually everyone. In parallel with this, on the left, recent decades have witnessed the disarming of an avant-garde that sought to supplement and complete political revolution by social revolution. But the remarkable thing is that this general embrace of the principles of 1789 has not eliminated division. Indeed, paradoxically, a strengthened allegiance to the ideals of liberty and equality has had the effect of accentuating the revulsion felt toward the extreme measures with which Robespierre's name remains associated. The Republic—lawful, liberal, peaceable—that ended up being established is unanimous in its detestation of the guillotine, committees of public safety, coups d'état, and terror. Robespierre is a reprobate in the view of most people today, something official memory is reluctant to admit. This has not prevented him, however, from attracting a not inconsiderable number of loyal supporters. For with the restoration of the rights of man to a central place in the life of the nation, Robespierre, who early on was the most fervent, rigorous, and implacable proponent of these rights, came also to be seen as the champion of fundamental principles. Even if the specter of 1793, the year of the Revolutionary Tribunal and the Law of Suspects, cast him down into the circle of the damned, the man whom popular opinion now gladly regards as a precursor of totalitarianism, the same logic of republican consensus nonetheless raised him up again as a prophet of the triumphant justice of democratic values. Far from disappearing, as one might have expected, the old divisions were simply recomposed.

Is this to say that we are condemned to replay the Revolution all over again, and, by giving it new life, to perpetuate the quarrel between Robespierrists and anti-Robespierrists, on the one side glorifying the advocate of universal suffrage and the right of all to life and liberty, and on the other bringing new charges against the unrelenting prosecutor of anyone presumed to be an enemy of the people? Not at all! Fortunately, the situation opens up another possibility. It places us in a position to understand that it is as pointless to take sides in this unresolvable dispute as it is futile to try to settle it. Neither of the two camps can hope to prevail. Instead they are doomed to coexist, because they defend causes that are equally justified in reason. The very irreducibility of the quarrel allows us to go beyond it, by granting each one its rightful share of the contradiction.

Examining the course of history over the past two centuries permits a more detached perspective. The slow and difficult consolidation of democracy in Europe has taught us that it is the responsibility of the state to acknowledge the existence of two competing forces that pull it in opposite directions, the one arising from what its founding principles require and the other from what its political system will tolerate. The apparently innocent doctrine enunciated by the Declaration of the Rights of Man and of the Citizen, from which democracy draws its legitimacy, conceals a deeply radical tendency that threatens to blind it to the practical conditions of orderly government. The French Revolution gave the first warning of the perils of this sort of excess, of which Robespierre was the outstanding example. His greatness consists in the fact that, both as orator and actor, he embodied the attempt to give liberty and equality their most complete expression. His tragic fate was to embody the failure to make a viable system of government from these principles, and the resort to terrorist violence in order to fill the gap between idea and reality.

It has taken two centuries for us to learn the hard way how to arrange matters so that liberty and equality may live together in harmony. There can be no question that the means for doing this are exactly the opposite of the ones imagined by Robespierre and his companions. But now that they have been firmly established, we may finally do justice to the grandeur of this longing to achieve the impossible, without in the least ignoring the horrors that followed in its train. At the same time, we are better able to appreciate the creative dynamic of these rights, whose meaning and scope sensible conservatives nonetheless struggle to grasp. Recognizing the Revolution's ambition, measuring its cost—these two things must go together if we are to profit from the progress that has been made in the interval.

Marc Bloch, appealing for an enlargement of patriotic feeling in *Apologie pour l'histoire, ou métier d'historien* (1949), famously rebuked two classes of his fellow countrymen who, he claimed, will never understand the history of France: those who cannot permit themselves to be stirred by the memory of the crowning of French kings at Reims, and those who feel no emotion on reading accounts of the Festival of Federation. It may fairly be said, in retrospect, that he made things easier for himself by seeking to reconcile the cause of the ancien régime and that of the Revolution on the basis of their most amiable symbols. It is a harder thing to reconcile admiration for the founders of the Republic and abhorrence of the terrifying violence of Year II. And yet Bloch's motivation was sound. We must press on, however arduous the journey that lies ahead may be, not losing sight along the way of the cleavage he rightly identified.

The moment has come at last when we are able to avoid a confrontation that can only lead to the impasse over means and ends in which the legacy of the Revolution has until now been stuck, and which made the path to democracy in France so torturous and so obscure for the people who led the way. Democracy has come to be established almost in spite of them, without their having been aware of it. For some, celebrating the ends made it unnecessary to consider the means, which were excused as a concession either to brute necessity (no omelette without breaking eggs) or to the adversity of circumstances; for others, denouncing the means sufficed to invalidate the ends, which were seen to amount to nothing more than a lethal fantasy. The truth is that the ends were just and the means were horrifying. The two parts of this truth need somehow to be conciliated—a difficult task, for they correspond to contrary ways of looking at the world, which naturally tend to diverge rather than come together, to such a degree that they cannot help but continue to nourish opposite points of view; but in each case a point of view capable in principle of giving a fair hearing to its opposite, the one learning to temper the pursuit of ends by taking means into account, and the other learning to qualify its devotion to means by recognizing the desirability of the ends. Eventually, the two sides could find a way to agree to disagree—exactly the willingness that was most lacking in the Jacobins, who in this respect resembled their adversaries.

The French face a choice with regard to a past that has for so long and so violently divided them: whether to let it slip away into oblivion in the hope of making a fresh start, this time on the basis of a standardized liberal order—in a world shaped by European unification and globalization, the temptation to proceed in this direction is strong; or to reappropriate a turbulent history by overcoming it—a more demanding alternative, to be sure, but also a more promising and indeed a more realistic option, especially if one believes that the imprint of such tragic beginnings is indelible and their memory destined to go on haunting France far into the future. All the more reason, then, to try to come to terms with the Revolution by trying to make sense of the dual character of this enigmatic man, Robespierre, in whom is concentrated the most problematic part of the French past—the part that is at once the most inspirational and the most repellent.

Thought and Action

Let us be clear about one thing from the outset. It is futile to try to say who Robespierre was, as Marc Bloch demanded in another memorable apostrophe, imploring friends and enemies to declare a truce: "Robespierrists, anti-Robespierrists, we've had enough; for pity's sake, simply tell us who Robespierre was." A natural and perfectly reasonable demand, but impossible to satisfy. No one will ever be able to tell us who Robespierre really was. To begin with, his persona was constructed around an impenetrable secret. The share of mystery is great in every stage of his career, from the initial participation in the Revolution—which nothing about him, an apparently rather conventional and well-mannered provincial lawyer, would have led anyone to expect—until the moment that the tide of events finally turned against him, on 9 Thermidor. We are, and we will remain, reduced to speculating about his motives. The most that we may say with any confidence is who he was not. In this regard, at least, the protracted battle between his admirers and detractors has been of some use. It has efficiently stripped away all that is legendary about the man, disposing of both the hagiographical clichés and the teratological fantasies inspired by the piety of some and the animosity of others. We have before us a demythologized Robespierre, still no less inscrutable in his deepest motivations, but now fully intelligible in respect of his outward behavior. We may be thankful to his most recent biographers for having provided us with trustworthy information.[1]

But the most solid material on which we can rely, in order to appreciate how vital Robespierre's role in the Revolution really was, remains the impressive mass of his speeches and writings, which by itself sets him apart from the other figures of the period. In what follows, I shall concentrate on analyzing this singular corpus. My object is not to produce yet another portrait of the man, but rather a view of his intellectual and political development between 1789 and 1794, which, I trust, will illuminate the meaning of the events themselves. For it was through the figure of Robespierre that all that took place during these tumultuous years was best expressed; all that constituted the motive force of events; all that caused prodigious efforts to establish the reign of happiness and liberty to end up in a murderous quandary. Robespierre's life, and the manner of his death, hold a lesson that goes well beyond his own time. It resonates down through the present day, which has seen the reemergence in another form of the question that the tragedy of the Revolution had left open—a question to which governments have struggled to find an answer ever since.

1. In this connection one cannot praise too highly two recent works, *Robespierre* by Hervé Leuwers (Paris: Fayard, 2014) and *Robespierre: La fabrication d'un monstre* by Jean-Clément Martin (Paris: Perrin, 2016), the first more classically biographical, the second more concerned with locating Robespierre politically in the context of revolutionary events. They complement each other by illuminating, in a remarkably precise, balanced, and nuanced way, the career of a man whom two centuries of polemical historiography had ended up making almost impossible to understand.

Confronted today with the need to reformulate it in the light of changing circumstances, we discover that the fate of Robespierre is more relevant than ever.

It has been said that there are two Robespierres: the one "incorruptible," the other a "tyrant"—words that in his time meant "hero" and "monster," respectively. The two images correspond to the two stages of his revolutionary career: opponent of the monarchy, then ruler in his own turn. In the first phase he earned a reputation for moral integrity, under the Constituent Assembly, by his unwavering defense of principles and of the rights of the people; within the Convention, he incarnated the Mountain's intransigence in the face of the Girondin faction. Later, with the elimination of the Girondins in the aftermath of the insurrection of 31 May–2 June 1793 in Paris, he became a member of the Committee of Public Safety two months later, on 27 July, at the height of his popularity. The esteem in which he was held caused him to be perceived as dominating the Committee—so completely that responsibility for the whole of the dictatorship of the "Twelve" came to be imputed to him alone, with the result that, following his arrest on 27 July 1794, he furnished the ideal scapegoat for the system of terror that had grown up in the interval. Henceforth his name was to remain inalterably associated with the image of a killing machine. The problem historians face, and more generally all those who reflect upon the legacy of the Revolution, is how to connect these two phases of Robespierre's career, which is to say the two faces of the man they have bequeathed to posterity. How did the one lead to the other? What is the link between them, if indeed there is one?

The answers that I give to these questions belong to the realm of ideas. I use the term "ideas" in a broader and somewhat less familiar sense than the one it usually has, closer to the notion of forces, where mental representations are inseparable from the actions to which they give rise. The guiding thread that leads us from the intrepid orator of the Constituent Assembly to the master of the Convention, I will try to show, is to be found in a style of thought that animates both the individual and the society of which he is a part. It is not only Robespierre's own way of thinking that needs to be taken into consideration, but also a way of thinking that enveloped and went beyond him, representing, as it were, the mentality of the Revolution itself. Robespierre was not a thinker in the conventional sense. He did not elaborate a distinctive and coherent doctrine built up from specific concepts and organized in a system. He did no more than pass on received ideas, ideas that he shared in the main with the majority of his colleagues. The Revolution conceived of itself as a rupture, a redirection of the course of history in the name of an idea. Its intention, ultimately, was to substitute an order designed in accordance with reason for an order inherited from tradition. For this purpose, it could draw upon a body of propositions expounded by natural law theorists. But under the pressure of events, and of the urgent decisions they required to be made, looking to books for solutions was not an option. As a practical matter, the most that could be done was to adjust whatever could be borrowed from them at a moment's notice to the needs of the situation at hand, without any concern for scholarly fastidiousness. This was the attitude that Robespierre and his fellow revolutionaries brought to bear in their various ways. The Declaration of the Rights of Man and of the Citizen, ratified on 26 August 1789, was its first characteristic monument.

There is of course some Rousseau in Robespierre. Rousseau was the only modern thinker for whom he had the highest regard, though probably more as a model for living than as an intellectual authority. There is also some Montesquieu, some Pufendorf, some Mably. But this alone is not enough to explain how Robespierre's austere eloquence was able to hold the attention of so large an audience during this period. What mattered above all was his ability to combine the ideas that he drew from these authors with the very spirit of the events that were just then in the process of unfolding. His manner of expression communicated the promise of the moment with a clearness and a precision that gradually elevated him to a preeminent place among his peers. Robespierre embodies the French Revolution in its most original aspect, the one that made it the Revolution of the Rights of Man—a decisive juncture in the transition from immemorial submission to divine authority to the idea of power legitimately created and exercised by human beings. Robespierre is the interpreter par excellence of this moment, its most systematic and most radical spokesman. From this there followed his incomparable prestige, uniting personal virtue, particularly self-abnegation in the service of the people, with unfailing intellectual steadfastness.

The tragedy of Robespierre is that his dedication to noble purposes ended up leading him astray when the moral supremacy that came from it brought him to power under the dramatic circumstances of 1793. Increasingly he found himself trapped by an untenable vision of popular government lastingly established on the ruins of the old monarchy. Some aspects of this vision were of his own invention and had the effect of isolating him; others derived from a common way of thinking that he more than anyone else helped to impose. By unraveling them, it will be possible to discern both the causes of his downfall and the reasons why his enemies later became entangled in the same difficulties—difficulties that were to be long-lasting and whose persistence was to constitute the distinctive mark of French political history. Throughout the entire course of its development, the Republic was to be plagued by the urge to embrace a theoretical radicalism that thwarted all attempts to give it practical effect.

The indelible imprint left by the Revolution consists in just this. The possibility that a regime of liberty founded on reason and rights might fail was incomprehensible to the very persons who sought to bring it into existence, convinced as they were of the self-evident correctness of the principles they imagined to justify their undertaking. As a consequence, the failure was fated to repeat itself. From this situation there arose a dilemma, whether to carry on in the pursuit of the Revolution's ambitions or to admit the justice of objections to its premises. This tension between two ways of "finishing the Revolution" was to be permanent—finishing it either by seeing it through to the end, on better terms and in the hope of more favorable circumstances, or by forswearing once and for all so many pretensions that had regularly been invalidated by experience. Thus a division was to be perpetuated in various forms, similar in inspiration, between an idealism blind to the conditions under which it could be realized and a realism utterly unaware of the ideals it was meant to achieve. It is true that this chronic tendency of French history seems now at least in part to have been dispelled. France appears to have found a way, if not to resolve the dilemma, then at least to make it more tractable. But it could just as well be the case, as we will see, that this dilemma is merely assuming a new form in the context of events that have permitted some measure of reconciliation. At all events, it has yet to be resolved.

There is not only a retrospective interest, then, in reexamining the historical origins of a peculiarly French predicament. We also have to consider the Revolution's formative influence on political modernity, the implications of which we are yet far from having fathomed. The career of Robespierre, from his ascent to his fall, is uniquely instructive in this regard. It offers the singular possibility of grasping from within—within a way of thinking placed in the service of action—the sources of a rift that has divided the French people down to the present day. Still today, no one divides France more than Robespierre.

CHAPTER ONE

The Man of the Revolution
of the Rights of Man

OF ROBESPIERRE BEFORE THE REVOLUTION, what is there to be said—except that it is futile to look there for insight into the Robespierre of the Revolution?

The thirty-one-year-old lawyer who came to Versailles in the spring of 1789 as a deputy of the Third Estate from Artois in no way stood out from the other representatives of his order. His childhood was rather ordinary for the period; even his unhappiness on being orphaned at an early age was not particularly unusual. He received a sound classical education, studying for twelve years as a brilliant scholarship student at the Collège Louis-Le-Grand in Paris. There followed a respectable career at the bar in Arras, soon marked by a few notable successes, accompanied by a promising start on a literary career, which gave him the opportunity, as a young member of the local academy and a man of the Enlightenment, to take part in the debates of the day. Like so many others, Robespierre was caught up in the excitement surrounding the elections to the Estates General held at the beginning of 1789, but the two polemical booklets he published in this connection, *À la nation artésienne sur la nécéssité de réformer les états provinciaux* and *Les Ennemis de la patrie démasqués par le récit de ce qui s'est passé dans les assemblées du tiers état de la ville d'Arras*, were aimed at a local audience. They aroused nothing comparable to the response that Sieyès's *Qu'est-ce que le tiers état?* and Pétion's *L'avis aux Français sur le salut de la patrie* met with in the National Constituent Assembly. Robespierre was only one of many minor provincial notables among the 1,100 members of the Estates General. Nothing in his career up to that point seemed to mark him out for a leading role in the long-awaited "regeneration" of the kingdom.

The events of 1789 were to reveal Robespierre to himself. It was his destiny to grasp the motive forces of the Revolution better than anyone else, to make himself its spokesman and to reveal its meaning, as it were, to the actors themselves. If there were anything worth searching for in his past, rather than improbable psychological motivations associated with emotional deprivation or social resentment, it would be the roots of his disposition to impersonality, a talent for self-abnegation that allowed him to identify himself wholly and unreservedly with the revolutionary impulse. Several of the traits his biographers commonly mention converge in this direction: a profound moral solitude; the sense of a separate destiny; an indifference to everyday comforts bordering on asceticism; and, not least, the lack of emotional attachment displayed by a chaste bachelor who enjoyed the company of women without feeling a need for them, any more than he sought to cultivate friendships with men. All these things inclined him to devote himself single-mindedly to a noble cause, assuming the burdens of public service without regard for his own personal interest; inclined him, in a word, to self-sacrifice. Even so, the events of 1789 made him another man, as though he had undergone a conversion. Very quickly he grasped the significance of what was taking place. He felt himself to be in the presence of one of "those unique revolutions that mark an era in the history of empires and that decide their destiny," as he put it that April in *Les Ennemis de la patrie*. He threw himself into his work on its behalf utterly and completely. He was now determined to live for nothing else until the day he died.

He found himself at once at the forefront of the struggle to win recognition for the "rights of the nation" and the "will of the people," even if his name was not yet familiar to observers. On 20 June he was the forty-fifth signer of the Tennis Court Oath. Seats in the galleries of the Constituent Assembly, convened on 9 July, were highly coveted in these tumultuous early days. Robespierre's first reported interventions in parliamentary debate already gave a glimpse of what was to be his constant line and permanent theme, marked in the first place by intransigent opposition to the established authorities: "[W]hat does it matter to us what the ministers say, what the ministers think? It is the will of the people that must be inquired into; the force of the people resides in themselves; it is in the incorruptible probity of their representatives." It was also marked by a dread of "the unprecedented conspiracy formed against citizens themselves" and a corresponding indulgence of the popular violence that resulted from it ("a few heads chopped off, of course, but the heads of guilty people"). Above all, it was marked by a reverence for principles that needed to be stated as clearly as possible. This became manifest during the debate over the Declaration of the Rights of Man, when Robespierre, speaking with regard to religious liberty and freedom of the press, inveighed against attempts to qualify the expression of these rights in their purest form: "[A]ny restriction, any exception in the exercise of rights must be entrusted to the Constitution. The Declaration of the Rights of Man must be clear, decisive, definitive, and without any modification."

But it was with the publication of *Dire contre le veto royal*, an undelivered speech to the National Constituent Assembly that appeared in the form of a booklet in September 1789, that the core of the doctrine that Robespierre was later to tirelessly and unwaveringly defend was fully formulated for the first time. With unsurpassable clarity he expounded a radicalism unaware of its own power, but no less implacable for that, that was to propel the Revolution forward. Robespierre did not attack the monarchy as such. For the time being it was a question, not of challenging it, but of examining what it involved and what retaining it implied. The word, he reminded his readers, "refers solely to a state in which executive power is confided to a single person." Under a constitutional monarchy, the duty of the executive is to apply the laws through which a nation governs itself—laws that are the expression of the general will, which in a large nation must be expressed through its representatives. Consequently, to grant a veto power of any sort to the executive means that "the man appointed by the nation to execute the nation's will has the right to thwart and fetter the wills of the nation," which is to say that "the nation is nothing and that one man is everything." For Robespierre, this was abhorrent. He could not bring himself to accept the tactical resignation of those "very good citizens" among his colleagues who voted to approve a temporary (or "suspensive") veto as a lesser evil by comparison with an absolute veto, knowing that they constituted a minority in the Assembly. For his part, he declared, he felt that "it was not good to compromise with liberty, with justice, with reason, and that an unshakable courage, an inviolable fidelity to great principles was the only resource suited to the current situation of the defenders of the people." With these words his persona was fixed.

The manner in which Robespierre justified his position makes it possible to discover the fundamental proposition that was to determine both the course of the Revolution and Robespierre's career within it, inasmuch as he identified the two things. One cannot help but be struck, in hindsight, by the blindness of the self-proclaimed patriots for whom

Robespierre spoke to the implications of the premises from which they argued. If in fact, as he wrote, governments are established only by and for the people, so "that all those who govern, and therefore kings themselves, are only the agents and delegates of the people," what then was left of royalty in the usual sense? For in that case it had been wholly emptied of its spirit—the supernatural unction and continuity of tradition. Robespierre's statement of basic principle therefore led directly to a republic. But this was not yet understood; for the moment, the very idea remained outside the realm of the thinkable. The force of monarchical heritage in France was sufficiently great to sustain the illusion that accommodation was possible. One could still cling to the fiction, at this stage, that it was only a question of redefining the basic assumptions of government and the attributions of its various powers by reconciling the ancient prerogatives of royalty with modern law. On this point Robespierre could quote his favorite author, the "divine" Rousseau, who had made the case in the *Contrat social* (1762) for joining a popularly elected legislature to a monarchical executive. Robespierre himself long persevered in this conviction, as we will see, until finally events exposed him to the charge of being a halfhearted republican. He was, in his way, a moderate. He did not by any means envisage the total overthrow of established institutions. In this, his thinking reflected the ambiguity of the circumstances under which the revolutionary experiment was first conceived. His apparent moderation, in calling only for reform of the ancien régime, nonetheless contained the seeds of the utter destruction of an entire society and system of government. In September 1789, unbeknownst to himself, Robespierre was the bearer of an explosive radicalism.

Once the dissident assertion of a will to provide France with a Constitution was amplified by the popular uprising in Paris and the storming of the Bastille in July, to say nothing of the rage that mounted throughout the country with each passing day, the logic of the situation imparted a spiraling momentum to events. The Constituent Assembly, established on 9 July, faced a problem of legitimacy. The self-declared metamorphosis of the deputies of the Estates General into representatives of the nation had not gone uncontested. A defense of this change of institutional identity, in response to the complaint that the task this body had set for itself went beyond the mandate that had been confided to officials elected in accordance with rules laid down by the ancien régime—namely, to communicate the grievances of their orders and their communities—takes up a considerable part of Robespierre's text. How could so substantial a work as a Constitution, he asked, be "the result simply of individual opinions that the representatives [*commissaires*] of local assemblies throughout the land [*assemblées bailliagères*] have written down in informal registers, composed in haste?" The remedy for this unsatisfactory state of affairs could only be an appeal to the primary truths concerning society and the aims of political association enunciated in the Declaration of the Rights of Man and of the Citizen. In taking cover behind this document, Robespierre's colleagues caused the precariousness of their position to be overlooked, while appointing themselves as its interpreters, in order to extract from it, by reasoning alone, a Constitution in complete conformity with natural law. Faced with the uninterrupted force of royal authority, which no one then disputed, reference to the rights of man furnished the Assembly with an independent and higher source of legitimacy.

In this way a weakness was converted into a strength—a far greater one, in fact, than the deputies themselves imagined at the time. A few of them did perceive, however, that the nature of the mission they were entrusted with carrying out had changed. They had been elected to patch up the decayed monarchical edifice; but now "a revolution as marvelous as it was unforeseen," as Robespierre put it, which promised to give back to the people "all the inviolable rights of which they had been deprived," suddenly placed them in a position to refashion the old system from top to bottom. It was no longer a question of being content with correcting a few flagrant abuses or of "slavishly copying" the example of England and its institutions, "born in times of ignorance." Instead the Constitution needing to be devised could be nothing less than "the masterpiece of the leading lights of this century" and "a model for Europe." Just as the work of the Constituent Assembly had begun to gather a self-sustaining momentum, what was at stake had become vastly enlarged. A marvelous and unforeseen revolution had become the Revolution of the Rights of Man, with Robespierre as its foremost exegete.

The fierce competition for legitimacy between the king and an Assembly basing itself on rights was the driving force of the Revolution in its earliest phase. The virulence of the debate over the royal veto makes this clear. For it was not a matter simply of converting a de facto power into a de jure power. It was a matter of embedding in the immense legitimacy, both historical and sacral, that the royal government continued to enjoy an ahistorical and desacralized legitimacy—though no one yet detected the contradiction between them, so massively did the abiding prestige of the former outweigh the rationalist charms of the latter. Even the most resolute defenders of the rights of the nation were under no illusion as to the monarchy's advantages. They could not imagine anything other than a negotiated settlement between the existing authority and the new one that was now emerging.

Paradoxically, it was the initial timidity of the French Revolution that gave rise to the extremism of its later phase. The perceived impossibility of attacking royal power head-on forced the revolutionaries to adopt a strategy of indirection that was to prove to be much more subversive. Instead of challenging the government on grounds of principle, something that was then still inconceivable, they sought to undermine it. A feeling of inferiority in relation to so formidable a power led them to try to create a countervailing force in the hope of wresting concessions from the monarchy. They found this force in the form of a popular movement whose vital usefulness was to provide a reason over and over again to excuse its excesses. Through a relentless determination to work out the implications of a logic of rights, they managed in spite of themselves to destroy the monarchy—and with it, the foundations of the old order—so completely that they found themselves confronted with the colossal task, likewise unanticipated, of having to establish a new system of government. Robespierre is the most striking personification of this dynamic.

The imbalance of power underlying the struggle between rival legitimacies was to have the greatest consequences, as much in the real world as in the realm of symbolism, for the revolutionaries' conception of democratic government. It pushed them to look for a practical way, in keeping with the theoretical implications of a doctrine of rights, to more or less entirely subordinate executive power to the will of the people. Under the pressure of events, this prevented them from soberly considering the nature of executive power and its proper functioning, something that Necker only got around to doing several years later in *Du pouvoir exécutif dans les grands États* (1792). The revolutionaries were always inclined to see it as a potential danger against which no precautions were too great—a conviction that was to leave a lasting mark on republican thinking in France, well beyond the Revolution. Robespierre is once again typical in this regard. His dread of conspiracies was equaled only by his dread of abuses of executive power, which furnished him with one of his strongest arguments against the royal veto. Possible abuses of legislative power count for very little, he held, when they are weighed against the means available to "[a] monarch cloaked in enormous power, who has at his disposal armies, tribunals, the police forces of a great nation." Was it not rather this power that an authentic government of the people ought to be concerned above all to limit and monitor? To his mind, the question answered itself.

Robespierre's protest against the royal veto—to which, again with the benefit of hindsight, we are able to attribute a prefigurative significance—seems to have passed almost unnoticed in the flood of opinions, articles, and booklets inspired by debate in the Assembly. But when Robespierre rose to speak on the subject of the king's acceptance of the Declaration of the Rights of Man, on 5 October, his main purpose was to draw attention to himself. If he provoked "murmurs" from some deputies, according to newspaper reports, he was "heartily applauded" by others. He seized the opportunity to vigorously affirm the ideas that he had developed earlier in his *Dire contre le veto royal*: "No authority is entitled to raise itself above a nation. No authority that emanates from the nation is entitled to censure a Constitution it gives to itself." His vehement rejoinder to the king's qualified approval of the Declaration of the Rights of Man is revelatory. "We are told that the principles of the Declaration are approved in principle; but we are told that they admit of different applications. This again is a great mistake. These are principles of justice, of natural law, that no human law can alter. . . . How could we wrongly apply them?" Here we have a glimpse of his axiomatic view of constitutional government. Given the premises, the consequences inexorably follow, so long as the reasoning is sound and uncontaminated by parasitic considerations. This is what makes the result irrefutable—and what a Constitution must assure.

The fifth of October was also the day that the women's march on Versailles forced the king and the Assembly to return to Paris, decisively changing the conditions of parliamentary debate. Removed from the hermetic atmosphere of Versailles, the Assembly's deliberations were henceforth to unfold under the immediate influence of popular feeling and in direct contact with the seething anger of the streets. This month of October was the moment when Robespierre first came into full public view, resolved to persist in the line of conduct that he had set for himself and from which he was never to deviate. Circumstances gave him the occasion to develop two themes that were to form the basis of his future popularity: hostility to martial law and rejection of any rule of suffrage based on tax qualification.

Bread shortages in Paris sparked protests and fueled rumors that speculators and monopolists were responsible for the growing famine and increasingly uncontrollable violence. One unfortunate baker was summarily hanged and decapitated. The Commune of Paris asked the Assembly to provide it with the means of reestablishing order: martial law, bread, and soldiers. Armed force was authorized in order to disperse the crowds. Robespierre, one of the few who opposed the measure, was emphatic in his dissent. To adopt martial law, he argued, amounted to saying that "the people are in revolt, they have no bread, we do not have any, they must be sacrificed." The alternative he proposed was to "go back to the cause of the disturbances." Behind this wave of discontent, he suspected, were people who foresaw it, perhaps even stirred it up, and who in any case counted on being able to turn it against the revolutionary movement. Stamping out "this formidable conspiracy against the safety of the state" required creating a permanent tribunal within the Assembly itself—charged with judging "crimes committed against the nation"—in order to hunt down the plotters. In the event, Robespierre's proposal came to nothing. But in it we can see the advent of one of the driving forces of the Revolution, which Robespierre, more than anyone else, orchestrated, namely, a delusional overestimation of the strength of the opposition to the Revolution. This had two corollaries: an underestimation of real difficulties and an unshakable belief in the necessity of resorting to ever more drastic measures in order to combat the extraordinary power of these dark enemies.

On 22 October, the question of the right to vote was placed on the day's agenda for debate on the Constitution. The Constitutional Committee of the Assembly recommended that it be reserved to citizens paying direct taxes equivalent to the value of three or more days of work. Robespierre, coming after Abbé Grégoire and Duport, spoke against the proposal. His argument was clear and compelling:

> All citizens, whoever they may be, have the right to claim all the degrees of representation. Nothing is more in conformity with your Declaration of Rights, before which every privilege, every distinction, every exception must disappear. The Constitution establishes that sovereignty resides in the people, in all the individuals of the people. Each individual has therefore the right to concur in the law by which he is bound and in the administration of the public interest, which is to say his own interest. If not, it is not true that all men are equal in law, that every man is a citizen.

This opinion, though it was very poorly received, helped to call attention to a courageous champion of the "cause of the poor," who "relies on the Declaration of the Rights of Man." One newspaper reported that the "cries of a part of the Assembly forced M. Robertspierre [*sic*] to step down from the tribune, to the great regret of the other part, which listened to him with the most lively interest." In a letter, Robespierre complained that his voice had been stifled by the "clamor of the aristocratic party," which "in the tumult" prevailed "as though by violence."

But the battle had only just been joined. Unrestricted suffrage was to be one of his favorite topics. He returned to it time and again, seizing every opportunity to condemn, if only indirectly, the distortion of "political equality" and to affirm the universality of rights. Thus the following year, on 23 October 1790, he categorically stated, "No one, not even the legislator, may impose limits beyond which one is no longer a citizen. Men are citizens by nature, by the very fact that they have the right to exist on earth, a right prior to legislators and to laws, who do not have the right to take it away from them." This trenchant formulation won him Marat's approval. Writing in *L'Ami du peuple*, he saluted "the only deputy who appears to be acquainted with noble principles and perhaps the only true patriot who sits in the Senate." Robespierre gave the most detailed and polished version of his argument in a speech that he was unable to deliver and that circulated, once again, in the form of a booklet, in April 1791. He went on the offensive once more during the crucial debate on final revisions to the draft Constitution on 11 August 1791, an occasion that assured his words would have added impact. His tireless advocacy of equal opportunity in this regard was to remain one of his incontestable claims to fame in the eyes of posterity. Robespierre was one of the first defenders and founders of universal suffrage, arguing on the basis of a coherent system of thought from which he endeavored to draw implications in every direction.

No doubt the systematic character of his undertaking was not yet perceived toward the end of 1789, but press accounts make it clear that his very ability to arouse opposition made him a figure to be reckoned with. His interventions in parliamentary debate were reported, discussed, and often denounced. He was seen as one of a small group of deputies given to exaggeration whose minority status nonetheless did not prevent them from enjoying a certain notoriety, because through their speeches the agitation in the streets came to reverberate within the Constituent Assembly. In this connection the strategy that Robespierre adopted, and once again never deviated from, was plain: he did not speak so much to convince his colleagues as to make himself heard outside the Assembly by the people—the Revolution's true "sovereign." He did not take part in the very active business of the Assembly's various committees, whose work was held in high regard by some observers. His domain was the tribune, and if his appearances there became more frequent it was above all in order to reach the public, in the first place through the spectators who filled the visitors' galleries. He saw himself as their spokesman, while seeking at the same time to win their approval. In Robespierre, disinterested conviction was to remain forever bound up with a desire for popularity.

This strategy was strengthened by its translation into something like institutional form with the formation of political clubs. Robespierre was associated from the beginning with the most prominent of these, the Society of Friends of the Constitution, meeting at the monastery of the Jacobins in the rue Saint-Honoré and composed, in its own words, of "all the patriotic deputies of the National Assembly and the most illustrious citizens of the capital." The Jacobin Club constituted a second tribune, in effect, hospitable to speakers hoping to reach a popular audience who had a hard time making themselves heard in the Assembly in the face of resistance from unreceptive notables. Robespierre was elected its president in April 1790, even though at this time his authority was modest by comparison with that of the club's leading figures, Mirabeau, Barnave, Le Chapelier, and Duport, all of them deputies from the moderate wing of the patriotic camp. It was only gradually that Robespierre came to the fore, against the background of a schism between centrists who urged compromise, the indispensable condition of establishing a constitutional monarchy, and radicals who unconditionally upheld the principles of the Revolution.

Mirabeau's death on 2 April 1791 deprived the faction favoring compromise of its most eloquent and most influential voice. The political situation then dramatically changed with the staggering news of the king's flight to Varennes, on the night of 20–21 June, which threw the choice facing the revolutionaries into stark relief: whether to maintain at all costs the fiction of a king "representing the nation" as the keystone of its institutions, or to acknowledge the irremediable weakening of royal legitimacy—but in order to do what and go where? Before the chasm opened up by the radicals' challenge to the monarchy, the moderate majority stepped back. Almost all of the deputies left the Jacobins, on 16 July, and formed a new club, the Feuillants, dedicated to promoting the political ideals to which they had been committed from the beginning. Robespierre found himself isolated, together with five of his colleagues, including Pétion and Buzot, as well as the militant faction of the Jacobins, which had supported the Cordeliers in presenting a petition demanding the removal of the king—the step that provoked the departure of the club's moderate elements. The following day, 17 July, the National Guard fired on a crowd of petitioners gathered on the Champ-de-Mars, martial law having been declared in the meantime, killing some fifty people. A wave of repression set in. Danton and Marat went into hiding. Robespierre himself took refuge in the house of an admirer, the cabinetmaker Duplay. When the storm had passed and he reappeared in the Assembly, Robespierre became the acknowledged leader of the Jacobins, who with the temporary eclipse of the popular clubs had become the trustees of the spirit of the Revolution. A month earlier, on 21 June, in an impassioned speech at the Jacobin Club, he had openly accused "almost all of [his] fellow members of the Assembly of being counter-revolutionaries, some out of ignorance, some from terror, others because of resentment, owing to wounded pride, and still others from an excess of self-confidence, often because they are corrupt." Following the crisis of 17 July, he adopted a conciliatory tone, seeking to calm emotions while at the same time continuing to proclaim the legality of the Jacobins' position. The dividing lines were now clear. From here on, when he spoke to the Assembly, everyone knew that he enjoyed the support of all those whom the Jacobins represented, profiting from the society's roots in a far-reaching popular movement (without having to take blame for its excesses) and from the communications of the Paris chapter with a network of affiliated provincial societies—in short, a revolutionary France that could no longer be ignored. Among the Jacobins in Paris, Robespierre was, if not the only legislator, then at least the most eminent of those who were determined to have the ear of the people, who saw themselves as their spokesmen, who did not separate their cause from that of the part of society that was least able to make its voice heard. This way of aligning the interests of the people and of their representatives was a key element of the system on which his authority was to be based.

The Logic of Principles

At bottom, Robespierre's message was as simple as it was constant: what mattered was the Declaration of the Rights of Man and nothing but the Declaration of the Rights of Man, in its entirety. He was indefatigable on this point, to such an extent that it would be tedious to list all the occasions on which he recurred to it. This topic also permitted him to develop his thinking about current affairs and to address questions that at first sight appeared to be of minor importance. For him the principles of the Declaration were the raison d'être of the Revolution, next to which everything else paled in comparison, not least the outbursts of violence that accompanied it and that he was constantly at pains to downplay. On 11 February 1790, in response to charges of "barbarism" that had been leveled not only in France but also across the Channel, in the English

Parliament, he expressed himself in terms that could without exaggeration be called eschatological:

> Leave it to the English, whose incomplete, imperfect, aborted, aristocratic Constitution has cost them rivers of blood and seventeen civil wars, to reproach us for burning a few châteaux and torturing a few conspirators in the name of man, reanimated in the fullness of his rights and recreated in the image of God, disfigured [until now] by ignorance and tyrants.

But the grandeur of what, in his eyes, was nothing less than an attempt to renew humanity also justified focusing attention on its failings, however minor. As one sympathetic journalist put it, silently referring to Robespierre's colleagues, "one never strays from principles without [incurring] grave dangers." This was no small matter for a man who was confident of his ability to set them back on the right course. Thus, for example, having declared himself in favor of "unlimited freedom to hunt," as against reserving the right for "landowners only," on 20 April, Robespierre returned to the rostrum of the Assembly two days later to protest against the prison sentence mandated for offenders:

> In the name of justice and humanity I speak out against the decree of your committee; and it is with the Declaration of the Rights of Man in hand that I register this complaint. One of the articles provides that the same crimes will be punished in the same manner, without distinction between persons; why does your committee openly violate this sacred principle, why does it oblige us to violate it ourselves, why must the Assembly sanction one of the greatest abuses of the ancien régime, distinguishing in punishments between poverty and affluence?

Always it was principles that had to be answered to. In February 1790, Robespierre did not hesitate to make his voice heard, in the event to no effect, in a very complicated matter concerning the loss of rights by certain German princes over lands in Alsace; or to respond to colleagues who were surprised to see him involving himself in a dispute over the Treaty of Ryswick and the public law of Germany, where what was at issue, he maintained, was "neither public law nor a treaty, but the law of peoples."

Robespierre's almost professorial manner of intervening in debate on topics large and small, his compulsion to make demands and correct misunderstandings, gradually set him apart from the other members of the Constituent Assembly, as much in the eyes of his admirers as in the eyes of his detractors. In February 1791, his old friend from school and university days, Camille Desmoulins, who had in the meantime become perhaps the most brilliant of the revolutionary journalists, praised the "pure and disinterested patriotism" of "our dear Robespierre." "When he speaks, it is less an orator who stands up to discourse on various subjects than a book of law that is opened up, not always [a book] of the written law, but of the uncreated law that is engraved in every heart. It is a living commentary on the Declaration of the Rights [of Man] and the embodiment of common sense." In elevating him to heroic status, Desmoulins sought to distinguish him from the mass of his colleagues, and to set his achievements above theirs. "Yet I do not believe that any of the bills he has proposed has ever been approved. Robespierre has almost always been a patriot, the perfect lawmaker, and I defy anyone to show me, from among the whole collection of decrees, [even] a half-dozen that could not be improved." Robespierre was to explicitly insist on this "unremitting inflexibility" in the *Adresse aux Français*, written in a frenzy during the crisis of 17 July 1791 to justify his conduct:

> The principles that I have brought to the assembly of the representatives of the people and that I have constantly supported (as all of France will attest) are those that the National Assembly has solemnly recognized, in the Declaration of the Rights [of Man], as the only legitimate basis of any political Constitution and of any human society. I swear that I have never regarded this Declaration as a mere theory, but indeed as [a statement of] universal maxims of justice, inalterable and indefeasible, applicable to all peoples.

His adversaries, for their part, were not slow to denounce the irresponsibility of a man holding forth in the Assembly as though he "held a chair in natural law," instead of accepting, among the more prosaic constraints of the legislator's duties, the overriding obligation to take into account the realities to which principles must be applied. Both sides were agreed in emphasizing the gap between principles and their application, except that they gave opposite interpretations of it. When the monarchist Clermont-Tonnerre, one of the most astute critics of Robespierre's cult of principles, declared at the end of his uncompromising study of the Constitution of 1791, *Analyse raisonnée de la constitution française*, that "the Declaration of Rights is a constant and complete condemnation of the majority of its institutions," he expressed an opinion with which Robespierre could only agree—with the difference, of course, that he saw this state of affairs as the result of the self-seeking behavior and the ill will of his fellow lawmakers, whereas Clermont-Tonnerre attributed it to their powerlessness in the face of events. Whereas Robespierre doubted neither the possibility nor the necessity of correcting the Constitution in order to make it fully conform to the maxims of the Declaration, Clermont-Tonnerre judged the enterprise impractical and the approach actually mistaken. The implications of this disagreement were to become clearer with the passage of time, giving shape to a profound dilemma that the Revolution bequeathed to its heirs. It is still with us today.

I do not intend to survey the full range of issues on which Robespierre expressed more or less considered opinions, whether orally or in writing, from the composition of military courts to the election of bishops and the principle of equality in the sharing of inheritances. He intervened in parliamentary debate more than a hundred times in 1790, and as many times again, only in a still more assertive fashion, during the first nine months of 1791, up through the final session of the Constituent Assembly on 30 September. It was during these last months that his influence began to grow. His argumentation became more forceful, his style more polished. He carved out a singular place for himself in the Assembly, where the hostility that he aroused, the interruptions to which he was subjected and the patience with which he endured them, served only to increase his popularity. He was sustained in his defiance by the sense of living through a unique moment in history, whose immense significance his colleagues did not sufficiently appreciate. It was in this spirit that he exhorted them to show themselves equal to the mission that had been entrusted to them—a mission that he described in frankly sacral terms, for example in the speech of April 1791 against the silver mark that he was unable to deliver to the Assembly but whose printed version caused a great stir within the various political clubs: "Eternal Providence has called upon you, and you alone since the beginning of the world, to establish on earth an empire of justice and liberty, aided by the most brilliant luminaries who have ever illuminated public reason, under the almost miraculous circumstances it has pleased [Providence] to bring together." It is true, however, that the appeal to the Enlightenment offset to some degree the role assigned to Providence.

The culmination of Robespierre's ascent in the combative and turbulent atmosphere of the period came in May 1791, when he composed some of the bravura passages that have survived as his greatest achievements in the minds of his admirers, on the right of petition, freedom of the press, the death penalty, and, not least, the ineligibility of sitting deputies for reelection to the next legislature—the occasion of one of his rare successes within the Assembly. The debate over the revision of the Constitution, in August, offered him a few more opportunities to vigorously plead the cause of principles, but they were only ways of giving further emphasis to themes that had already been developed at some length.

Rather than take up each of these points in turn, it will be more useful, for the purposes of this essay, to examine the overall view of social and political organization that emerges from them. Its most striking characteristic is the moderation that colored the radicalism of Robespierre's attempt to demonstrate the universality of rights.

To begin with, his intransigence in defending the rights of the nation did not go so far as to make a republican of him at this stage. He took the continuation of the monarchy for granted, considering it the sole possible regime for France in its present situation. Speaking before the Jacobins in April 1791, he brushed aside accusations of wishing to undermine it: "Overturn the monarchy! As if I were mad enough to wish to destroy the government, the only government that befits a great people and that can assure its rights and prosperity." Setting republic against monarchy presented a false opposition, he emphasized in July, more resolutely still— this at a tense moment when the king's flight had posed the question of whether he should be removed. The words "republic" and "monarchy" were only "vague and idle" terms, he maintained, incapable of defining a form of government. "Every free state in which the nation counts for something is a republic," so that "a nation may be free with a monarch"; from this it followed that "republic and monarchy are not two incompatible things."

The difficulty with this formalistic respect for the monarchy, as I say, is that it empties the institution itself of all substantive content, by reducing it to nothing more than a "repository of executive power." On this point Robespierre was categorical and adamant. The king cannot be said to represent the nation, he declared on 18 May 1790; the king was merely "the agent of the nation, appointed to execute the nation's will"—a claim that caused an uproar in the Assembly and forced him to justify himself. He explained that he had in mind only "the supreme duty, the sublime office of carrying out the general will." The following year he reaffirmed this position during the debate on the revision of the draft Constitution, on 10 August 1791, with Roederer's support: "M. Roederer has spoken to you a truth that has no need even of being proved, that the king did not represent the nation and that the idea of representation necessarily supposes a choice made by the people, and you have declared the crown to be hereditary. The king is therefore not the representative of the people. Chance alone gives him to you, not your own choice." What, then, could this accidental monarch still embody, this stranger to the declared wishes of the nation who is nonetheless sovereign and invested with the power of giving effect to its wishes? At most, even allowing for the immensity of its power, a precarious authority. The tension was unbearable, as events would soon make clear. For the moment, we should pause to consider the effects of this state of affairs on Robespierre's conception of government in general. It led, on the one hand, to a thoroughgoing mistrust of executive power and, on the other, to an unreasonable faith in legislative power as the expression of the nation's will.

The king, as the symbolic repository of executive power, could still be tolerated. But the ministers! "It is not the king I fear," Robespierre said to the Jacobins on 10 April 1791, "but the continual tendency to put arbitrary power in the hands of [his] ministers." In the weeks that followed he continued to warn against this "ministerial system," which, if unchecked, would erect a new despotism on the ruins of the old one. As early as May 1790 he had been alert to the perils of entering into armed conflict with foreign powers, an opportunity that in his view was desired by the government as a means of enlarging its prerogatives. Thus he argued in favor of reserving the right to declare war to the representatives of the nation, who "will always have a direct and even a personal interest in preventing war." It was this same preoccupation that stimulated his thinking on the organization of a National Guard. Although he was unable to address the Assembly on this subject, it was to bring him one of his first notable public successes a few months later, in December 1790, among the members of the political clubs, beginning with the Jacobins.

The subject has a number of aspects. In the first place it presented him with the occasion to make the case once more, only now from a different angle, against the distinction between active and passive citizens, by defending the idea that all citizens have an equal right to be admitted to the National Guard, given each person's right to provide for his own defense. But Robespierre took advantage of this opening to develop another argument to which he attached great importance, concerning the nation's need to protect itself against possible encroachments by executive power. "Any nation that is home to a numerous and disciplined army under the orders of a monarch, and that believes itself to be free, would be mad not to equip itself with a powerful safeguard." The object of a National Guard—a "new institution," he emphasized—was to make "the executive powerless to turn, against public liberty, the immense forces with which it is perpetually armed," without itself posing a danger either to liberty or to the executive. Alongside the danger presented by the government's temptation to resort to force, however, as Robespierre urged on several occasions, there was the insidious and permanent menace of corruption, a matter that ought to be of special concern to the nation's representatives. In August 1791 he came back to this topic in the course of the debate over revisions to the proposed Constitution, in connection with the proposal to allow ministers to address the Assembly, which he opposed. One could not take too many precautions, he explained, considering that "the executive will always have sufficient means to exert a ruinous power over the integrity and the freedom of the deliberations of the legislative body." This view of the executive as practically a foreign power, forever liable to turn against its masters and, as a consequence, never separate enough to be controlled, made any positive opinion of its function all the harder to entertain now that the nation had come to be regarded as the exclusive source of all legitimate authority. No one cultivated this sense of foreboding as assiduously as Robespierre. Here, as elsewhere, his purpose was to expose the logic of the principles at work. It was this logic that was to guide the revolutionary process. And the dynamics of this process were to make the executive unthinkable.

With regard to the legislature, confrontation with the royal government, whose legitimacy was tacitly admitted without anyone being quite able to define it, made it all the more urgent to affirm the independence of the people's representatives, as well as their identification with the nation itself, from which they derived their own legitimacy. Robespierre was unyielding; indeed, it was one of the convictions that governed his conduct from start to finish. As he put it in May 1791, explaining his opposition to making the present members of the Constituent Assembly eligible for reelection, "Everywhere the people do not exert their authority and do not manifest their will by themselves, but through representatives, if the representative body is not untarnished and almost identical with the people, liberty is destroyed." The ideal of incorruptibility he sought to realize, which could arise only from this unimpaired union of the people with their representatives, is what made him a man of the Assembly, whatever its name might be; that is where he wished to be—he knew of no other place to be. He was to remain faithful to this allegiance to the end.

At bottom, however, quite apart from Robespierre's sense of his own vocation, it was obvious to him, as to the majority of his colleagues in the patriotic camp, that the paramount power—the power through which the sovereignty of the people is expressed—resides in the legislature; the execution of its laws is secondary, so long as the loyalty of the executive is assured. Robespierre missed no opportunity to stress the preeminence of the representative body. During the debate over the Civil Constitution of the Clergy, in June 1790, he had caused a stir by taking issue with the draft version of the first article, arguing that "the first and most important duties of society are not those of ministers of religion, but rather those of legislators." He took pains to draw the consequences of this principle. Given that "no power must be raised above the representative body of the nation," it followed, for example, that deputies accused of misconduct could not be tried by the courts; they could be judged only by their peers.

The most original and crucial application of this principle led to the idea of a supreme court of appeal. The purpose of such a court would not be to decide individual lawsuits, but to determine the conformity of statutes currently in force with prior rulings. As Robespierre put it, a *tribunal de cassation* "is in no way a judge of citizens, but the protector of laws and the censurer of judges. In a word, it is placed outside and above the judicial realm in order to keep [the law] within its proper limits and in obedience to the rules that the Constitution has made binding upon it." Who could be better qualified, then, to determine whether the law has been upheld than the legislator himself? "It can only be the person who makes the law who is in a position to say that the law has been misunderstood and violated." Hence Robespierre's proposal to locate a court of appeal within the legislature, entrusting its responsibilities to a specialized committee. In practice the idea proved unworkable and eventually was abandoned. Nevertheless it had a certain logic that was not easily dismissed. Moreover, it called attention to a constitutional problem that was much more difficult to solve than established procedures would have led one to suppose.

The moderate character of Robespierre's radicalism in this first phase of his revolutionary career with regard to political questions is also found in connection with social issues. He was as cautious in the matter of the inequality of material conditions as he was intransigent in the matter of the universality of rights, declaring it to be "a necessary and incurable evil" in his speech of April 1791 on the silver mark. Even if it could not be remedied, however, one could at least indicate where one's sympathies lay. Robespierre did not hesitate for a moment, frankly telling the noble deputies, "I do not at all envy you the privileged share that is yours." What he absolutely rejected was the tax-based qualification enjoyed by the majority of the members of the Assembly, fearing that this inevitable inequality might once again become a source of political advantage. What was the point of destroying the "feudal aristocracy," only then to fall back under the yoke of a new aristocracy? "And what an aristocracy! The most unbearable of all: an aristocracy of the rich." However likely it may have seemed to him that this gloomy prospect would come to pass, he felt bound to remind his listeners that it was within their power to bring a more promising future into existence. At the root of "this extreme inequality of fortunes that concentrates all wealth in a small number of hands" were "bad laws" and "bad governments." Accordingly, there was reason to believe that good laws and good governments, devoted to the welfare of all, not only of a few, would correct at least the most shocking abuses of the reign of pecuniary privilege.

Liberty in All Things

Robespierre's optimism on this point only lent more importance to the struggle for the establishment of personal rights and public freedoms, his chief subject in speaking before the Constituent Assembly and the source of his popularity and of his claim to posthumous glory, which, in the eyes of his steadfast admirers, blots out all the rest. And it is true that his speeches and interventions on this topic form a corpus that is remarkable for its breadth and coherence. If it were possible to isolate this body of work from what followed—imagine that he had died at the end of 1791— his place among the great figures of liberal thought would be guaranteed.

We need not come back to the question of suffrage, which occupied so much of his attention at the outset of his parliamentary career. It involves a certain view of society, based on the rights of man, in connection with which I have already laid sufficient emphasis on the basic principle that guided Robespierre, namely, that the "holy equality of rights" is indivisible. Either it applies to all or it does not exist. Here again it is worth noting that Robespierre's radical inclinations were subject to a very traditional sort of limitation. The "all" of whom he speaks, rich and poor alike, did not include women. He was not one of those daring spirits, such as Condorcet, who felt that simple logic required that the universality of rights comprehend the female sex—to say nothing of female citizens who campaigned for the right to vote, a cause that held no interest for Robespierre.

Not unnaturally, considering Robespierre's professional training, he attached great importance to reforming the judicial system and strengthening the guarantees with which it must be provided. One notes in passing the high opinion he had formed of the lawyer's calling and of his guild. His intervention on 14 December 1790, objecting to the proposed removal of ministerial officials and lawyers as part of a restructuring of the legal profession, contained a discreet autobiographical note that is all the more revealing as he seldom spoke of his past. Robespierre praised the "happy and profound traces of liberty, and of the virtues it produces" that are still to be found at the bar, and stressed the role that these "magnanimous sentiments" have long fulfilled. They "have contributed in no small way," he continued, "to bringing about a revolution, which has taken place in government only because it was prepared [beforehand] in people's minds." Having emphasized the indispensability of moral rectitude in public affairs ("Genius, proud and independent, does not achieve its successes unaided; inflexible probity knows neither the suppleness of intrigue nor the art of solicitation"), he proceeded to denounce what he saw as the monstrous error of the recommendation made by the Constitutional Committee:

> [It] seeks to denature, to degrade offices that are as precious to human-
> ity as they are intimately associated with the progress of public spirit
> and the triumph of liberty; to turn a school of patriotism, in which the
> true friends of justice and humanity are led by their courage in defend-
> ing the cause of individual persons to [embrace] the still more impor-
> tant duty of defending the cause of the people in public assemblies, into
> a school of baseness and venality.

His two most memorable speeches on this topic concerned the intro-duction of jury trial in civil cases and the abolition of the death penalty, respectively. The first, delivered on 7 April 1790, was as much a rousing hymn to the spirit of the Revolution as a statement of his position on a particular aspect of judicial organization. The Assembly had approved the use of juries in criminal matters. Many of his colleagues opposed the extension of this practice to civil matters, citing the complexity of the rel-evant law. As against this, Robespierre argued that the primary advantage of judgment by juries rested on a distinction between facts and law. The law may well be complicated and its application difficult, but the deter-mination of the facts of a case is no more difficult in civil matters than criminal matters. And there was good reason, he maintained, to believe that trust in a verdict reached by one's peers—which is to say "ordinary citizens, chosen by the people, who will soon resume their place among the many, where they themselves will be subject to the same powers that they have just exercised over me"—will be greater than in one influenced by the *esprit de corps* of the magistrature, "a peculiar spirit, a spirit of haughti-ness, pride, and despotism that attaches to every corporate body invested with great power." But this technical pleading also offered Robespierre the opportunity to dismiss the arguments from political prudence that had been put forward by other speakers. "What is our political situation?" he asked. "That of a people who are making great strides toward achieving liberty for themselves, with a noble enthusiasm that overcomes all obsta-cles, at perhaps the only moment that will be given to them to provide themselves with all the beneficent institutions necessary to strengthen this liberty." He concluded with an impassioned appeal on behalf of the boldness required by divinely inspired circumstances:

> Moreover, no matter what anyone may say, I know of nothing so dangerous as this pusillanimous spirit, which always sets imagined inconveniences against sacred rights that must be established.... Woe be unto us, if we do not have the courage to be completely free, [for] half-liberty necessarily leads to despotism. Woe be unto us, if we create obstacles, just when they have all been removed from our way.... History, reason, everything tells us that nations have only a moment to become free: for us that moment has now come; it is you whom eternal Providence has destined to turn it to advantage for the regeneration and the happiness of peoples! Courage, reason, a religious respect for the right[s] of men and for the decrees of the Supreme Legislator, these things ought to form the principle of your [decrees]—the sole rule of conduct appropriate to your situation.

This lyrical peroration, though it was not enough to compel the conviction of his colleagues, nonetheless gives us a fleeting glimpse of the exalted sense of urgency, usually expressed in a much more controlled way, that animated his mission.

A year later, on 30 May 1791, when he rose to speak on the question of whether or not the death penalty should be retained, he had recently managed to achieve one of his very few successes in the Assembly. Two weeks earlier, on 18 May, he had played a decisive role in making incumbent deputies ineligible for reelection to that body in its next term, with the self-interested support of the right side of the chamber. Desmoulins observed that the two motions made by Robespierre (part of a bill that also concerned the participation of current deputies in the next government) were until then "the only two from this eloquent and incorruptible citizen that have ever met with approval." On the death penalty, Robespierre's argument is unsurprising. It restated the two points pressed by Enlightenment reformers against the "barbarism" of ancient penal laws, namely, that the death penalty is unsound in theory and ineffective in practice. Yet it is instructive for showing the extent to which Robespierre subscribed to the liberal view of a necessary limitation on the power of society. The object of the social contract being the preservation of individual rights, the "power of all" must reasonably be prohibited from depriving any one person of his life, even were he guilty of a crime, limiting itself to the right to hold him under arrest. This view is also very far from the notion of unlimited sovereignty, another possible reading of the social contract. Sovereignty is meaningful only if it is placed in the service of personal liberties, and this is what must guide its exercise. At all events Robespierre once again found himself in the minority: the death penalty was not abolished.

Liberty in all things meant, first and foremost, freedom of the press. The subject came to prominence at the beginning of May 1791, in the wake of the debate on the right of petition, which Le Chapelier, reporting on behalf of the Constitutional Committee, sought to reserve exclusively for active citizens, with the additional restriction that the right could only be exercised individually. A few weeks later the same argument was made on behalf of the much more famous "Le Chapelier law," outlawing guilds and trade unions in the name of a strict separation between the individual domain and a collective domain governed by the general will. Robespierre, bizarrely, uttered not one word about this law. On the framing of the right of petition, by contrast, he had spoken out forcefully. To his mind the point at issue turned on the false distinction between active and passive citizens, and he let no occasion pass to drive the point home, despite the accusations that were brought against him of incitement to revolt. Indeed, he reveled in his defiance: "I declare therefore that I adhere still to the principles that I have ceaselessly upheld in this forum; I shall adhere to them unto death." And then he reiterated his commitment to the universality of citizenship: "Our constituents are all the French people, and I shall defend all of them, above all the poorest." How could those who have the greatest need of the right to express their demands be deprived of it? Lest there be the slightest doubt about what this meant, he reminded his colleagues that "the Assembly, in its capacity as legislator and representative of the nation, is incompetent to take away from citizens this indefeasible right of man and of the citizen." He was no less severe with regard to the prohibition of petitions drawn up in the name of a collective body, holding that a "collection of individuals" has no fewer rights than an individual, and that a gathering of individual opinions in no way supplants a political authority speaking in the name of all.

In this connection, the more general question of a right to freedom of speech naturally came up for discussion. The Jacobins seized upon it, and Robespierre made it the subject of an important address, which, though it had manifestly been intended for delivery before the Assembly on 9 May, was printed and distributed by the society instead. He later recycled parts of it during the debate on revision of the Constitution, in August, notably the appeal to the authority of the American example concerning freedom of the press, a convenient way of deflecting criticism from those "who would be tempted to find one's opinion extraordinary and exaggerated." Robespierre's opinion was simplicity itself: "Freedom of the press cannot be separated from freedom of speech. The two things are sacred, like nature; they are both necessary, like society itself." The main part of his speech was devoted to the need for the legislator to be constantly on guard against approving restrictions that, in the apparently justified interest of combating abuses of this freedom, would open the way to its destruction. "Freedom of the press must be complete and unqualified, or it does not exist." What was fundamentally at issue was the advancement of knowledge, itself a consequence of the "commerce of thought that each man has the right to engage in with all minds, with the entire human race." It was a matter of public liberty, since, as he later insisted, in August, "in every state the only effective brake on abuses of authority is public opinion." Any restriction must therefore be very carefully weighed. It was in this spirit, for example, that he opposed a motion to prosecute the circulation of obscene images, protesting, to no avail, "those partial laws that under one pretext or another undermine the freedom to publicly announce one's thoughts." He reaffirmed it further by rejecting the power of municipalities to inspect theaters: "Public opinion is the sole judge of what is in conformity with the good."

Robespierre also held that the rights of man, supposed to be indivisible, applied to "men of color"—or, at least, "free men of color." Here we come up against the limits of a commitment to universalism, even one as resolute as his. If he inveighed against the scheming of the "party of the whites" who sought to strip free blacks of their rights, again during the fierce debate on the colonial problem that roiled the Assembly in May 1791; if he raged against the mention of the word "slave" in a decree issued by the Assembly as a dishonor and a stain upon the reputation of this body, still he did not go so far as to call for the abolition of slavery—no more than Grégoire or Pétion did, his allies in this battle. Was this a matter of unspoken conviction or of tactical shrewdness, considering the consequences of such a measure? Even if the word does not occur in his peroration, it is difficult not to imagine that the institution of slavery is referred to there: "Keeping your colonies is a matter of great importance; but this same interest is related to your Constitution; and the supreme interest of the nation and of the colonies themselves is that you preserve your freedom and that with your own hands you do not overturn the foundations of this liberty. Ah! May you lose your colonies if you must keep them at this price." A variant of the last phrase is commonly, but wrongly, attributed to him: "Rather that the colonies be lost than a principle." This

was in fact due to another speaker. Robespierre concurred, again to the
grumbling and noises of approval aroused by his earlier remarks: "Yes, if
it be a question of having either to lose your colonies or to lose your happiness, your glory, your liberty, I repeat: may you lose your colonies." If he
attached so much importance to ensuring that the word "slave" not appear
in a law passed by the Assembly, was it not because, to his way of thinking,
the institution itself had no place in the territories where the Constitution,
the fruit of its own labors, was meant to be applied?

Robespierre exhorted his colleagues, in the speech on freedom of the press,
to take up a task that well summarizes the philosophy that inspired him:
"Let us make laws, not for a moment, but for centuries; not for ourselves,
but for the world; let us show that we are worthy to lay the foundations of
liberty." In characteristic fashion, the speech itself combines a view of the
events then unfolding and a principle of action. Robespierre never ceased
to tell his fellow revolutionaries what their efforts were meant to accomplish, and to remind them of their obligation to do their utmost to see this
task through to a successful conclusion. Laying the foundations of liberty
required them to be equal to the challenge before them, casting aside petty
calculations of self-interest, so that the unique opportunity presented by
this unprecedented disruption in the long history of oppression and arbitrary rule would not be missed. Liberty having no other guarantee than
itself, and half-measures infallibly promising the return of despotism, they
were called upon to perform their duty as conscientiously as possible.

It was from this moment forward that the view of Robespierre as an
exemplary figure gradually began to take shape. In turn it was the idea
of Robespierre as a model to be imitated that was the real source of his
popularity. There is something mysterious about this popularity, as many
historians and biographers have rightly observed. The accusation of demagoguery, which recurs like a leitmotif, both among his adversaries and in
the newspaper editorials of the period, is unconvincing. It is in fact quite
clear that Robespierre was the opposite of an ordinary demagogue, the
sort of rabble-rouser that Paris was filled with during these years, in both
patriotic and popular quarters. Robespierre was an orator, but certainly
not a great one. He had neither an imposing appearance nor a commanding voice—all witnesses are in agreement about this—nor, above all, a cap-
tivating style, as his writings make clear. His impeccable but cold rhetoric
and his dense style of argumentation were scarcely suited to stirring up
and exciting crowds. The content of his speeches no doubt escaped most of
his listeners, who applauded their basic thrust and their conclusions more

than their substance. Nor did his distant manner and imperturbable air of respectability mark him out as a leader of men. He had loyal supporters, but no troops. And yet, despite all these qualities, which might have earned him the esteem of a discerning few, but nothing more, he emerged triumphant at the end of the closing session of the Constituent Assembly, on 30 September 1791, to the exuberant acclaim of a crowd that had gathered to present him with a wreath symbolizing civic virtue. He had become a popular figure.

It is quite true, as one of his adversaries, angered by what seemed to him "a ridiculous apotheosis," was at pains to point out, that not "a single decree, a single law on any matter" was directly attributable to Robespierre. But if his contributions to the work of the Assembly had been minor, he embodied the spirit by which it had to be guided if it was to remain faithful to the principles that guaranteed its legitimacy. Time and again he corrected the Assembly's course, reprimanding its members for their many deviations. It was this inalterable sense of direction, anchored in an unswerving devotion to the sources from which the revolutionary dynamic sprang and thrown into relief by his colleagues' chronic inclination to compromise, that set him apart from them, not least in the minds of people who could hardly have been moved by the demonstrative austerity of his rhetoric. His unfailing resoluteness of purpose and the clarity of his message were enough to win their ardent support.

Robespierre refused to be led astray. He inspired trust and built up a loyal following on the basis of his moral authority. On 30 September 1791 he became the man of the Revolution of the Rights of Man in the eyes of the most committed members of the patriotic cause, the man who drew attention to the gap between what the Revolution promised and what it had so far achieved. At this moment, he may well have appeared to be the one who was most capable of making the Revolution's promise a reality.

CHAPTER TWO

I, the People

IN THE AUTUMN OF 1791, Robespierre was still very far from being seen as the embodiment of the people. In the view of the old Assembly he was only one man of note among many, a self-assured and long-winded speaker, adulated by some, detested by others, whose notoriety nonetheless did not give him any particular influence over the deliberations of the new legislature. The office of public prosecutor in the Paris Criminal Tribunal, to which he had been elected in June 1791 as part of the restructuring of the judiciary, did not obviously destine him to play a leading role in the life of the nation—unlike, for example, his friend Pétion, thrust into prominence by his election as mayor of Paris in November that same year. Surely he did not imagine being content with holding this office; indeed, he never really performed its duties, and abruptly resigned his position, on 10 April 1792, not quite two months after he had finally been sworn in. He was determined to go on having a say in public debate. There remained to him the forum of the Jacobin Club, where he regularly spoke and where he could hope to enjoy the power over opinion to which he aspired—from now on to the exclusion of all else. It was from there that his future career took flight.

Robespierre was in no sense a rabble-rouser, not now or later. He was a firm defender of the Constitution, in keeping with a carefully considered plan of action, hints of which could already be found in his last interventions at the Constituent Assembly. Having located the peril facing the nation in the king's court, his ministers, and "the ambition of a few schemers," Robespierre urged his colleagues to swear an oath "never to agree to compromise with the executive on any article of the Constitution." On the eve of the closing session, he spoke out against a bill introduced by Le Chapelier aimed at limiting the activity of the popular societies, arguing that they were now more indispensable than ever, because they helped to "propagate knowledge, the principles of the Constitution, and that public spirit without which the Constitution cannot endure." As against his adversaries, who claimed that the Revolution was now finished, and so that what mattered above all was to assure the smooth functioning of the existing government and its protection against external interference, he argued that the Revolution could be said to be finished only when the Constitution had finally been made secure. For in the meantime the Constitution had encountered opposition on several fronts, both at home and abroad—and even within the Assembly itself, where Robespierre detected "the rise of a Machiavellian system that threatens it with impending ruin," a system that consisted of "speaking in praise of liberty only in order to suppress it with impunity." Now more than ever, then, the Constitution demanded the active supervision of citizens devoted to the public good.

As critical as Robespierre had been of many of the draft Constitution's provisions, once the final version was adopted he regarded it as a vital achievement that had to be defended at all costs in view of the dangers surrounding it. This is what led him to say that he did not understand the majority view in the Assembly that the Revolution was "finished." If the Revolution was nothing other than "the efforts of the nation to preserve and conquer liberty," the attempts by enemies of every sort to overturn its results or to pervert them meant that it would have to be carried on as long as necessary. Here, however, he saw fit to rely on scrupulously legalistic argumentation. It was in this spirit that he took part in the great debate over going to war against the Austro-Prussian coalition, in late 1791 and early 1792, which was to set him against Brissot and cause a momentous split within the Jacobins. It was also in this spirit that he threw himself into journalism, in the spring of 1792, after having resigned his post as public prosecutor. His newspaper, which appeared in May, after the declaration of war against Austria on 20 April, was aptly entitled *Le Défenseur de la Constitution.*

Progress and Prudence

It would be a mistake to suppose that Robespierre was willing to tolerate the lame compromise arrived at by the Constituent Assembly with regard to the Constitution, or that he shared the illusions of his moderate colleagues regarding its durability. To the contrary, he had a very precise idea of how to improve it. Speaking before the Jacobins on 2 January 1792, he had wondered ironically whether this "Constitution, said to be the

daughter of the Declaration of Rights, so strongly resembles its mother."
But the right way to strengthen this resemblance was not to act precipi-
tously. In the first issue of *Le Défenseur*, he urged his readers to be patient:
"[L]et us have the strength to bear its imperfections for a time, until the
advance of knowledge and public spirit will have led us to the moment
when we will be able to eliminate them in a spirit of peace and harmony."
For, as he put it in a striking phrase that reminds one of the man of the
Declaration of the Rights of Man, "[I]f the defects of the Constitution
belong to men, its foundations are the work of Heaven; and it carries
within itself the immortal principle of its perfection." Enlarging upon this
theme, he went on to say:

> The Declaration of Rights, freedom of the press, the rights of petition
> and peaceful assembly; virtuous representatives, stern toward the great,
> unrelenting toward conspirators, lenient toward the weak, respectful of
> the people, ardent protectors of patriotism, scrupulous guardians of
> public decorum . . . —under their auspices, peace and abundance are
> reborn; nothing more is needed to force royalty to walk along the path
> the sovereign's will has marked out for it, and to bring about, smoothly
> and imperceptibly, an era in which public opinion, enlightened by the
> age and the crimes of tyranny, will be able to pronounce on the best
> form of government suited to the interests of the nation.

This irenic vision expressed his resolve to persevere in the role he had
indefatigably carved out for himself since 1789 as defender of revolutionary principles and spokesman of the people. One suspects that he saw
himself as their tutor in this apprenticeship to virtue, which began with
a warning against any undue haste that would sow confusion about what
remained to be done. "We will therefore have the courage to defend the
Constitution," Robespierre continued. "We will defend it all the more
ardently in proportion as we are more keenly aware of its defects." The
perils of going backward, at a moment of "stormy crisis," made it essential
to guarantee that the country would go on moving forward.

It was for this reason that he refused once more to take sides in what he
considered to be a false dispute. "Does the solution to a great social problem reside in the words *république* and *monarchie*?" The abstractions they
stand for, he maintained, have nothing to say about the actual form that
governments should assume. "I would rather see a popular representative
assembly and free and respected citizens with a king than an enslaved
and degraded people under the yoke of an aristocratic senate and a dictator." Again he expressed his opposition to an impetuous and shortsighted

radicalism: "Why should it matter to me that supposed patriots hold forth the imminent prospect of covering France in blood in order to rid ourselves of royalty, if it is not national sovereignty and civil and political equality that they wish to establish on its ruins?" The same motive led him to sharply rebuke an unfortunate publicist who came before the Jacobins to expound Voltairean views on the Catholic priesthood's abuses of the sacrament of confession: "One must not directly oppose religious prejudices venerated by the people; one must allow people's minds time to mature, so that insensibly they are raised up above prejudices."

And it was for this same reason, finally, that he objected to the war advocated by an influential part of the patriotic camp for the purpose of dispersing the menacing groups of émigrés that had gathered at the northern and eastern frontiers, from Brussels to Frankfurt, with the blessing, if not actually the collusion, of the masters of these lands, notably the Court of Vienna. Robespierre turned his attention to the problem on returning to Paris from an extended visit to his native province of Artois after an absence of two and a half years. Addressing the Jacobins, on 28 November 1791, he was not entirely unmoved by the ambient warmongering. But two weeks later, on 11 December, having considered the matter more carefully in the meantime, he gave an extemporaneous speech aimed at rallying minority opinion, cautioning against armed conflict on prudential grounds: "The most dangerous course of action is to declare war." His chief argument, stated at the outset, was simple and powerful: "By declaring war, you deprive yourself of this precious resource: the means of mistrusting executive power." He expanded upon this theme in the days and weeks that followed. While admitting that there were disadvantages to remaining at peace with hostile neighbors, he was adamant that "[w]ar is the greatest scourge that can threaten liberty under the circumstances in which we find ourselves." For this was not a war like others: "[I]t is a war of all the enemies of the French Constitution against the French Revolution"—and these enemies were to be found as much within France itself as outside its borders. Going to war could only have the effect of strengthening both external and internal opposition. The ensuing debate turned into a highly personal duel between Robespierre and Brissot, the leader of the war faction among the Jacobins, who moreover was a deputy in the new legislature, a second and more public forum where Robespierre no longer had a voice. The growing bitterness between the two men widened an ominous rift within the patriotic camp, with dramatic consequences.

Robespierre dealt with the question in the course of a series of speeches at the Jacobin Club that culminated, on 10 February 1792, in an interminable address (running to forty-five printed pages) "on the means of saving the state and liberty." The style was more polished, and the range of topics treated broader than in the earlier speeches, but the thrust of his argument remained the same. He was not animated by pacifism as a matter of principle. What mattered was having a clear view of the political situation and the motivations of its major figures. It was not by chance, he maintained, that the king's court and his ministers sought war. "War is always the first wish of a powerful government that desires to become still more powerful." Nor was there anything in the least mysterious about this. "I therefore sum up, discouragingly, and in sorrow," he had said by way of conclusion a month before, on 11 January. "I have proven that war, in the hands of the executive, [is] only a means of overturning the Constitution." Rather than rush off to war abroad, the first concern must be to maintain peace at home. Now that "disturbances are breaking out in all parts [of the country]," it was plain that the most numerous and determined enemies of the constitutional order were not at the frontiers, but "in our midst." It was this unsettled state of affairs, of which Robespierre gave an impressive summary, that the government counted on being able to exploit in order to free itself from the shackles of popular oversight, by conjoining foreign war with civil and religious unrest. These were the forces, allied with the aristocrats against "the cause of the people and patriots," that had to be stamped out before any thought could be given to marching against foreign enemies. The list of reactionaries was a long one, from insubordinate priests to corrupt government officials, to say nothing of unnamed "egotists" who sought equality with their superiors but not with their inferiors. Only once this task had been carried out would it be possible to contemplate an authentic "people's war" against foreign enemies.

In addition to warning against the opportunity that war unavoidably presented for the arbitrary use of power, in one form or another, even to the point of imposing a military dictatorship, one of the most significant aspects of these speeches is the remarkably shrewd and realistic conception of political progress they develop. This is especially true of Robespierre's speech of 2 January 1792, in which he dashed the glorious hopes that Brissot had held out a few days before. Brissot had been warmly applauded for describing the offensive war he favored as a "crusade of universal liberty," which would cause the peoples of Europe to join together in enthusiastically embracing the principles of the French Revolution. A "magnificent prediction," Robespierre replied with mordant irony, that contradicted "truth and common sense." For "[i]t is in the nature of things that the march of reason makes slow progress." In effect, Brissot assumed that one nation's suffering could be imposed on other nations, something Robespierre thought utterly futile. "The most extravagant idea that can arise in the mind of a politician is to believe that the nation has only to take up arms against a foreign people in order to make them adopt its laws and its Constitution. No one welcomes armed missionaries." Peoples must be left to develop in their own ways. The paths some have followed may well be taken as examples by others, of course, but only in relation to their current stage of development. "The Declaration of Rights is by no means a ray of sunshine that enlightens all men at the same moment." No doubt it was permissible to hope that "over time our revolution will influence the world's destiny," but it was puerile to believe that its effect could be instantaneous.

Robespierre's sensitivity to the turmoil of the present moment led him to reflect on what he called the "natural course of revolutions," of which the French Revolution was an instructive example.

> In established states, as almost all the countries of Europe are, there are three powers: the monarchy, the aristocracy, and the people, though in fact the people have no power. Should a revolution occur in any of these countries, it can only be gradual; it begins with the nobles, with the clergy, with the rich, and the people support them when their interest agrees with theirs in resisting the dominant power, which is that of the monarch. Thus it is that among us it was the high judicial courts, the nobles, the clergy, and the rich who gave the Revolution its first impetus; the people came to it later. They regretted what they had done, or, at least, they wished to stop the Revolution, when they saw that the people could regain their sovereignty; but they are the ones who began it, and without their resistance and their miscalculations the nation would still be under the yoke of despotism.

From this analysis of the social mechanism that guided the Revolution in France there followed a lesson concerning the state of forces in play in the other nations of Europe—a warning to privileged groups who cooperated with their governments "in order to escape the Declaration of Rights." Far from the warm welcome prophesied by Brissot, France could expect only renewed hostility.

Confronted with another argument advanced by Brissot to reassure the patriotic camp with regard to the perils he had pointed out, namely, that "the people are there," Robespierre again counseled caution. "No doubt they are," he retorted, "but you cannot ignore the fact that the insurrection you refer to here is a rare remedy, uncertain, extreme." In addition to being "terrible," this remedy for treachery—treachery that Brissot had no qualms about encouraging in view of the reaction it would provoke—was unpredictable in its results. Brissot supposed that the people are well-informed about the targets and purposes of such an uprising. On this point Robespierre appealed to Rousseau ("The people always desire what is good, but they do not always perceive what is good") and added, "their natural goodness makes them liable to be duped by political charlatans." What Brissot imagined to be a guarantee was nothing more than a highly risky wager. In short, the war party was the party of chance. A better policy, Robespierre held, was to try to fortify popular sovereignty within the framework of existing institutions through vigilant supervision of the behavior of the executive and the conduct of the people's representatives.

Robespierre's thinking was rooted so deeply in this way of looking at things that at first he did not appreciate the implications of the fall of the monarchy in August 1792. In keeping with his legalistic scruples, he had taken no part in the insurrection. But several days later he described it, in what was to be the last issue of the *Défenseur de la Constitution*, as an illustration of his thesis. "The insurrection of 10 August 1792 has [certain] advantages over that of 14 July 1789 which announce the advance of knowledge since the first period of the Revolution." The tumultuous uprising of the people of Paris, in 1789, was the work of passions, an essentially negative undertaking. Its object was "to shake off an ancient despotism, rather than to conquer liberty, the idea of which was still confused and the principles unknown." In 1792, by contrast, the people "rose up, with impressive composure, to avenge the fundamental laws of their violated liberty. . . . Three years earlier they had executed the proclaimed principles through their first representatives; [now] they exercised their recognized sovereignty and deployed their power and their justice, in order to assure their safety and their happiness." What is more, whereas in 1789 "they were aided by a large number of those who were called great men," in 1792 they had no need of anyone's help. "They found all their resources in knowledge and strength; alone they protected justice, equality, and reason against the enemies of these things." Thus it could be hoped that this second insurrection would prove to be decisive, making it possible to bring the Revolution of the Rights of Man to a successful conclusion. Robespierre could not conceal his unbounded admiration for what had been achieved so far: "Thus began the finest revolution ever to honor humanity; more precisely, the only one to have had an object worthy of mankind, that of founding polities at last on the immortal principles of equality, justice, and reason."

In overturning his habitual way of thinking about the monarchy in France, the shock of the event was to propel him in an unforeseen direction. He was unsurprised by the rise in tensions since the outbreak of war in April. Far from being the triumphal expedition forecast by Brissot, the first military operations ended in reverses that exposed the disorganization of the army, weakened by the desertion of officers from the nobility who took refuge abroad. Charges of treason and conspiracy began to be exchanged on all sides. Robespierre set himself apart in this regard, beginning on 23 April, three days after war was declared, with the sensational announcement of the discovery of a "plan for civil war" that he would soon be able to make public. In the event the announcement was without consequence. I will come back to this in due course. For the moment it is enough to observe that the promise to imminently unveil dark secrets of conspiracy was to be a hallmark of Robespierre's oratory from now on. But there was no mystery about the target he had in mind; the campaign he openly conducted against Lafayette in the following weeks made it perfectly clear. In the person of this general, who claimed to command the Legislative Assembly and who represented himself as a protector of the king, he detected the emergence of the specter of "military despotism." Against the background of public anxiety over impending disaster at the nation's frontiers, unrest in Paris increased with the growing tensions among the Court, the government, and the Assembly. On 11 July, the Assembly declared "the fatherland in danger." The question of the king's overthrow was publicly posed and debated. Compounding the anger and fear of the moment, the menacing proclamation issued on 25 July by the commander in chief of the Austro-Prussian armies, the Duke of Brunswick, and made known in Paris three days later, promised the "total destruction" of the capital in the event that the king and his family were harmed. In this feverish atmosphere, Robespierre gave a major speech at the Jacobin Club on 29 July whose vigorous tone scarcely masked an underlying ambiguity, if not actually a real difficulty.

His principal point was that the removal of the king was not enough; indeed, it was likely to be dangerous in the absence of legislative reform. Those who preached insurrection, Robespierre clearly implied, had not given sufficient thought to the cause of the "extreme evils" that afflicted France. This cause, he maintained, lay mainly in the transgressions and the corruption of the incumbent deputies. The reality was that the "power of the legislative body is infinitely greater than that of the king, since it may avail itself of the force of the people and surround itself with public opinion." In the event, the nation's representatives had made the worst possible use of this power, for "the great crisis to which we have now come is none other than the conspiracy of a majority of the people's delegates against the people." The fact that the French had to struggle at once against external enemies and their own government is what gave the situation its unparalleled drama. Robespierre emphatically insisted on the point: "It is necessary that the French people support the weight of the world and, at the same time, vanquish the monsters that torment them. It is necessary that they be among peoples what Heracles was among heroes."

It was necessary in any case to overhaul a system of representation that had been irreparably damaged. For this purpose, Robespierre argued, "[a] national convention is absolutely indispensable." But real reform required that lessons be drawn from experience. The first was that all citizens must take part in electing the new assembly, thus "erasing these harmful distinctions that reckon the virtues and the rights of man according to their share of taxation." Still, universal suffrage was not enough. It was necessary, in addition, that citizens meeting in assembly from time to time be able to judge the conduct of their representatives and deliver their opinions "on all that concerns public happiness." Experience had shown the dangers of "representative despotism." The source of all the country's ills was "the [state of] absolute independence in which the representatives have placed themselves with regard to the nation, having never consulted it." Since what was at issue was executive power, the main thing was to reduce "the immense means of corruption at its disposal." But with regard to the holder of such power, Robespierre proved to be remarkably evasive. While not ruling out the removal of the king, he stressed the very considerable uncertainties to which this would lead, and which he made no attempt to resolve. How and by whom could the king be replaced? "What would it matter," he asked, "if the phantom called king were to disappear and despotism were to remain? Louis XVI having been overthrown, into whose hands would royal authority pass? Into those of a regent? Of another king or of a council?" These questions were all the more crucial as it could be foreseen that this "great change . . . will provoke new political storms." Where were the pilots, both "resolute and able," who would be needed to steer the ship of state to a safe harbor? Robespierre rejected out of hand the suggestion that the exercise of executive power be confided to the legislature. "In this confusion of all powers I see only the most unbearable of all despotisms. I know of nothing so frightening as the idea of an unlimited power, handed over to a numerous assembly that is above the law, even were it an assembly of wise men."

He stood firm, reminding his listeners of the soundness of his arguments, by contrast with those of an assembly that had fatally been led astray. "The happiness of France was truly in the hands of its representatives. A few months ago, before the declaration of war, I demonstrated that the Constitution was all they needed to prevent the evils that threatened the state and liberty." Now that these evils had come to pass, it was necessary to seize the opportunity to remedy the most flagrant defects of the Constitution while at the same time recovering its original inspiration, which ought never to have been abandoned. Robespierre's perseverance in this line of argument left the fate of the king and his power undecided. In connection with legislative reform, a further sign of his steadfastness, Robespierre advocated that the Constituents' exemplary "disinterestedness" be reaffirmed by excluding from the next assembly the members of the two previous ones. He therefore was willing to deny himself a place in the very National Convention he sought to bring into existence. But the role left to him in that case would have suited him marvelously well, to judge from the surpassing importance he attached to it: "What matters is that there remain, among the people, men of integrity and discernment, strangers to public office, who may enlighten and supervise the trustees of their authority."

Circumstances were to decide otherwise, by snatching away any chance that the continuity of government in which he placed his hopes would come about. The insurrection of 10 August and its aftermath upset the existing order without any feasible alternative having been devised in the interval. The question that Robespierre had left unanswered, how executive power should be recast, was to catch up with him in a way that he scarcely anticipated. Unlike Brissot and his allies, he had grasped the destabilizing implications of a state of war, but he had still underestimated the impact that it was bound to have. Although he was more aware of the crisis facing the country than most in his camp, and more alarmed by it, he was slow to appreciate the depth of the divisions that were now making themselves felt. Paradoxically, his hostility to the "revisionist faction," which in the summer of 1791 had managed to save the monarchy by spreading the fiction that the king had been abducted, blinded him for a time to how unpersuasive this fiction was. The truth was that royal legitimacy, following the flight to Varennes, hung by a thread. Robespierre's speech of 29 July 1792 showed that he had finally come to his senses. "Is it really Louis XVI who reigns? . . . Stripped of public confidence, which alone gives kings their strength, he no longer has any power of his own." Nevertheless the mere presence of this royal phantom closed off discussion of the legitimacy of the nation's supreme authority just when war had rendered the problem acute. The king's sudden irrelevance exposed a yawning abyss into which two bombs left behind by the Constituent Assembly as a fatal inheritance were belatedly to explode: the religious dissension sown by the Civil Constitution of the Clergy and the social tensions created by the inflationary effects of the *assignat*, a promissory note first issued by the Assembly in 1790 that circulated as legal tender for the next six years. Now it was a question, not of defending principles against the clever and the powerful, but of taking responsibility for an enormous burden of a different sort. The task of exercising power in the name of the people turned out to involve much more than merely pleading their cause. Delivered from the monarchist threat, the man of the Revolution of the Rights of Man now had to face up to the formidable challenge of laying foundations for a new kind of regime that would be fully consistent with the principles of equality, justice, and reason—and this under the most trying circumstances imaginable.

Another Man

Robespierre was no longer the same man. The battle against the war, which turned into a battle against a majority of the Legislative Assembly in the first months of 1792, had changed him; or rather, it hastened the crystallization of novel attitudes and ideas that gradually became preponderant in his thinking. If Robespierre continued to look at things from the same perspective and to argue in the same terms for a while longer, his speeches during this period were increasingly preoccupied with an idealized image of the people, and of himself as their spokesman, together with a corresponding image of the political combat he was engaged in, which became bound up with one another so completely as to detach him from reality in a way that turned out to be fatal.

This mystifying tendency to romanticize the people was by no means something new. The first hint of it may be found in a speech of December 1790 on the National Guard, when Robespierre protested against a decree of the Constituent Assembly that effectively barred passive citizens from serving in it. "[D]esist from slandering the people and from blaspheming against your sovereign, by ceaselessly representing [the people] as unworthy of enjoying their rights, as wicked, barbarous, corrupt; you are the ones who are unjust and corrupt. . . . It is the people who are good, patient, generous." This idyllic image would have been nothing more than a harmless piece of rhetorical overstatement were it not for the political significance that Robespierre attached to it:

> The people ask only to be left undisturbed, ask only for justice, for the right to live. Powerful men, the wealthy, crave distinctions, riches, sensual pleasure. The interest, the desire of the people is that of nature, of humanity; it is the general interest. The interest, the desire of the wealthy and of powerful men is that of ambition, pride, cupidity.

The purpose of the Revolution being to establish the reign of the general will, it was above all the business of the people, if not the business of the people alone, to see that this was done. Associated with this purpose was a matter of the highest importance: the moral regeneration of humanity. Six months earlier, Robespierre had already stated the principle that guided his thinking on this point during the debate on the Civil Constitution of the Clergy in June 1790. To a prelate who invoked "the corruption of the age" as a reason for reserving episcopal election to the clergy, he replied that there was only one remedy for "what is called the corruption of the age," namely, the "principle that the morality that seems to have disappeared in most individuals is found solely in the body of the assembled people and in the general interest." The wishes of the clergy represented only its own interest, whereas "the wishes of the people represent[ed] the general interest." But his argument extended much further than this particular case. To the virtue he ascribed to the people as a whole, he assigned the mission of restoring morality to the world by political means.

Robespierre returned to this theme many times, so often, in fact, that it came to be considered inseparable from his larger ambition. It was at the heart of his philippic against the silver mark in April 1791. There he had invoked the testimony of "all those whom the instinct of a noble and sensitive spirit has drawn closer to it and made worthy of knowing and loving equality"—note the shrewd arrogance of this formulation—in order to assure his listeners that "there is nothing so just nor so good as the people, so long as they are not provoked by an excess of oppression"—another qualification meant to provide an excuse in the event of violent outbursts that could not easily be justified by appeals to justice and goodness. At this point Robespierre was still careful not to claim that he was himself one of the people; he limited himself to magnifying the sentiment that drew him nearer to them and that permitted him to say, "[I]t is among them that one finds, beneath an outward manner that we call coarse, honest and upright souls, and a common sense and a vigorous spirit that one would long search for in vain among the class that despises them." The division among classes was also a moral division: "The people demand only the necessities of life, they ask only for justice and to be left in peace; the wealthy lay claim to everything, they seek to encroach upon everything and to dominate everything." And this division of appetites was mirrored by a political division: "The interest of the people is the general interest, that of the wealthy is the particular interest." Thus the people are the soul of "this glorious Revolution that must cause the world to shake in order to regenerate it," as Robespierre replied to Abbé Raynal, who had permitted himself, secure in the prestige of his reputation as a prophet of liberty, to denounce, in a letter to the Constituent Assembly, the anarchy and disorder caused by popular protests. The people, Robespierre emphasized, were at once the "object, cause, and support" of the Revolution. Raynal had repudiated the people, portraying them as "a horde of brigands that must be subdued," failing to understand that such disturbances as they caused were "the natural effect of every revolution and the necessary crisis of liberty."

This argument was given its definitive form in the *Adresse aux Français* of July 1791. There Robespierre held that "this interesting and numerous class, designated until now by the word *people*, is the natural friend and indispensable guardian of liberty," because its condition renders it impervious to the many impulses that lead the privileged classes to pursue their particular interest and therefore to promote inequality. The people are "neither corrupted by luxury, nor depraved by pride, nor carried away by ambition, nor agitated by all the passions that are opposed to equality." Destitution causes the good of all to be obvious to them: "[T]heir temperament, their weakness, and their very poverty make justice and the protection of the laws necessary to them." Here we encounter perhaps the earliest version of the argument that caused the industrial proletariat to be seen a few decades later as the class responsible for achieving human emancipation everywhere, by transforming its radical alienation into a community of shared liberties.

Even if Robespierre cannot be said to have been a protosocialist or Marxist, his vision of the people spontaneously joining together on behalf of the general interest was immediately to have serious political consequences. Not only did it prevent the people from being seen as they really are, animated by diverse and often contradictory interests and passions, but it also fixed a goal for the Revolution: to create a society in which the longings of its citizens would be indistinguishable from the general interest as a consequence of the potentialities that the people contained within themselves, if only they would be permitted them to express them—in

other words, a society from which everything that is not of the people
has been eliminated. But while the equality of the rights of each person
has as its correlate, in the abstract, the general power that is exercised
in the name of all, Robespierre was silent with regard to how, as a practical matter, this power could be brought into being. In postulating the
existence of a social actor that happens to be the "most numerous class,"
in which the theoretical aggregation of individual potentials is realized,
he sidestepped the most difficult question of all—the political question of
what sort of regime is required by a society based on rights and what sort
of constitutional mechanisms are proper to it. What is more, he failed to
take seriously not only the universality of rights, which applies equally to
individuals who are not of the people, but also, and above all, the consequences of granting these same rights to all citizens, each of whom wishes
to be free to pursue his own ends. Here we come to a tipping point, where
the ambition of giving the rights of man their fullest extension threatens
to give rise to a system of unprecedented oppression.

The intensification of this intellectual blind spot was inextricably inter-
twined with a change in Robespierre's personality, the innermost secret of
which it is futile to try to penetrate, but whose manifestations can rather
easily be detected. One thinks in this connection once more of the people.
I stressed earlier his caution in declaring allegiance to their cause before
the Constituent Assembly, taking care not to claim that he himself was
one of the people. In the debate with Brissot over the war, however, he
emphatically repudiated his former position. Brissot thought it a clever
move to call him a "defender of the people," so that the surprise of "hearing
him slander and debase the people" would be all the greater. In his speech
of 2 January 1792, Robespierre replied condescendingly, "Be aware that
I am in no way a defender of the people; never have I pretended to this
pompous title; I am of the people, I have always been that, I wish only to
be that; I despise anyone who claims to be something more than that." The
pride this false humility strains to conceal is too flagrant to warrant further
comment. Robespierre's insistence on identifying himself with the people,
when everyone knew he was not one of them, was meant to set him apart
from Brissot and his ilk and to establish his own exceptionalism—a status
that he began to cultivate in this same speech by calling attention to the
solitude that was his lot from the beginning:

> [I] was the one who knew how to displease all those who are not [of]
> the people, by defending, almost alone, the rights of the poorest and

most unhappy citizens against the majority of legislators; I was the one who constantly set the Declaration of Rights against all these distinctions calculated in proportion to the level of taxation. . . . ; I am the one who defended not only the rights of the people, but their character and their virtues . . . ; I am the one who consented to appear overwrought, obstinate, even arrogant, in order to be just.

Arrogance as a means of being just: the hauteur was justified by the nobility of the intent, which made it invulnerable to criticism. This egotism only came to be magnified in the months that followed.

What might be called Robespierre's Jacobin moment, in which he was unencumbered by any official duties and free to wholly dedicate himself to winning the battle of public opinion, was decisive in setting him on his future course. It was then that he established his political base, while at the same time molding it in his own image and impressing upon it his own sense of personal destiny. The fact of the matter, of course, is that he had lost the debate over the war, the central episode of this period. He had not managed to persuade; he found himself in a minority among the elite of the patriotic camp, his usual supporters, even if his isolation should not be exaggerated. But from this controversy, by once more turning the appeal to popular sentiment against the dominant view—his opponents, led by Brissot, represented the majority opinion in the Legislative Assembly, where they were to prevail—he emerged, again owing to his steadfastness in opposition, with his prestige not merely intact, but actually fortified. This is what enraged Guadet, who on 27 April denounced Robespierre as "a man who, whether [by] ambition or misfortune, has become the idol of the people." An echo of this idolatry, attested by many witnesses, both friendly and hostile, may be heard in reading reports of the turbulent meetings of the Jacobins. Robespierre, as a minority voice, benefited from the noisy support, unconditional and sometimes deafening, of the audience in the public galleries; these spectators played an important role in the course of the Revolution, one wishes more were known about them. Another one of Brissot's allies, Réal, had accused Robespierre, a few weeks before Guadet, on 2 April, of "exercising in this society, perhaps without knowing it, and surely without wishing it, a despotism that weighs upon all the free men who compose it." Strong words—but they give some idea of the depth of feeling that the power of opinion in Robespierre's favor aroused among his opponents.

A few days earlier, on 26 March, there had been another incident involving Robespierre and Guadet, again a significant one. The pretext was

Robespierre's use of the term "Providence" in the draft of a speech in which he called for a reexamination of the question of war in light of the new situation created by the death of Emperor Leopold II of Austria. The term was unacceptable to Guadet, a freethinker, who objected that there was no point in "working so courageously in order to free people from the slavery of despotism" if it meant "placing them under the slavery of superstition." This presented Robespierre with another opportunity to engage in one of those exercises in self-justification that were now becoming common with him, in which the recollection of his deeds—or, as in this case, the restatement of his convictions—was inseparable from an obsessive concern with himself. For Robespierre, beneath what might have appeared to be mere quibbling over words there was a symbolic issue of considerable importance, setting Rousseau's deism against the unbelief of the *philosophes*. Hence the vehemence of his riposte, which manifestly startled his listeners. He began by brushing aside Guadet's objection: "Uttering the name of the divinity can in no way lead citizens into superstition." To his mind, this name encompassed the "eternal principles on which human weakness steadies itself before throwing itself into the arms of virtue." He then embarked upon an impassioned profession of faith, reasserting the supernatural character of the Revolution but then suddenly veering off into a personal confession of unexpected intimacy. The idea of an eternal being—a being "that has an essential influence on the destinies of nations, that seems to me to watch over the French Revolution in a quite particular way"—was "a heartfelt sentiment, a sentiment that is necessary to me; and how could it [not] be necessary to me, subjected [as I was] in the Constituent Assembly to passions of every kind and every manner of vile intrigue, and surrounded by so many enemies, [for it] has sustained me? Alone but for my soul, how could I have borne labors that are beyond human strength, had I not raised up my soul?"

Robespierre's indictment of atheism was to figure prominently in his career from this point onward, culminating in its institutionalization as the cult of the Supreme Being. What interests me for the moment, however, is the remarkably personal manner in which it was first expressed. It is not a philosophical conviction that speaks; it is a heart that opens up and confides. It is the "I" of a "sensitive man" to which Robespierre gave voice, in what amounted to an indirect glorification of his heroic solitude in the face of so much hostility and corruption. One may well wonder whether this kind of exhibitionism, altogether unusual for the period, was not one of the most powerful sources of the fascination, and indeed the sway, that his personality came to exert and that was manifested by the "frenzy," the "transports," and the "ecstasy" that we are told punctuated his interventions.

What seems clear is that Robespierre was by no means immune to the effusive praise that was heaped upon him. A craving for popularity took root in him and flourished. To be sure, preliminary indications of this aspect of his character can be found in earlier speeches. It was already well established in the *Adresse aux Français* of the summer of 1791, where the transition from self-justification to self-celebration was given a rhetorical foundation in victimhood. The most remarkable instance is Robespierre's portrayal of himself there as a victim of the obligation to sing his own praises: "A profound malice is directed against a man, a kind of accusation that forces him to justify himself in respect of things that are advantageous to him and thus to arouse the hatred and envy of those who bear him ill will." A victim, too, of the obligation to remind his listeners that the "blessings of the people" are purchased only "at the cost of the hatred, calumnies, and vengeance of all the powerful enemies of reason and humanity." But it was in the spring of 1792, when the growth of unrest and the approach of war began to sow doubt in people's minds, that this propensity asserted itself almost to the point of taking hold of his whole being. It reached its height in Robespierre's speech of 27 April, in which he responded jointly to Brissot and Guadet—the latter, it will be recalled, having reproached him for welcoming and encouraging popular idolatry—by inviting Guadet to apply the ancient law of ostracism to him. It will also be recalled that Robespierre was the one who had inaugurated hostilities with the sensational request a few days earlier, amidst the general nervousness created by the declaration of war on 20 April, that a date be set when he would disclose "a plan of civil war presented to the Assembly by one of its members." This had the effect of casting suspicion on his adversaries in the war party, with the further result that first Brissot, then Guadet, each in his own way, attempted to discredit the promised revelations in advance. When the day came, however, there were no revelations. The large crowd that had gathered at the Jacobin Club out of curiosity was treated instead to an altogether different spectacle. As one witness summed it up: "One was eager to know on what facts so important a denunciation could be based. Futile hope! Instead of laying them out, M. Robespierre delivered his own panegyric." Yet another helping of celebratory self-justification intended for public consumption—which did not prevent his audience, in spite of the deception, from receiving it with rapturous delight.

This speech, a carefully prepared anthology of sorts, merits closer examination than I am able to give it here. Let me simply point out a few salient features. It is remarkable, to begin with, for the insight it provides into the ways by which what is, after all, only the psychology of one individual can take on a political dimension. The whole rhetorical construction depends upon a central mechanism: denial. It is this device that opens the speech and closes it. There was nothing personal at issue here, Robespierre assured his listeners, nothing to do with himself: "[T]he cause of the people is the sole object of this entire dispute." He hastened to draw the lesson at the very outset: "Beware of thinking that the destinies of the people are attached to a few men." Once more Robespierre disclaimed all responsibility for the dispute. It had its origin in the attacks directed against him on all sides: "The newspapers of all the parties leagued against me try to outdo one another in slandering me." He did not complain about it, as he was fond of saying; quite the contrary, "I very much like it that they accuse me." The phrase was meant ironically, but no doubt it revealed a bit more than he wished—something like: I am very pleased to have to justify myself before the "court of public opinion," the only "truly sovereign" tribunal. Moreover, how could he fail to respond when "these sorts of attacks are directed less against persons than against the cause and the principles that they defend"?

Robespierre's claim to have no personal interest in the matter quickly gave way to a plea in his own defense. The unfortunate Brissot had made the mistake of questioning his right to criticize his opponents: "What have you done to earn the right to find fault with my conduct?" Robespierre at once seized upon this welcome opportunity to recapitulate his past achievements. He began by repeating a favorite theme: "I have spoken of myself only when I have been forced to repel calumny and to defend my principles." No less instructive was his recollection of the conversion that he claimed to have experienced on the occasion of his arrival at the Estates General in 1789: "The spectacle of these great assemblies awakened in my heart a sublime and tender sentiment that forever bound me to the cause of the people." Robespierre's listeners could not have helped but help recall Rousseau's conversion: "From that moment I understood the moral and political truth proclaimed by Jean-Jacques, that men sincerely love only those who love them; that only the people are good, just, magnanimous, and that corruption and tyranny are the exclusive prerogative of all those who scorn them." By invoking Rousseau, Robespierre was able to discredit his adversaries while reminding them that they owed their political position in the first place to the Legislative Assembly—"What have I done? Oh! Something important, no doubt. I gave Brissot and Condorcet to France." To what did these men owe their election if not the "great example of disinterestedness" that originated with him and on account of which the Constituents had renounced their own eligibility for reelection? But his main line of attack consisted in likening them to the *philosophes*, who, while they "combatted and ridiculed the priests," also "courted the great and adored kings"; above all, "they persecuted virtue and the genius of liberty in the person of Jean-Jacques, the sacred image of whom I perceive here, of this true philosopher, who, alone of all the famous men of that period, in my opinion, was worthy of these public honors that in the meantime, through intrigue, have been prostituted to political charlatans and contemptible heroes." In this way, several birds were killed with one stone. What amounted to a review of the busts lining the hall of the Jacobin Club concerned as much the past as the present—not only Voltaire, Rousseau's enemy, but also Mirabeau, formerly an ally who had had ended up being repudiated in death for his embrace of corruption and tyranny. Following Rousseau's illustrious example, Robespierre portrayed himself as a victim, persecuted by the disciples of those who had persecuted the only true friend among the *philosophes* whom the people could depend on, and for the same reasons. "You dare to accuse me of wishing to mislead and flatter the people! But how could I? I am neither the messenger, nor the mediator, nor the tribune, nor the defender of the people: I am one of the people myself!" Here we find the same assertion of popular identity brandished against Brissot earlier, only now it takes on its full philosophical, moral, and political meaning.

One of the criticisms of his conduct for which Robespierre was evidently determined to exact retribution involved his recent resignation as public prosecutor. This decision had given rise to rumors, exploited by his enemies, among them even the suspicion of collusion with the "Austrian committee." Rejecting these gross slanders furnished him with an opportunity to clarify the role he intended to play in the future. He had stepped down, he explained, when he realized that it would leave him "no time for the duties of public service [more] generally." In this regard he had merely obeyed his civic conscience: "I prefer to maintain the freedom to frustrate the plots hatched against the public's safety." He had acted in accordance with his duty as a citizen, namely, to "sacrifice one's particular interest to the general interest." Explanation then abruptly assumed the aspect of prophecy, while again striking an intensely personal note, when Robespierre declared that his unqualified devotion to the fatherland extended even to the point of making the ultimate sacrifice: "The heaven that gave me a soul passionately fond of liberty and that caused me to be born under the domination of tyrants, the heaven that prolonged my existence until the reign of factions and crimes may call upon me to trace with my own blood the path that must lead my country to happiness and liberty; gladly do I accept this sweet and glorious destiny." This was not a new premonition; he had already mentioned it on several occasions, most notably after the crisis of 17 July 1791. But here again it acquired additional significance as the organizing principle of the image he wished to project of himself—a principle closely linked with another consideration: the duty owed to future generations. He had spoken of this duty earlier that year, on 11 January, in a speech on the war ("Sweet and tender hope of humanity, nascent posterity, you are in no way foreign to us; it is for you that we confront all the blows of tyranny."); its invocation in the speech of 27 April naturally accentuated the portent of his death as a martyr. What would it matter if he were to succumb to the condemnation and the lies of his enemies, so long as he could count on "the belated assistance of time, which must avenge a betrayed humanity and oppressed peoples"?

Robespierre concluded this unflagging defense and illustration of himself with a superb disclamatory pirouette: "There you have my apology— no doubt I have said enough for you to see that I had no need of one." He had elaborated it at such length, in other words, only to show its perfect uselessness! Additionally, and in the same manner, he held out an olive branch to his opponents that strongly resembled a declaration of war. It began, after all, with an unmistakable threat: "I could wage offensive war no less effectively than defensive war"; and it closed with an ultimatum: "If you reject [my proposal], keep in mind that no consideration, no power can prevent the friends of the fatherland from fulfilling their duties."

No matter that this piece of egocentric eloquence was enthusiastically received—there were calls for it to be printed at once and distributed to the public—there were skeptics within the patriotic camp and even among Robespierre's usual supporters. Unsurprisingly, the pro-Brissot press heaped ridicule upon his habit of celebrating a cult "of which he was at once the priest and the god," by burning "an insipid incense on his own altar for an hour." But one sympathetic journalist, Gorsas, felt obligated to issue a warning: "We invite M. Robespierre to mistrust himself. We invite him to persuade himself that, as he is not a god, he may sometimes be mistaken; we invite him above all to dispel an impression that every day becomes more deep-seated in certain minds, that he seeks to win over the people by never forgetting to apostrophize them in each one of his speeches." A resounding article in the *Révolutions de Paris* took the warning a step further, in the form of an "Adresse à Maximilien Robespierre" (apparently written by the newspaper's editor, Sylvain

Maréchal). It began by observing that "this same man about whom there
had only been opinions [has now] become a problem, even in the eyes of
a rather large number of patriots." The reason for this, the author went
on to say, now addressing his subject directly, was that the atmosphere
of the clubs and "the vapors from the incense that is burned there for you
[have gone to your head]." This climate revealed "the secret of the chink in
your armor," namely, "a weakness for praise administered in large doses."
Whence the apostrophe: "Robespierre, the patriots are not pleased that
you make an exhibition of yourself." And the further insistence on deplor-
ing so unseemly an "eccentricity":

> The patriots who wish you all the best, who esteem you and who would
> love you, if your pride did not place a barrier between you and them,
> cannot refrain from saying: what a shame that he does not have that
> old-fashioned bonhomie, the usual companion of genius and the vir-
> tues! Robespierre is sometimes eloquent; he abounds in noble ideas
> and fine sentiments; his motives are admirable. If only he could forget
> himself a little more!

It will be plain, then, that the metamorphosis of Robespierre's personality had hardly gone unnoticed. Indeed, all the grievances against him
that were to be articulated during the great confrontation with the Girondins in 1793, and then during the latent conflict among the Montagnards
that culminated in Thermidor the following year, are to be found on this
occasion in the spring of 1792. Later they were to assume the same form;
only the words were different.

From Psychology to Politics

In order to make sense of this disturbing transformation, let us begin by
trying to determine whether its significance has not been overstated. The
author of the unsigned editorial in the *Révolutions de Paris* himself wondered, by way of conclusion, whether he had not granted too much importance to "the follies of an individual's amour propre." The answer that has
generally been given, even by those historians who notice this aspect of
his character, is that no very great weight should be assigned to it. I maintain, to the contrary, that it had a central and decisive influence on Robespierre's behavior. We are not dealing here with a personal characteristic
that interacts and blends with a multitude of others so thoroughly that
it has little consequence of its own. In this case an element of individual
psychology acquires a political dimension to the extent that the spectacle

of oneself becomes a collective identifier and determines one's course of action—a course that might have remained merely potential, but that circumstances were to make real.

The innermost impulses that gave rise to Robespierre's conduct are inseparable from a body of ideas that coalesced with them to form a system. It is not the development of his personality from childhood that concerns us here; it is how the events of the Revolution and the cause to which he had devoted himself combined to transform his personality at a crucial moment, and what they caused it to mean for others. It would be a simple matter if this tendency to self-celebration derived merely from the common vanity of someone seeking to create a favorable image of himself. But something altogether different is at work here, I believe, an extension of the self through its projection and dissolution in something greater than itself. Robespierre did idealize himself, to be sure, through his idealization of the people, but his identification with this idealized people was total and absolutely sincere. In no way can he be seen as an ordinary demagogue who cynically flatters the people solely for his own benefit. Robespierre's disinterestedness was complete and beyond question. He was animated by a sort of sacrificial narcissism; his aspiration to disappear behind a higher calling, which had the effect of magnifying his own exceptionalism, blinded him to himself. But this glaring contradiction is precisely what allowed him to personify the impersonality of revolutionary ideals in its purest form, what allowed him to be admired as an unrivaled example of the individual citizen's devotion to the public welfare. Inevitably, however, this same contradiction led to a profound difference of opinion: some saw only an honorable will to self-abnegation, considering Robespierre an example to be generally imitated; others only a self-serving infatuation with the image of a solitary seeker of justice.

It is impossible not to hear an echo of Rousseau's *Confessions* in all of this. Robespierre was not content simply to uphold Rousseau's reputation as a political theorist. Rousseau had impressed him no less forcefully as a model for living, the first to dare to portray himself "in every way true to nature." It was this unforgettable example that no doubt inspired Robespierre's attempts at self-justification and the image that he sought to present of himself. But there was an essential difference. The transposition of his impersonality to the political sphere transformed its meaning, so that it became the soul of a revolutionary struggle. Whereas Rousseau's singular truth was the truth of a private man, alienated from his peers and cut off from society, Robespierre affirmed his solitude in the midst of a public battle for the regeneration of mankind. His ambition was to entirely efface the private man to the benefit of the public man, who wishes only to work on behalf of the general interest, undistracted by the least egotistical motivation. If the tendency to self-promotion served to glorify his matchless virtue, the guiding intention by contrast was to dissolve his personal heroism by merging it with the naturally virtuous unity of the people. In this lies the fatal contradiction that was to decide his destiny in large part, as well as the fate of the Revolution that he came to dominate.

The effects of this contradiction were many and powerful. On the one hand, the self-image that he constructed in a hall of mirrors with allies and adversaries alike ordained him to be the master of the Revolution. It made him the embodiment of the principles that the Revolution ought to inculcate in every citizen, the exemplar of a kind of selflessness that would bring about the fusion of individual wills in a sovereign union of the people. It endowed him, in other words, with the authority of a guide. Whence the recurrent accusations of dictatorial behavior that were to hound him in the months to come, charges that were as inevitable as they were misconceived. Robespierre's self-image was part of his innermost being, as curious as this may have appeared to observers at the time. History provides us with no other example of someone who succeeded in objectively exercising a kind of dictatorship without subjectively putting himself in the position of a dictator, which is to say, as a practical matter, without providing himself with the means of actually exercising dictatorial power. His language was dictatorial, not his person.

On the other hand, this self-image, of which he became the prisoner, ruled his behavior. His identity, based on an identification with the people, virtuous by definition, initially asserted itself as a way of interpreting persons and events and acting upon them. It was not only a driving force, but a powerful filter as well, setting him apart from his colleagues. He wished only to be himself—precisely in order not to be someone who was trapped by the particular circumstances of his existence, incapable of looking beyond his own interests, and for that reason "corrupt" from the point of view of the public good. A typical remark in this connection occurs in the speech of 27 April 1792, where he dismissed suspicions that he was taking part in a concerted campaign of some sort: "My opinion on everything having to do with this subject is [my own], independent, isolated; my cause and my principles have never depended, nor do they depend now, on those of anyone." It is tempting to ascribe such a claim to the pride of a private man, and reasonable moreover to suppose that his privacy furnished a basic predisposition—but only as the basis for something quite different, namely, the reputation for incorruptibility of a public man determined to obey only the voice of the general interest, who held himself aloof from others in order to hear this voice more clearly. This is what distinguished his personal authority from that of ordinary political leaders, who are accustomed by contrast to exploit popular sentiment for their own private purposes. Robespierre dominated by the power of his austere rhetoric, never allowing himself to get carried away.[1]

Inwardly, this solitary disposition imposed a rigid and blinkered way of looking at the world. Faced with the incomprehension, the malevolence, and the hostility of men animated by unpatriotic passions, Robespierre's isolation made it all the likelier that he would meet with a violent end, the victim of his own inflexibility. Outwardly, notwithstanding this inevitable adversity, or perhaps because of it, his isolation allowed him to indicate not only the direction needing to be followed, but also the goal needing to be attained. By its very nature, this goal left no room for compromise. Between virtue in the service of the public welfare and corruption that knows only selfish interests, there was no middle ground. Accordingly, the opposition encountered by a man devoted to virtue could only be suspected of arising from shameful motives. And as the hold of corruption is immense, fierce resistance had to be anticipated in the form of malign intrigues, secret plots, and permanent conspiracies aimed at thwarting high-minded efforts to give new life to the nation. There was no guarantee that corruption would not triumph in the end, by crushing a vast uprising of the people and indefinitely postponing the achievement of the mission undertaken by the Revolution. True patriots knew they were putting their lives on the line.

Here again Robespierre's tendency to suspicion, his inflexibility in the face of contradiction, and his sacrificial melancholy can be seen merely as personal idiosyncrasies, the oddities of a psychology that generations of

---

1. Marat had judged Robespierre well in this respect. Desperately in search of a candidate dictator, Marat was greatly disappointed by a conversation with him in January 1792. The exchange served only to strengthen the impression he had formed of Robespierre from a distance. "This interview," he wrote in the 3 May 1792 issue of *L'Ami du peuple*, "confirmed me in the opinion I had always had of him, that he combined with the intelligence of a wise senator the integrity of a genuinely good man and the zeal of a true patriot; but also that he lacked the foresight and the daring of a statesman." Speaking before the Convention's Committee of General Security in May 1793, Marat was still more specific: "I believe that ambition has never come near Robespierre's person, unless it is that of holding forth from the rostrum. He has been accused of contemplating a tribunate, a dictatorship, but he is so little suited to being a party leader that he avoids any group in which there is turmoil and pales at the sight of a drawn sword." See Jean-Paul Marat, *Œuvres politiques, 1789–1793*, edited by Jacques de Cock and Charlotte Goetz, 10 vols. (Brussels: Pôle Nord, 1989–1994), 10:6538.

biographers have labored to interpret with uneven results. But that tells us nothing about the impact these traits came to have on the course of events, about the mobilizing fascination they exercised, about the urgent sense of conviction they inspired among a great number of actors who felt no temperamental affinity with Robespierre himself. These traits must be detached from the peculiar psychology of one man and placed in a broader context. They acquired a larger significance by virtue of the fact that they were bound up with a political vision to which they gave practical expression. No doubt Robespierre felt he had to act as he did in order to present himself as the preeminent incarnation of the spirit of an evolving revolution. But had he contented himself with displaying these extraordinary characteristics, and nothing more, he would have remained but one actor among others.

CHAPTER THREE

From the Authority of
Principles to the
Struggle for Power

IT WAS ALTOGETHER as though the event had suddenly changed his personality. In the aftermath of the storming of the Tuileries Palace, on 10 August 1792, Robespierre was no longer the same man. The orator, the man of principles who had kept his distance from the insurrection (though no doubt he had prior knowledge of it), was transformed into a man of action—not in the streets, but in the Legislative Assembly. There he was in his element. On 11 August, he was elected to represent his municipal electoral ward (or neighborhood "section") in the Commune of Paris, the new power that had emerged from the popular movement. On 12 August, he became the Commune's spokesman before the Assembly and quickly established himself as its most prominent voice, if not actually as its chief source of inspiration. Shortly thereafter, as head of the electoral assembly charged with nominating deputies from Paris for election to the Convention, the successor to the Legislative Assembly, he arranged matters with consummate tactical skill. The noble appeals of the past to disinterestedness were now forgotten. He was determined to play a leading role in the work of the Convention and to place his allies in positions of influence. It was as a party leader, imperious and wily, that he now set to work. The hour of the man of power had come.

The August uprising appears to have persuaded him of the providential character of the Revolution, not least for having magnified its historic significance, which now could favorably be compared to the landmarks of antiquity. Thus on 14 August, speaking on behalf of his Paris district, the

Section des Piques, Robespierre proposed that a monument be erected to the memory of those "citizens who died on 10 August 1792 fighting for liberty." In support of this motion he went on to say:

> Let us manage to reckon what we are worth. What are the acts of hero-ism that expelled the petty tyrant of a small country next to the tri-umphs that we achieved over despotism and intrigue in order to avenge the cause of all humanity? Others have established more or less just governments; you alone, people of France, have fought to establish on earth the immortal reign of reason, justice, and equality.

How could one fail to see the sign of divine intervention in this unfore-seen upheaval that altered all calculations, pushed back the boundaries of what until then had seemed possible, and forced the revolutionaries to reconsider what a regime based on liberty might actually look like? How could one resist putting one's body and soul in the service of the new movement that had emerged, when one felt called upon to carry out the mission of guaranteeing the rights of the people? In Robespierre's eyes, the people had at last demonstrated both their power and their wisdom. "Far from having become boisterously and aimlessly agitated," he wrote in his *Adresse aux représentants de la Commune* of 1 September, "they sol-emnly reclaimed the exercise of their rights, and [in all of the forty-eight Paris sections] appointed delegates invested with full authority to ensure public safety and liberty. A grand and sublime conception, without which the insurrection would have flowed out as a torrent, leaving no trace." In other words, they were able to give lasting political form to what might otherwise have been an uprising of no consequence—another triumph due solely to the will of the people, who work "miracles" and who ask no more of their representatives than that they maintain "direct communication" with the nation, forming a "union" that will allow the great undertaking assigned to them to be accomplished. Thus strengthened in his convic-tions, and all the more sure of his vocation, Robespierre took his seat at the Convention on 21 September 1792.

This meant resuming his role in opposition, to begin with, only now the challenge facing him was still more daunting. For obtaining a pre-ponderant influence in Paris was one thing; representing the whole of the country was another. If his adversaries in the *faction brissotine*, beginning with Brissot himself, had been ousted from the capital by the maneuvering of his side, they were elected in the provinces. What is more, they com-manded a majority in the Convention, thanks to the support of a large number of moderate deputies from the departments, who were at the very least preoccupied, if not frankly terrified, by the turn of events in Paris since the storming of the Tuileries. The massacres committed in the prisons from 2–5 September on the authority of hastily convened people's courts, which the new authorities did nothing to stop, whether owing to impotence or to silent complicity, cast a terrible shadow over the popular movement. Was that the "just vengeance of the people" that Robespierre had invoked on behalf of the Commune on 15 August? At the heart of the attacks that were at once brought against Robespierre at the opening session of the Convention was the question whether a divorce between the capital and the departments was imminent. This was the price to be paid for the preeminence he was acknowledged to enjoy, notwithstanding the omnipresence of Danton, the other great figure of the Parisian revolution. Scarcely had the Convention accomplished its most pressing task—decreeing the abolition of the monarchy and proclaiming the Republic—than the storm broke. On 25 September, the Protestant cleric Lasource, deputy of the Tarn, denounced "the despotism of Paris," called for the reduction of its influence to "a one-eighty-third share like each of the other departments," and warned against a dictatorial party in the assembly that was bent on exploiting the capital's disproportionate power. To this a deputy from Marseille hastened to add that the leader of this party was none other than Robespierre. Robespierre defended himself by asserting his usual claims to virtue and by protesting his complete lack of ambition—"far from being ambitious, I have always combatted the ambitious." He then denounced in his turn the plan of his adversaries to form a "federative republic" and asked that it be formally recognized that the "French republic will form a unique state, subject to uniform constitutional laws." On this point he was to prevail: at the end of the session, the Convention decreed that the Republic is "one and indivisible." With this first skirmish, the main lines of the great clash to come were drawn. The division that had manifested itself within the Jacobin Club during the preceding months was now carried over into the Convention, and what began as a battle for public opinion was rapidly transformed into a struggle for power, with fateful consequences.

None of this came as a surprise to Robespierre. The guiding ideas he had worked out furnished him with a natural explanation for it, which he presented as part of a "statement of principles" that prefaced the new edition of his newspaper, retitled *Lettres de Maximilien Robespierre à ses commettants* [Letters of Maximilien Robespierre to His Constituents] since he was now once more a deputy. So long as the monarchy still existed, he observed, "the nation seemed to be divided into two parties, the royalists and the defenders of the popular cause." With the abolition of the royal system, Robespierre went on, one might have thought that the cleavage would melt away. Not at all—it merely assumed a new form.

> Now that the common enemy has been brought down, you will see that those who were lumped together under the name of patriots will necessarily be divided into two classes. Some will seek to constitute a republic for themselves, others for the people. . . . The former will try to modify the form of government according to aristocratic principles and in the interests of the wealthy and government officials; the latter will try to establish it on principles of equality and in the general interest.

This political problem having finally been clarified, the moral implication was plain as well. If "the soul of a republic is virtue, which is to say love of country, that magnanimous self-sacrifice by which all private interests are combined to form a general interest," the patriotic class would inevitably be split between those who accepted the underlying principle and agreed to the sacrifice it entailed, and those who would rather protect their own interests, the "egoists" and the "corrupt." The upshot of this, Robespierre calmly concluded, was that there "are now only two parties in the Republic, one of good citizens, the other of bad citizens, which is to say one of the French people and the other of ambitious and greedy men." Evidently the struggle between these parties could only be a fight to the death.

Otherwise his fundamental philosophy had not changed; indeed, the substantive program he envisioned for the Republic is striking for its eminently liberal character. To his mind, the principal challenge had been met, since the Republic's foundations—"holy equality and the indefeasible rights of man"—had been laid with care, and the plan of the edifice largely sketched out. "[S]uch is the beauty of several of its parts that have remained intact," he said, "it may be that there is less for the new architects to do than is generally supposed." What was not settled, and required not only further thought but also imagination, was the fundamental problem posed by government in the strict sense. Its solution—"perhaps the masterpiece of human reason"—had hardly been "inquired into seriously even once in [the history of] the world." Robespierre started from the assumption that the "chief object of constitutional laws must be to protect public liberty against the usurpations of those who govern." For if "government is instituted to enforce the general will . . . , [each of] those who govern has an individual will; they are naturally inclined to [advance] their particular interest" (note that the possibility that citizens might be inclined to behave in the same fashion is not contemplated). Given this much, the conclusion naturally followed: "It is therefore necessary that the law cease-lessly remind [those who govern] of the common interest and that it be capable of identifying the magistracy with the republic." This argument is wholly consistent with the views that Robespierre had expounded two years earlier with respect to the responsibilities of a National Guard. The legislator's first concern "must be to guarantee the rights of citizens and the sovereignty of the people against the very government that they must establish." What makes the problem so difficult to solve is that the gov-ernment must nonetheless always possess "the force necessary to subject citizens to the yoke of the law." But this ancient imperative, until then the bane of political theory, had now somehow to be reconciled with the modern imperative of conferring upon the people "the force necessary to preserve its liberty." At bottom, the problem of republican government was how to find a way to do just this.

Curiously, in the same editorial, Robespierre wavered between an opti-mistic minimalism and a pessimistic maximalism. At first he imagined a swift outcome: "[W]e are in a rather fortunate situation, having been able in the space of a few months to consolidate the liberty of our country by means of a just government, without even having the right to pretend to be politicians of the first rank or legislators of extraordinary talent." But his tone became less assured once, having made a closer analysis of the sit-uation, he ran up against the vicious circle to which any attempt to found a new regime on the basis of revolutionary principles is bound to lead: "[I]n order to form our political institutions, we would need to have the morals that one day they ought to give us." Prophetically, he had put his finger on what ultimately was to be the stumbling block of the Revolution.

What to Do About the King?

For the time being, the need to equip the Republic with a Constitution took a back seat to political infighting. The pressure exerted by the major-ity in the Convention upon the deputies from Paris and the authorities of the Commune was unrelenting. On 28 October Robespierre responded with a major speech delivered before the Jacobins "on the influence of calumny on the Revolution." He attacked a "new faction," worthy heirs of Lafayette and the Feuillants, that pretended to reign by restraining "free republicans" and by deceiving the country about what was happening in the capital. "Are they less powerful than their predecessors? They are much more powerful. They accuse us of marching toward dictatorship— we who have neither army nor treasury nor official positions nor party;

we who are obstinate (like the truth), inflexible, uniform—I almost said unbearable (like principles)."

The nature of the offensive mounted by those whom Robespierre called "the well-mannered people of the Republic" became clear the following day, at the Convention, in the form of a bill of indictment drawn up by a man of talent and experience who was well acquainted with the difficulty of the exercise and who had already come into direct contact with Robespierre at the Jacobin Club a few months earlier—the novelist Louvet de Couvray, author of *Les Amours du chevalier de Faublas*. Even though Louvet's principal target was Robespierre, he did not omit to associate him with the "disruptive Commune," of which Robespierre was alleged to have made himself the leader, and with Marat, the "man of blood," from whom Robespierre had taken care to distance himself, but whose incendiary demagoguery he had nonetheless taken advantage of; proof of their secret complicity, Louvet claimed, was the manner in which he had arranged for Marat to be elected to the Convention. The strength of Louvet's philippic was its skillful cataloguing of the ways in which the Robespierrist faction had gained ascendancy among the Jacobins and subsequently acquired de facto control of Paris after 10 August. In effect, this party had succeeded in harnessing an idolatrous cult to the celebration of a fictive people: on the one hand, the presentation (and self-presentation) of Robespierre as "almost a god"; on the other, the identification of "a few hundred citizens" who formed the Jacobins' membership with, first, the people as a whole, and then with the people as a sovereign body. Because the idol had "time and time again attested the force, the greatness, the goodness, the sovereignty of the people, even claiming to be of the people himself," the effect of this self-identification was "to render [him], as it were, unattackable," since whoever dared to challenge the "adored leader" would immediately find himself persecuted "for having insulted the people." A crude but effective ruse, Louvet emphasized, for it was precisely this ruse that all brought "all usurpers" to power, "from Caesar to Cromwell." In Robespierre's case, the will to domination was realized, after 10 August, with his seizure of control over the Commune and the tyranny he exercised over the electoral assembly. Louvet's indictment followed automatically: "Robespierre, I accuse you of obviously seeking supreme power."

A rhetorically brilliant close, but the obviousness could not have been more doubtful. The implausibility of the evidence adduced by Louvet provided Robespierre with yet another of the oratorical triumphs on which his singular authority was based. Louvet made the mistake of interpreting his motivation as a quest for power in the ordinary sense, a claim that

Robespierre had no trouble demolishing piece by piece. A dictatorship without an army, without money, without an administrative apparatus? Marat? Marat's own words were enough to dispel any suspicion of collusion. The "despotism of opinion" exerted over the Jacobins? It was nothing other than "the natural influence of principles." This influence was "in no way the property of whoever enunciates them; it belongs to universal reason and to all men who wish to hear its voice." The insurrectionary Commune and its emergency measures? It is here that the new Robespierre appears, freed from his earlier cautiousness and led by his faith in the people to insist on their revolutionary dynamism. His speech culminated in this famous apostrophe: "Citizens, do you want a revolution without a revolution?"

Yes, no doubt, there were arrests, suspensions of civil rights, unlawful proscriptions, but what was the Revolution if not a break with the framework of existing law? "All these things were illegal, as illegal as the Revolution, as the fall of the throne and of the Bastille, as illegal as liberty itself." Yes, no doubt, only the people of Paris took part, but that was because "a great nation cannot rise up in a single movement," and the citizens who rebelled "must be regarded as tacitly acting on behalf of society as a whole." Yes, no doubt, "some apparent or real disturbances, inseparable from so great an upheaval" did occur, but "the world, posterity, will see the sacred cause and the exalted result of these events; you must look at them in the same way." Swept along by his compulsion to justify everything that had been done in the name of liberty, Robespierre then added this striking denial: "And do not think that I have invoked these eternal principles because we need to draw a veil over a few reprehensible actions." He went on to excuse the September massacres on the infallible ground that they proceeded from a "popular movement," claiming moreover that they were responsible for the death of only one innocent victim, the others being silently relegated to the hell of the "enemies of liberty."

All the arguments that were to be employed by the revolutionary rhetoric of the next two centuries are found in this speech, from the conjuring trick of describing action by a minority as the expression of a majority will to the pardoning of arbitrary, indeed monstrous means by appeal to the nobility of the ends sought. For the time being, at all events, Robespierre's decision to consolidate a revolutionary bloc by uniting it with its most radical wing, even if this meant absolving its least respectable elements of blame, set him on a vertiginous course leading to rupture with the established order and the heritage of the ancien régime without any new constitutional structure having been firmly put into place. Where did the illegality of liberty stop so long as a legal framework in which all liberties would have their place had yet to be constituted—a framework that would be all the more constraining as it could only derive from a competition among liberties? Robespierre's motivations for plunging into the tempestuous seas of radicalism without any shore on the horizon are destined forever to remain obscure, reducing us to mere guesswork. It is tempting to interpret them as a consequence of the need to make ever more extravagant promises to followers whom, in reality, he was following, in order to continue to appear to be their guide. The course of events and the manner in which Robespierre was led to explicitly dissociate himself from ordinary demagogues are enough to invalidate a purely political reading of this sort. A more persuasive alternative is to locate the causes of his behavior in the fiction that drove him forward all the more implacably as it blinded him to himself—this fiction of a people, united and just, who therefore in the end were bound to form a united and just polity.

Robespierre's clear, even overwhelming exoneration of the charge brought against him by Louvet must have done much to convince him to press his advantage when the so-called Louis Capet affair presented him with a propitious opportunity to go on the attack. Once the monarchy had been abolished, there remained the thorny question of what was to be done about the king. Should he be tried? Sentenced? To what punishment? Brissot's followers and the moderate republicans in the Convention favored a compromise solution that would allow Louis XVI's life to be saved, at the end of a trial conducted in strict accordance with regular procedure, in order to neutralize royalist sentiment, deeply rooted in a large part of the population, by showing leniency as far as possible. This position exposed them to suspicions that they were seeking one way or another to restore the monarchy—a situation that Robespierre and his followers moved at once to exploit to the fullest, and all the more urgently in view of their conviction that the king's execution was essential if royalist prejudice were to be eradicated. It seems probable that Saint-Just and Robespierre acted in concert to launch the offensive, the former through an address to the Convention on 13 November and the latter through an article published three days later in his newspaper. Robespierre's conclusion was clearer than his demonstration: "The National Convention must declare Louis a traitor to the fatherland, a criminal toward humanity, and punish him as such." The speech delivered by Saint-Just, making his first appearance before the Assembly, a stunning performance, was remarkable for its unyielding lucidity. Establishing the Republic required doing away with the tyrant who embodied its negation. Louis had to be judged not as a citizen, but as a "foreign enemy." "This man," Saint-Just declared, "must either reign or die."

Always anxious to have the last word, Robespierre amplified Saint-Just's argument in a very accomplished speech on 3 December. The matter of Louis XVI did not come under the head of ordinary justice, he explained; it was an extraordinary case in which the law that regulates the relations of citizens among themselves does not apply. This law supposes that a social pact has already been established. But here it was the very establishment of such a pact that was in question, against the background of a state of nature where the right of a nation to defend itself against "an enemy that conspires against it" took precedence. This meant having to push the logic of revolution to its limit. "The right to punish a tyrant and the right to dethrone him are the same thing. The one does not allow of different forms than the other: the trial of the tyrant is insurrection; his judgment is the collapse of his power; his punishment is what the liberty of the people requires." For the same reason, the prohibition of the death penalty (which, it will be recalled, Robespierre had advocated in the Constituent Assembly) did not apply in this case: "Louis must die in order that the fatherland may live." The following day he summed up his argument in still more energetic and direct terms, in the course of a stormy session, asking that it be "decreed in principle that no nation may give itself a king" and concluding, "in accordance with principles," that Louis XVI must be sentenced "at once to death, pursuant to an insurrection."

The difficulty is reckoning how much of this long and bitter debate, which did not come to an end until 21 January 1793, when the king was finally put to death, was due to intellectual conviction and how much to tactical maneuvering. It is clear that Robespierre had discerned the advantage that could be drawn from embarrassing his adversaries before the Rubicon of the king's execution had been crossed—an advantage that he thoroughly exploited in order to discredit them. Did not these delays, these quibbles, these equivocations over terms and conditions betray a secret intention to restore the monarchy? In his speech of 3 December, Robespierre suggested they did. Word of his accusation got around, and on 19 December he requested permission to address the Convention for the purpose of "denouncing a plot against public order." Speaking at the Jacobin Club a few days later, he described the nature of the conspiracy in much greater detail. The aim of Brissot and his followers, he explained, was to try people's patience to the point that a state of "great agitation" would provide the Convention with "grounds for leaving Paris" in view of the spreading unrest. "It is plain," he had said on 7 December, again addressing the Jacobins, "that the men who dominate us wish to found a new tyranny on the wreckage of the monarchy."

Robespierre did not succeed in obtaining approval for the immediate action he demanded. Louis XVI was found to be entitled to a proper trial. Robespierre nonetheless did manage, as the battle went on, to modify the balance of power within the Convention. The manner in which the members of the Assembly consulted among themselves when the time came to vote (on the king's guilt, appeal to popular opinion, and execution) showed that the influence of those Jacobins who had taken the name of "the Mountain" had grown appreciably in relation to that of Brissot and his allies, preponderant at the outset, who came to be identified with the Gironde.

In the meantime the tensions of the debate had precipitated the emergence of two distinct parties. Arguments became heated, and hatreds, implacable hatreds, took root on both sides. One of the harshest speeches was delivered to the Jacobins on 12 December by Robespierre, who set out to prove that "the nation is in the hands of rascals and that we have a detestable government led by a scoundrel." The scoundrel in question was Roland, the Minister of the Interior, to whom he transferred the animosity that formerly he had reserved for Lafayette. To Roland, supposed to have obtained for the *faction brissotine* a monopoly on power, he imputed the intention of "slaughtering the patriots." Predictably, this intemperate accusation led on to a solemn promise of sacrificial communion: "We will perish with you under the sword of the Brissotins." Robespierre's infamous outburst occurred in his speech of 28 December, in which he vehemently rejected the moderates' proposal that an appeal be made to the people with regard to the judgment of the king, taking care to distinguish the vast majority of the members of the Convention from the "twenty or so rascals" whom he held responsible for this nefarious plot. Their aim, he explained, was to "lead us back to despotism through anarchy." In this they were worthy heirs of the "schemers" of the Constituent and the Legislative Assemblies, whose misdeeds he then rehearsed at length. History was in danger of repeating itself—a recurrent theme in Robespierre's interpretation of events from now on. "I am frightened," he said frankly, "by the resemblance that I perceive between two periods of our revolution." The hydra of corruption did not cease to sprout new heads. It was in this speech that he employed a formula that was often to be misunderstood: "Virtue is always in the minority on earth." In its original context it had a very restricted purpose, namely, to challenge the principle of majority rule. I shall come back to this point. For the moment it is enough to observe that it is so consonant with the overall thrust, not only of this speech,[1] but also of Robespierre's mission, that it is tempting to see it as having a more general import. For it reflects the tragic willfulness of what was almost surely his deepest conviction. The battle for virtue needed all the more to be fought as it was lost in advance, given corruption's power of coming to life again; but no less did it give him new life as well, a means of transmitting his glorious lessons to posterity. The formula also reveals the perils of the very attitude it expresses: a readiness to exploit the political advantages of denunciation in order to reaffirm his own reputation for virtue, combined with a propensity to invent imaginary enemies as the occasion demanded.

Both these things are to be found here. One cannot help but be struck by the disproportion between the impassioned claims of parliamentary debate and what was really at stake. Was it absolutely necessary that the king be put to death in order for the Republic to be securely established? The question will be endlessly disputed, of course. The pity is that its implications could not have been assessed and debated more coolly at the time. The reckless accusations brought by Robespierre and his followers concerning the ulterior motives of Brissot's faction—a desire to restore of the monarchy, to institute despotism, even a dictatorship—lend plausibility to the idea that what was at issue was not any real substantive disagreement, but a pure struggle for power. What fundamentally separated Girondins from Montagnards, and what later historians were to invest with such great significance, was far from clear at this stage. What mattered was the Montagnards' growing reliance on the sans-culotte movement that was then taking shape in Paris, and the Girondins' concern to stay in touch with developments in the rest of the country, particularly by maintaining contact with minor provincial notables who did not necessarily regard them as their natural spokesmen—many of the Brissotins were from Paris, while few of the Robespierrists were sans-culottes. There is much to be said, then, for the view that Robespierre was essentially a tactician and, above all, determined to obtain power by discrediting his rivals. But it misses the main point, namely, the man's conviction, which, though it was no doubt associated with tactical skill, involved much more than that. Robespierre's behavior was, and was to remain, fully consistent

1. Here Robespierre remarked, on a somber personal note, "I see clearly that the system whose dangers I have demonstrated will destroy the fatherland; and I do not know what sad presentiment warned me that it will prevail."

with the revised assumptions that the revelation of 10 August had led him to adopt.

To begin with, he was persuaded that the execution of Louis XVI was indispensable for "consolidating liberty by a great example given to the world," as he was forever fond of repeating. He saw the king's death as a point of no return, placing his hopes in the symbolic impact that it could not fail to have. He explained what he had in mind a few days after 21 January, in the third issue of the *Lettres à ses commettants*: "The tyrant has fallen under the blade of the laws. This great act of justice has staggered the aristocracy, annihilated royal superstition, and created a republic." A month later, he was still more explicit a month later with regard to his confidence in the effects of this founding sacrifice:

> The punishment of the tyrant ... has disenchanted minds of this superstitious prestige that for twenty centuries of servitude and ignorance surrounded royalty. Now that the people have looked upon him with scorn, this antique idol crushed, by their order, under the axe of the laws, what fresh tyranny could be imposed on them? How will the bourgeois aristocracy, for example, be able to hoist itself up on the shattered pedestal of nobles, priests, and kings?

Today we deserve no credit for knowing, with the benefit of hindsight, that the conjurative efficacy of such purifying rituals is limited. To be sure, they do leave their mark on the popular imagination—no one can doubt the profound impression that the death of Louis XVI on the scaffold left on French memory—but they seldom succeed in exorcising the demons of a nation's sacral heritage. More often than not, they feed them.

The faith that Robespierre placed in these rituals is in any case readily understood. Even so, it does not explain the spirit of vindictiveness that caused him to lash out against his opponents. Here it is necessary to take into account Robespierre's visceral hostility to persons in positions of power, in which psychological motivations were entangled with political beliefs. Making sense of them in combination is not easy, but we must try. From the beginning, Robespierre had been convinced of the supreme odiousness of the king's ministers. The harsh rule of a king whom "the chance of birth has given us" could be endured, even if the people in that case had little freedom. His hatred was directed instead at the officials who effectively exercised power mainly for the purpose of keeping it. Their outstanding characteristic was a talent for intrigue, pride, ambition, cupidity—in short, corruption in the service of particular interests, by contrast with the virtue of a government that is identical with service to the general interest. The cardinal sin of Brissot and his followers in Robespierre's eyes was their entry into the government, when they had been elected to represent the people as deputies in the Legislative Assembly. Later, owing to their majority in the Convention, they came to dominate the government. This was the last straw. Robespierre's adversaries in the Assembly, men such as Guadet, Gensonné, and Vergniaud, were only "rascals," but Roland, the principal minister, was entitled to the higher rank in infamy of "scoundrel." To Robespierre's mind, the caution and reticence displayed by the Brissotins in respect of Louis XVI's execution was a sign of their connivance with the aristocratic system, of which their participation in the government was the most visible proof. The king's death, and with it the destruction of the monarchical principle, was the prerequisite for eliminating all its false superiorities, chief among them "royal superstition." He expressed this idea in striking terms in the course of the article of late February 1793 that I quoted from earlier: "The punishment of the tyrant has realized the principles of equality, which until then were only sterile axioms." More precisely, it opened the door to their realization, for "all the vices to which tyranny gave birth did not disappear with the tyrant; those who had prostituted themselves to him [now] prostitute themselves to pride, ambition, and cupidity. A corrupt minority of the nation battles against the healthy majority; not without advantage, because it is composed of the most learned men, the most skilled in intrigue, the most able in the art of speaking and persuading." But this advantage could only be momentary once the minority had been deprived of the fulcrum provided by the royal incarnation of inequality. This meant that the days of Brissot's faction were numbered.

As a consequence of the constitutional undertaking set in motion by the uprising of 10 August, Robespierre expected that the king's death and the imprisonment of his ministers, who had perpetuated the vices of despotism, would lead to the establishment of a regime of equality—a regime in which the people, the assembly that represents them, and the government that puts the laws into effect would henceforth be one. Rather unusually, Robespierre published a piece in his newspaper by a fellow Montagnard, Dubois-Crancé, that grouped the reasons for the division of the Convention in two "sections." This was in mid-December 1792, in the midst of the king's trial.

The Jacobins seek a genuine and *unique* republic, founded on the purity of the principles of the Declaration of [the] Rights [of Man], in which the law alone dominates, never an individual. The respectable people [*les honnêtes gens*, as Robespierre mockingly called them] seek a leader, whose will *sometimes* makes up for the deficiency of the law, in order to keep *in line* those *factious persons* who would dare *to disrupt society*, by reproaching this leader either for his corruptive depredations or for his despotism.

Dubois-Crancé did not go so far as to accuse the Brissotins of plotting to put Louis XVI back on the throne. He castigated them for making possible the establishment one day of a new dynasty, "in the shadow of a republic, which, like that of *the United States*, would be divided into many small states and have a general executive council and a *permanent president*." No leader, no internal dissension. This is why, he went on to say, the patriots wanted Paris to remain the "center of administration," because the size and the mixed character of its population prevented any "dangerous *local* motive" from arising. Two weeks later Robespierre developed a similar argument, again in his newspaper, rejecting accusations made by the Brissotins in connection with unrest in the capital. "Everywhere, gentlemen, the people have the same interest and the same principles. Paris is only a kind of general meeting, a continuous and natural federation that is ceaselessly renewed by the citizens of this vast state." From this it followed that to cast blame on Paris amounted to nothing less than blaming "the French people, the human race, public opinion, and the invincible ascendancy of universal reason." One is tempted to smile at this rhetorical extravagance. But it must be taken seriously. It testifies to the force of Robespierre's compulsion to be identified in the public mind with something larger than himself.

For the same reason, he rejected the idea that there might henceforth be a majority and a minority in the Convention. Obviously he recognized that voting was divided along partisan lines, but he discounted its significance: "There is nothing permanent about a majority, because it belongs to no one party: it is revised with each free deliberation, because it belongs to the cause of the people and to eternal reason." Necessarily, then, it is a majority constituted by "the good citizens." The purpose of parliamentary procedure in a republic, in other words, was not to give expression to the contradictions of society and the relative strength of opposing opinions; it was to make manifest the unity of the people and to discover exactly in what their interest consists, through a process of deliberation and debate that, as with any approach to the truth, will be tentative and uncertain at first, but sure in its final result. This is precisely what the overthrow of the central figure of the royal system was meant to achieve, in Robespierre's eyes, by denying the "ambitious" and the "proud" the means of raising themselves above the people in order to rule over them. Inevitably, then, in this light, the reluctance of the moderates to approve the king's execution was seen to be ominous: it could only result from a culpable resolve to prevent the Revolution from coming to fruition. The government of the people, secure in their rights, would emerge by itself from the break with the past, so long as this rupture were ruthlessly carried out.

Girondins versus Montagnards

In principle, the king's trial having now been concluded, the Convention was finally free, four months after it first convened, to turn to its official mission: drawing up a Constitution for France, which is to say translating the Republic into a set of workable institutions. In the event, nothing of the sort happened. The political struggle between the two camps, from now on implacably opposed to each other, got in the way. The Mountain sought to press its advantage and block Brissot and his supporters from winning approval for their own draft version, a remarkably sophisticated document in its democratic ambition, presented to the Assembly on 15 February 1793 by Condorcet on behalf of the Constitutional Committee. It fell flat, a victim of general indifference and Montagnard suspicions. The condescending tone adopted by Robespierre that very evening, speaking before the Jacobins, illuminated a tactic on which henceforth he was increasingly to rely: detaching the mass of moderate and undecided deputies, known as "the Plain" (also, more commonly, "the Marsh"), from the core of doctrinally committed Brissotins. There was no need for alarm, he assured his listeners, without going into details: "[T]he defects of this draft have been keenly felt," the "aristocrats" are few in number, the majority of the Convention is "pure"; "if we are calm and deploy reason in all its majesty, I guarantee you victory. The moment of the triumph of the true patriots is at hand." When Buzot counterattacked, on 15 April, demanding that debate bear primarily on "the basis of government," considering the urgency of the situation, Robespierre this time had interesting things to say about the substantive points at issue—evidence of the continuity of his thinking, even if tactical considerations were not far from his mind. His programmatic vision had not changed in the least. "What is the basis of the Constitution and of a government? . . . What is the end aimed at by the Constitution? It is the happiness of men, and consequently the preservation of their rights, of their safety, their liberty, and their property; it is therefore necessary, prior to establishing a government, to properly determine the nature and extent of rights, whose preservation is the object of the government." The argument in favor of haste was specious: "The [true] means of moving quickly," he maintained, "are to lay down principles from which it remains only to draw the consequences." At this point Robespierre promptly returned to the political imperatives of the moment, recalling at length the prior debate on the subject in the Constituent Assembly, which allowed him to liken his present adversaries to the "privileged orders" of days past and to include them among "those who wish for a despotic Constitution."

Quite apart from the paralysis induced by the struggle for power, circumstances were scarcely conducive to dispassionate discussion in the first months of 1793. The complexion of the war had changed with the entry of England, Holland, and Spain. More men and more money were needed. The organization of the army was of more immediate concern than constitutional arrangements. Political conflict within the Convention began to spread beyond the capital, with growing unrest in several cities, notably Lyon. Resistance to conscription aggravated tensions in the provinces, culminating in early March with the uprising in the Vendée. The massive issuance of *assignats* compounded inflationary pressures, worsening other problems in turn. Food shortages became acute, particularly in Paris, giving rise to popular protests that the violently radical Enragés claimed to have instigated. Taking advantage of this unsettled state of affairs, the Mountain was able to eliminate Brissot's faction and, between 31 May and 2 June, carry out a coup d'état.

Robespierre had early on given thought to the problem of food supplies and responded to it by making an important adjustment to his stated policy on the subject. The new position was first formulated in an "opinion" delivered on 2 December 1792. Its novelty consisted mainly in translating the problem into the language of rights, which led him to introduce a right to subsistence ("the means of existence") that was to be the cornerstone of the formal declaration that followed. In other respects, as a practical matter, it was typical of what might be called the methodological centrism that served as one of his most effective political weapons—a talent for distancing himself equally from two tendencies, one to excess, the other to moderation. In this case, on the one side, he took a liberal position on property and freedom of commerce; on the other, he yielded to tax accessors' demands that a maximum price be set for the sale of grain and called for vigorous public intervention in the market, the terms and conditions of which remained unclear, even if they were supposed to conform to "rudimentary notions of common sense."

It is instructive to compare this approach with the distinctly more realistic analysis presented three days earlier by Robespierre's young disciple and friend Saint-Just. With regard to the source of the problems faced in assuring adequate supplies, Saint-Just correctly pointed to the inflationary effects of the *assignat*. "What, in France, has upset the system of commerce in grains since the Revolution is the uncontrolled issuance of the currency." But this dysfunction was part of a larger moral and political disorder, which Saint-Just went on to frankly describe: "Our food supplies have shrunk to the extent that our liberty has expanded, because we are so preoccupied with the principles of liberty that we have neglected those of government. . . . Everyone wants a republic; no one wants poverty or virtue. Liberty wages war against morality, so to speak, and wishes to reign in spite of it." Whence a program in several stages proposing immediate remedies, the first of which was that "the quantity of paper [money] does not increase." Nevertheless it was essential not to lose sight of the principal difficulty, namely, that "what is involved are the evils of a revolution." It was a matter, Saint-Just emphasized, of "making a republic out of the wreckage and the crimes of a scattered people's monarchy, of establishing trust, of instructing hard-hearted men, who live only for themselves, in virtue."

Robespierre's answer to the problem, a piece of self-serving reductionism building on Saint-Just's argument, had a fairly clear ulterior motive: if the solution was simple and yet the problem remained, the reason could only be that those who were in a position to solve it chose not to, for suspect reasons. Given that "the soil of France produces much more than is necessary to feed its inhabitants," it followed that "the present shortage is an artificial shortage." It was caused by withholding commodities and cornering the market, by monopolistic practices and speculation. Consequently, the means for correcting these abuses were "as simple as they are infallible." What is more, "they injure neither the interest of commerce nor the rights of property." It sufficed to put these goods, which had been diverted from their natural function, back into circulation: "Let [the] circulation [of goods] be protected throughout the length and breadth of the republic; but let the necessary precautions be taken to ensure that circulation occurs." It was only a matter of "forcing grain merchants to sell [their grain] at market." This was not a policy that Robespierre had any intention of putting into effect. His purpose was to expose the ill will of those who currently governed the nation while professing concern for his needy fellow citizens. Politics first!

In February 1793, however, popular distress once more assumed the form of violent unrest, complicating Robespierre's discourse about the people. Having been outflanked on its left by the Enragés, the Mountain now had to wage a war on two fronts. Some idea of the quandary in which the Parisian uprising placed him may be had by considering the laborious explanations he felt obliged to give, in his newspaper to begin with and then at the tribune of the Jacobin Club. On 11 February he was called upon, together with Marat, to pacify a delegation from the Paris neighborhood sections whose petition concerning food supplies the Convention had refused to hear. Writing a few days later in the *Lettres à ses commettants*, in a tone of controlled anger, he made it clear that these delegates were not to be confused with the people for whom they claimed to speak. They were schemers who trifled with the people while pretending to serve them. "The motives of the people are always pure," he explained. "They can love only the public good, since the public good is only the interest of the people. But the intriguers, as sly as [the people] are simple, as depraved as they are good, seek sometimes to take advantage of their virtues, indeed of their righteous indignation, it must be said, in order to deceive them and then to put them in chains." This sort of manipulation was all the more dangerous as it did not seek merely to exploit fleeting emotions; it also sought to distort revolutionary principles by taking them "to an absurd extreme in order to discredit them." To the "declared enemies" of liberty it was now necessary to add its "disguised enemies," whose treachery—this, the height of perversity—consisted in exaggerating the claims of liberty to a destabilizing degree.

The prompt publication of this new line of defense did little to improve his position. Robepierre's embarrassment was still more palpable when he took the podium to address the Jacobins on the evening of 25 February, only hours after the looting of grocers' shops in Paris. How was he to square the fact of reprehensible disturbances with his fundamental conviction that "the people are never wrong"—a conviction, Robespierre reminded his audience, that he first publicly expressed when he was "under attack and friendless," before the course of the Revolution had forced him to qualify it in certain respects. His answer assumed the form of a denial in two parts: first, it was not really the people who took part in the looting, despite the presence of a few "honest citizens," but instead "wealthy men" disguised as sans-culottes; second, it could not have been the people, since they never rise up for "mere commodities." Then he went a step further: "The people must rise up, not to provide themselves with sugar, but to crush the brigands." Message understood: no one was in any doubt about the identity of these bandits, at least not for much longer, since on 9–10 March the most radical wing of the sectionary movement mounted a second insurrection, this time without any further consequence, calling for the overthrow of the Brissotins. This allowed Robespierre to begin preparing his next move.

The outcome of the struggle was suddenly determined by Dumouriez's betrayal in the wake of the military disasters in Belgium. His defection to the Austrians, on 4 April, following his arraignment by the Convention, had the effect of undermining the credibility of Brissot and his followers, who had placed their trust in him. In retrospect, it vindicated Robespierre's defiant lucidity in respect of the war party. He lost no time in exploiting an unanticipated opportunity to the fullest. On 3 April, he had drawn up a merciless indictment against the "conspirators" associated with this "counterrevolutionary general," whose "scheme has been to involve us in a disastrous war and then to divert it to the detriment of liberty." For us today, who know the rest of the story, the outcome seems to have been preordained: "I declare that I regard as the first of the measures [needing to be taken] the issuance of a writ against those who are accused of conspiracy with Dumouriez, notably Brissot." For the moment, his demand was met with no positive response, but it set the tone for what followed: a battle to the death. It was destined to be promptly decided.

At this juncture it will be useful to pause for a moment and more closely examine the significance of the legendary clash between Girondins and Montagnards, so greatly did it influence the image of Robespierre that was subsequently to take shape. No aspect of revolutionary memory is more perplexing. It had its origins in the unfortunate label "Girondins," which gained currency following the publication in 1847 of Lamartine's magnificent *Histoire des Girondins*, but which was seldom used during the Revolution itself (hence my use so far of the more common term, "Brissotins"). It has the disadvantage of making the group seem as though it were something like a party, which it scarcely was. It is not difficult to see why, from 1848 onward, an anachronistic reading came to be superimposed in the light of the socialist workers movement. But interpreting what was an essentially political conflict in terms of the class struggles peculiar to capitalist society is of no help whatever in understanding what it involved. This is not the place to take up the topic in detail. Until a new generation of historians is able to reconsider the episode more objectively, undistracted by the misleading perspectives of the nineteenth century, it may be enough to emphasize that Robespierre was neither more nor less "bourgeois" than Brissot or Pétion; and that the Montagnards did not more or less represent the lower classes (as one should say, rather than the "proletariat") than the Girondins—the two sides had a different relationship to them, which is not the same thing.

Where the two sides fundamentally differed was in their assessment of the political situation and of the responses it required. Against the background of widespread hardship produced by the economic disorganization of the ancien régime, the popular movement in Paris, with its forty-eight wards and its many political clubs, occupied a central place in this calculation. As Saint-Just memorably observed in his speech of November 1792 on food shortages:

> There is a hidden vulture in Paris. What do they do now, all those whose livelihood used to depend on the custom of the rich? Destitution gave birth to the Revolution, destitution may destroy it. We must determine whether a multitude that, not long ago, used to live on the superfluities, the luxuries, the vices of another class can live simply on the correlation of their individual needs.

The Girondins (I resign myself to using the term from now on) attached priority to reestablishing order through the reassertion of public authority in a stable constitutional framework. As Vergniaud was to put it very well in his speech of 10 March 1793, denouncing the attempt to eliminate traitors through the reintroduction of the Revolutionary Tribunal that same day, the part of the Convention that he claimed to speak for "regarded the Revolution as finished, from the moment when France was constituted as a republic. From this moment onward, [my party] considered it necessary to arrest the revolutionary movement, to restore calm to the people, and to promptly make the laws necessary to make [this calm] lasting." This program assumed that the unrest in Paris could be curbed in the name of the majority of the country's citizens. Hence the exemplary significance attached to bringing the authors of the September massacres to justice. In opposition to this, the Montagnards drew up a plan—a very vague one, it is true, but nonetheless highly suggestive—for an egalitarian republic whose principle could be summed up in a phrase due to Marat: "There must come a time when the republicans will have no leaders." The plan depended on the support of the avant-garde represented by the forces of insurrection in the capital, discreetly drawing a veil over their excesses as necessary while at the same time listening more attentively to their economic demands.

To what degree this more inclusive orientation issued from an authentic concern for justice or from a need to lay the groundwork for the conquest of power is a question that is unlikely ever to receive a satisfactory answer. Nevertheless it is clear that the Montagnards' program was rooted in a vision of society, property, and economic liberties that was quite similar to that of the Girondins. Their differences had to do with the extent of government regulation and intervention, not with the rules of the game; there was, of course, an additional nuance in the case of Robespierre—a moral one, associated with his abhorrence of the corruption that he believed almost inevitably accompanied wealth. As for the strictly political accusations brought against the Girondins, they bordered on demagogic fantasy. The Girondin appeal to the people during the king's trial concealed no tendency to "royalism." Similarly, one searches in vain for any hint of "federalism" in Condorcet's draft Constitution; the specter conjured up by the term was intended simply to divert attention from radical activism in Paris. The idea that popular election of the executive and the division of legislative power between two chambers made the draft an "aristocratic" document was simply deceitful. The charge that it would bring about an "aristocracy of the rich" would seem somewhat more arguable, were it not for the fact that the accusers knew no better than the accused how to achieve material equality in a free society, as Robespierre himself, in less troubled times, had had the honesty to admit. What we are dealing with here, in short, is a witch trial whose prosecutors, to the astonishment of posterity, allowed themselves to be so carried away by the political passions of the moment that they saw nothing improper about it.

It is quite true, however, that the unfortunate Girondins did not have the political resources they needed, that their thinking on constitutional matters was inadequate to the task at hand, and that, more generally, they were not able to work out what the situation demanded of them. Their preoccupation with establishing a legal system and restoring the smooth operation of the agencies of government as quickly as possible prevented them from appreciating how deep-seated the causes of popular discontent were and how feeble were the instruments they relied upon to cope with it. The utter thoughtlessness with which Brissot and his allies had urged France to go to war was matched only by the pathetic naïvete with which they contemplated the swift institution of a republican sovereignty that would be both efficient and peaceable. Not that their adversaries were much more enlightened in this regard. But the Montagnards were at least able to recognize the exceptional character of current events and determined to combat the threats to public safety that followed from them. The very vagueness of their ideas about the power of the people opened up the possibility of a regime with emergency powers, indispensable for supporting the war effort, curbing civil unrest, and maintaining order in the country. This was certainly not a formula for regular government, something that in more settled times they would rightly have been expected to provide, but the very excessiveness of their aspirations qualified them to preside over a revolutionary government and justify recourse to its extravagant methods. The fact of the matter is that they saved the Republic from foreign invasion and internal dislocation, even if in the end they proved to be incapable of making it a workable regime. This is why the French Revolution should be thought of as a tragedy—proof of a terrifying inability to realize the highest and most noble of human ambitions, namely, the ambition of a people to govern itself. There are those today who wish only to remember the nobility of the ambition, and others who wish only to see its ignominious failure. These one-sided views are equally misleading. They must be combined in order to explain why it should have been possible, eventually and in spite of everything, to overcome the miscarriage of the Revolution without once more undergoing the ordeals that accompanied it. Girondins and Montagnards, in establishing the Republic, had jointly posed a question that neither of them was able to answer: how could the power of popular sovereignty be firmly established, firmly enough that the power of the king would be forgotten?

Which Republic?

There is something dreamlike about the two months of April and May 1793, in which the antagonism of the two parties was finally to be resolved by the vicissitudes of political conflict, the emergency measures dictated by a dire situation, and a series of insightful debates about constitutional organization. The threat from foreign armies massed along the country's frontiers was at its height, the counterrevolution in the Vendée continued to spread, and provincial uprisings multiplied. Food shortages in Paris became still more acute, and unrest increased to the point that the Convention decreed a maximum price for grain on 4 May. Two exceptional institutions devised under the influence particularly of Danton to deal with the growing menace—the Revolutionary Tribunal and the Committee of Public Safety—were put in place without the manner in which they were to operate having been fully worked out. Partisan struggle was initially concentrated upon the controversy surrounding Marat, against whom the Girondins had managed to bring an indictment for having demanded that they be punished as "accomplices of Dumouriez." He was acquitted by the Revolutionary Tribunal on 24 April and triumphantly reinstated in the Convention, where his rhetoric became more heated than ever. The Paris sections then called for the dismissal of the Girondin deputies, at which point the battle turned into an open confrontation between the majority party of the Convention and the Commune of Paris. The insurrection planned by the leaders of the Commune began on the last day of May. On 2 June the Convention finally capitulated, agreeing to issue writs for the arrest of twenty-nine Girondin deputies and two ministers.

It was in the midst of this paroxysmal tension that the Convention debated the Constitution. During the course of a single session, on 15 April, the Assembly resolved at last to examine the draft proposed by Condorcet two months earlier, and the mayor of Paris, Pache, came in person to present the petition of the sections calling for the dismissal of the Girondins. This was the context in which Robespierre presented two of his most important contributions to revolutionary thought: his own draft version of the Declaration of Rights, on 24 April, and his reflections on the Constitution, on 10 May.

The conflict between the two camps having spilled over into the constitutional sphere, it is important not to concede a monopoly in this domain to the "statesmen," as Marat pointedly called the Girondins, and to recognize that the party of the "true patriots" possessed its own doctrine concerning the creation of a republic of and by the people. Moreover, for Robespierre it was a matter of defending and illustrating his stature as a legislator by comparison with the two other members of the Montagnard "triumvirate" that his enemies accused him of forming with Danton and Marat. They too had the ear of the people—as much if not more than he did—but Robespierre, though he lacked the stunning eloquence of the one and the talent for scathing invective of the other, had the advantage that he alone grasped the end that had to be attained. He was the one who understood the revolutionary movement and knew which direction it needed to take. There could be no excuse for depriving the French people of the benefit of his unique authority, not at a moment when, besieged by all the tyrants of Europe, they were determined to resist on behalf of happiness and liberty. Thus it was that Robespierre, theoretician of the Revolution of the Rights of Man, came forward to present his most recent reflections on the subject, even if the chance that they would receive the attention they deserved was exceedingly small—and this while announcing a dramatic change of position that was fatefully to entangle him in the terrible machinery of revolutionary government.

That liberty was in danger of being converted into its opposite came as no surprise. Robespierre himself was well prepared. Consider his response to an intervention by Buzot on 19 April, during a debate on the Declaration of Rights that, over Buzot's objections, he had succeeded in ensuring would take place prior to the debate on the Constitution itself. Buzot demanded that the Declaration provide for the unrestricted freedom of the press. To this Robespierre replied that while his arguments were "reasonable in themselves," they omitted a crucial exception made unavoidable by "revolutionary times," for "revolutions are made in order to establish the rights of man. One must therefore, on behalf of these rights, use all means necessary to assure the success of revolutions. Now, the interest of the Revolution may require that certain measures be taken to repress a conspiracy founded on the freedom of the press." The implications of this remark were immediately grasped, there being no doubt about the identity of the conspirators he had in mind: for months he had ceaselessly railed against the disastrous influence of the newspapers acquired by the Girondins. He had once more accused them, two days earlier, speaking at the Jacobin Club, of "corrupting public spirit"—to the point that the convocation of local assemblies urged by some for the purpose of electing a new national assembly could not fail to work to the advantage of the "counterrevolution." "Because the people have been led astray," Robespierre concluded, "an effort must be made to instruct them." Robespierre was now willing, in other words, to approve the suspension of the very rights the Convention was laboring to define, so that their reign might be more surely established, by proscribing the undue influence of "the rich and the selfish," which was bound to fatally compromise their character.

It was this baneful prospect that his own draft was meant to forestall. He presented it to the Jacobins on 21 April (a preliminary version had appeared in the *Lettres à ses commetants* two days before), and then to the Convention on 24 April, vehemently taking issue with the spirit of the text adopted by the majority, based on Condorcet's draft. The question of property once more furnished Robespierre with an opening. It permitted him to lash out against those "base souls who value only gold," while exorcising the specter of the "agrarian law" and of the equality of assets. His objective was to show that the Girondins had unwittingly revealed the true nature of their dealings. "You have multiplied articles [in your draft of the Declaration] in order to ensure the greatest freedom for the exercise of property, but you have not said a single word to define its legitimate character, so that your declaration appears to have been made, not for ordinary men, but for the rich, for profiteers, speculators, and tyrants." Against this, Robespierre set the need to balance the individual right to property by a corresponding obligation to respect the rights of others. In the same spirit, he called for the establishment of a system of progressive taxation. And finally, for good measure, he lamented the neglect of the "duties of fraternity" among men and nations that form the basis of an "eternal alliance of peoples against tyrants"—another way of casting suspicion on the real intentions of his enemies. Still, these supplementary principles were enunciated only as part of a polemical preamble to the proposed Declaration itself, comprised of thirty-eight articles that Robespierre went on at once to review. His draft was meant to deliver an unmistakable warning to the Girondins, this "well-mannered" elite, putting them on notice that the meaning and aims of the Revolution were not theirs to decide.

The speech was warmly received and subsequently issued in printed form, but nothing more came of it. Curiously, Robespierre made no effort to defend his text during the drafting of the Montagnard Constitution of June 1793, which used it as the basis for its Declaration of Rights while substantially modifying it.

Robespierre's version came to acquire a legendary significance in the nineteenth century, serving as a banner for republicans to rally around during the early stages of the socialist movement, before the collectivist critique consigned its argument from individual rights to the hell of bourgeois values. It owed its fame to article 10, in particular, which consecrated the right to existence: "Society is obliged to provide for the subsistence of all its members, either by finding them work or by assuring the means of survival for those who are unable to work." In this way an idea he had expressed earlier, in his speech of December 1792 on food supplies, came to assume the status of a foundational principle: "The first social law is that which guarantees to all members of society the means of existence; all the other [laws] are subordinate to it; property has been instituted and guaranteed only for the purpose of strengthening it; it is only in order to live in the first place that one has property." These considerations no doubt explain why he went as far as it is possible to go in conceiving of collective solidarity within the framework of individualistic thought.

But Robespierre's proposal was no less radical in respect of democratic sovereignty. Article 14 stipulates that "the people may change their government and recall their representatives when it pleases them to do so." Robespierre could not prevent himself from introducing his political philosophy into a text that in principle was intended to formulate positive prescriptions. Thus article 19 says, "In every free state the law must, above all, defend public and individual liberty against the abuse of the authority of those who govern; every institution that does not suppose the people to be good, and the magistrate corruptible, is wicked." It is not until the noble internationalism of article 35 that the present age of nationalist strife looked forward to a time when proletarians would no longer pledge allegiance to the country of their birth: "The men of all countries are brothers, and the different peoples must help one another, according to their power, as citizens of a single state." This rhetorical escalation reaches a climax in the impassioned anathema of the final article: "Kings, aristocrats, tyrants, whoever they may be, are slaves rebelling against the sovereign of the earth, which is the human race, and against the legislator of the universe, which is nature." The flamboyant solemnity of this proclamation cannot have failed to make a great impression. It was meant to emphasize the difference between the sublimity of Montagnard ambitions, the only ones adequate to meet the challenge of the moment, and the small-mindedness of the undistinguished Girondin majority. This is not the place to enter into a long discussion of the philosophical coherence of Robespierre's conception. I shall limit myself to observing that here, on his view of the matter, the tension between a state of nature and a state of society, between individual independence and collective interdependence, is raised to its highest point—clearly stated in article 30: "When the social guarantee is lacking to a citizen, he reverts to the natural right of defending his rights himself."

This same 24 April (the day, it will be recalled, of Marat's triumphal return to the Convention), in what bore all the signs of a concerted effort, Saint-Just delivered a speech on the Constitution aimed at demolishing the Girondin draft, which he described as doubly defective, alleging that its conception of the legislature was "federative" and its conception of the executive "representative." To this Saint-Just opposed a system in which representation would be of the people as a whole, with a subordinate executive, in order to properly express the unsurpassed unity of the people and its government, the purpose being to abolish the "power of man," necessarily unjust and tyrannical, in favor of the only legitimate power, the "power of laws." Robespierre came back to the subject on 10 May in a speech that held no surprises for anyone familiar with his thinking. In it he rehearsed many of his favorite themes. "The first object of every Constitution must be to defend public and individual liberty against the government itself," since the personal interests of those who govern inevitably depart from the public good to which the people are devoted. Consequently, "it is in the virtue and the sovereignty of the people that protection against the vices and the despotism of government must be sought." The classic solutions for limiting the power of magistrates, beginning with a balance of powers, were ineffectual. New ones were necessary: short terms of elected office, strict separation of legislation from the execution of laws, division of duties, and, above all, limitation of the attributes of power. Never has the liberal determination to give the widest possible scope to individual initiative received more vigorous expression than Robespierre gave it:

> Shun the ancient obsession of governments with governing too much; leave to individuals, leave to families the right to do that which does no harm to others; leave to communes the right to regulate their own affairs, in all that in no essential way is connected with the general administration of the Republic. In a word, give back to individual liberty all that does not naturally belong to public authority.

Yet this was not enough in order to devise the proper arrangement of constitutional powers. It was necessary to prevent the other major source of abuses, namely, the "independence of the government" in relation to the citizens. Here the sovereign remedy was publicity, regarding which Robespierre developed arguments that were both meticulous and lyrical. To this must be added the need to make public officials answerable to the people by imposing upon them an obligation to account for their behavior in office and by allowing their actions to be challenged. But the stability of institutions ultimately depended on making sure that they remain faithful to their first principles. For this reason the Declaration of Rights had to be at the heart of public life: "The other laws are by their nature mutable and are subordinate to [the Declaration]. May it constantly be present in everyone's mind; may it illuminate our public code." The last article of his draft, which, strictly speaking, is more an exposition of constitutional principles than an institutional blueprint, explained what needed to be done if this instrument of enlightenment were to fulfill its highest purpose: "The Declaration of the Rights of Man and the Citizen shall be placed in the most conspicuous location in the places where the constituted authorities will hold their sessions; it shall be borne aloft, in pomp, in all public ceremonies; it shall be the first object of public instruction."

The advent of the republic of the rights of man was to be indefinitely delayed, however. The issue of public safety now came to the fore, and never relinquished its hold over debate thereafter. On 8 May, two days after his speech on the Constitution, Robespierre argued the case before the Convention, and then that evening at the Jacobin Club. The tone of his remarks was notable for its extreme harshness. He lumped together the insurgents in the Vendée, the foreign armies massed on the northern frontier, and the Girondins, seeing them as constituting an informal alliance, if they were not actually accomplices acting in concert. "There are now only two parties in France, the people and their enemies. All these rogues and scoundrels, who eternally conspire against the rights of man and against the happiness of all peoples, must be exterminated. This is the situation in which we find ourselves today. Whoever is not for the people is against the people, whoever wears silk knee-breeches is the enemy of all those without breeches. There are only two parties, one of men who are corrupt, the other of men who are virtuous." This aggressively Manichaean view was sometimes tempered by an appeal to legal authority whose sincerity is difficult to judge. Thus he went on to say that "existing law requires us to exterminate all our enemies." This may have been motivated by a desire to see a majority of the Convention swing over to the side of the Mountain, assuming enough pressure could be brought to bear by the Paris sections. After all, this was exactly what came to pass with the coup d'état of 31 May–2 June, albeit at the cost of a violent uprising that Robespierre had wished to avoid, not least for the collateral damage it was bound to entail.

He had had to make up his mind on this issue as the confrontation between the Girondin majority in the Convention and the Paris Commune intensified during the month of May. On the thirteenth, he once again defended himself before the Jacobins, presenting his views on the Constitution, not without opposition, to judge from newspaper reports. Interrupted by a member who "wished that attention were paid to public safety rather than to oratorical discourses," Robespierre explained that his policy was "compatible with the means of public safety"; indeed, it was "the most effectual and the most energetic"—with all due respect, he added, politely for once, to those who sought to "cast on [his] character a few shades of moderantism." But on 26 May, again speaking at the Jacobin Club, he took the fateful step of inviting "the people to rise up in the National Convention against all the corrupt deputies." Three days later the insurrection was underway and there was no need for further exhortation. He took credit for leaving the outcome to popular spontaneity, in another one of those strange self-pitying outbursts that celebrated victory by emphasizing his weakness:

> I am incapable of prescribing to the people the means by which they may save themselves; that is not given to me, exhausted as I am after four years of revolution and by the crushing spectacle of the triumph of all that is the most vile and the most corrupt. It is not for me to indicate

these measures, worn down as I am by a slight fever, and still more by the fever of patriotism. I have said: no other duty is left for me to fulfill.

But it was with commanding authority that he delivered the coup de grâce to the Girondins on 31 May in the Convention, where the Montagnards were joined on their benches by representatives of the Paris sections and the Commune. Robespierre's reply to Vergniaud, who had called upon him to conclude his remarks, was damning. "Yes, I will conclude, and against you. . . . My conclusion is this: all of Dumouriez's accomplices and all those who have been named by the petitioners ought to be prosecuted." He watched in silence at the session of 2 June, when the Commune's armed forces succeeded in extracting from the Convention a writ for the arrest of the Girondin deputies.

CHAPTER FOUR

Governing the Revolution

THE RULE AND THE EXCEPTION

WITH THE EXPULSION OF THE Girondins, the final stage of Robespierre's career got underway—the stage that was to decisively shape his historical reputation. Strictly speaking, it did not really begin until a little later, with his appointment to the Committee of Public Safety on 27 July 1793. This time the change of role was total, the metamorphosis complete. The man who stood in opposition to the government had now become a member of the government; the intransigent defender of principles now found himself responsible for applying them. It was no longer a matter of pleading the case of the people but of exercising power in their name. More than this, it was a matter of laying the foundations for a republic of the people.

This new phase is generally thought of as the culmination of a methodical conquest of power, the crowning of an ambition to rule as a dictator—whether to reprove this ambition or to glorify it as proof of a necessary and salutary heroism. On closer and unbiased examination, however, it becomes clear that things are far from being so simple. Nevertheless it must be kept in mind that, in this period of maximal tension, nearly everything is obscure and difficult to interpret. Robespierre defended himself against the charge of having sought election to the Committee of Public Safety, declaring on 11 August that it had been forced upon him "against [his] will." Why should we not believe him, even if this disclaimer cannot fail to remind us of the tactical denials and evasions he so often resorted to? It is consistent with what one knows of his vocation as a member of the revolutionary assembly and his faith in the authority of the spoken word.

Indeed, he was to take little part in the administrative work of the Committee and continued to hold forth regularly from the podium.

It is possible, after all, to see Robespierre's election as the result of a tangled configuration of political forces, in which he represented a sort of equilibrium point. The dominant force to emerge from the coup d'état of 31 May–2 June, in which true power resided, was the Paris Commune. But it was a power whose exercise could not be admitted, for to do this would amount to confirming the Girondins' charges of usurpation. At a time when the provinces and the large cities were deeply disturbed by the violence committed in the capital, it was essential that the Commune be able to take cover behind the Convention, which at least retained its functional legitimacy, even if the amputation it had performed on itself cast doubt on the actual extent of its representativeness. The Montagnard minority that had gained the advantage by eliminating the Girondin leadership needed, for its part, to have the support of the Commune in order to control what remained of the old moderate majority, which it did not dare eliminate for fear of forfeiting what was left of its claim to represent the country. The Mountain ruled by intimidation, but it could not do without the continuing presence in the Convention of the Plain, now frightened and reduced to silence, in order to preserve at least the appearance of adhering to lawful procedure. At the same time, however, if the Mountain wished to keep the upper hand, it had to be able to resist the radicals of the Commune and the Paris sections, whose members held a number of positions in the two principal ministries, War and the Interior. This was a role for which the executive prerogatives of the Committee of Public Safety ideally suited it. And so it came to pass: little by little, the Committee of Public Safety achieved ascendancy over the officials of the Commune and their intermediaries among the sections and the clubs.

There can be no doubt that Robespierre's appointment was decisive in this connection. The complicated predicament facing the Montagnards at the end of July 1793 left them with no alternative. After Marat's assassination at the hand of Charlotte Corday on 13 July, and confronted by the fading influence of Danton, whether this was a matter of his own doing or the result of the suspicions and rumors that swirled around him, Robespierre stood out as the indispensable man. He was a link to the Commune, without being beholden to it; he had the ear of the people; and he was a relatively reassuring figure for the deputies of the Plain (notwithstanding the vigor of his attacks against the Girondin "rascals," he had always been careful to show respect for the "great majority" of the Convention, whom he declared to be "pure"). Finally, and above all, his personal authority put him in a position to give the Committee of Public Safety the necessary political clout to deal with a dangerous situation without yielding to the pressures rashly brought to bear by the Enragés and the Hébertists. Robespierre's own judgment of the situation had changed. He had spoken harshly about the Committee at first, but then came around to the idea that it constituted a critical element of an unavoidably improvisational system of government. He was entitled to imagine that his membership had been imposed upon him, both from within and from without, inasmuch as he did not seek it.

Robespierre's change of heart was due in large part to the fact that in the meantime he had come to recognize the limits of the strategy he had initially hit upon for legitimizing the coup of 31 May–2 June, whose success depended on promptly drafting a Constitution and submitting it to the people for ratification. Events moved quickly. On 10 June Hérault de Séchelles presented the draft produced by the Committee of Public Safety. Debate in the Convention concluded two weeks later. The final version was approved by popular referendum on 4 August, with a relatively high degree of participation for the period—on the order of thirty percent, enough to vindicate Robespierre's policies (1.8 million votes in favor and only a negligible number against). Plainly, to Robespierre's mind, the symbolic value of the document's acceptance—celebrating the triumph over Girondin obstructionism—was more important than its content. While praising the constitutional order it brought into existence, "infinitely superior to all ancient moral and political institutions," he distanced himself from it, adding that he did not himself regard it "as a finished work." He had taken part in the Convention's debate, as he was obliged to do by virtue of the special authority he enjoyed, but he limited himself to occasional interventions, some of them nonetheless significant. On 14 June he tried to moderate the democratic ardor of the framers, emphasizing that what mattered was not establishing "pure democracy," but "a democracy that, in the interest of general happiness, is tempered by laws." Similarly, the next day, once more taking issue with those who argued for the most expansive possible form of democracy, he opposed the direct election of an executive council by the people. "The rock on which liberty normally founders in all countries," he explained, "is the excessive influence acquired over time by an executive council, which, for the very reason that it controls all the forces of the state and that it does not cease to employ them, soon comes to dominate all [other] authorities." With regard to taxation, on 17 June, he hastened to correct an inadvertent error in his own draft two months earlier, which provided for an exemption for the poorest citizens. That would only create "a class of proletarians, a class of isolated individuals." It was necessary instead to "consecrate the honorable obligation falling upon every citizen to pay his share." Recalling the combat—his word—that had been waged in the Constituent Assembly against the proposal that mention be made in the Declaration of the Rights of Man of the "duties of man," he reminded his listeners of the imperative need to remain faithful to this principle.

The so-called Montagnard Constitution of 1793, cobbled together in haste from various existing drafts, was meant to be judged on its ultrademocratic intentions rather than its practical plausibility. It was, so to speak, a promise made in order not to be kept. But however welcoming the response, it was of little help in meeting the challenges that loomed ahead. Even granting that this "rallying point of the people" may have had a certain effectiveness in mobilizing political support, it was incapable of coping with the extent and the multiplicity of the dangers facing the nation. A legitimate government was not enough. What was wanted was a government with exceptional powers, as Robespierre rather quickly became convinced. Military reverses requiring a reorganization of the army, provincial protests on a vast scale needing to be contained, the counterrevolution in the Vendée needing to be suppressed, ever worsening food shortages, political divisions undermining popular movements and even the Mountain itself—the dramatic accumulation of threats of all kinds called for bold and immediate action. One has the impression, reading his speeches during these weeks, that Robespierre had given very careful thought to the problem and that he underwent something very much like a conversion, though not, it would appear, without moments of dejection—as when, addressing the Jacobins on 12 June, he confessed his "inadequacy" and announced his intention to submit his resignation. But how can we tell whether or not he was being sincere? Once again, put to the test of extraordinary circumstances, he discovered the necessity of what he rejected or disapproved of in principle—and, precisely because the circumstances were exceptional, the discovery did not call his principles into question. The very executive power whose place in the Constitution he had unsuccessfully argued against, and which he had sought thereafter to limit as far as possible, he now worked diligently to make a cornerstone of revolutionary government while seeking to disguise his role as far as possible. In short, practice overruled theory.

This deep ambivalence is no doubt what explains his astounding tirade of 11 August, when he described the Committee he had just joined—against his will, he said—as nothing less than a "den of thieves." There he saw "things that I would never have dared suspect. I have seen, on the one hand, patriotic members who seek in vain to serve their country well and, on the other, traitors who plot within the Committee itself against the interests of the people. Now that I have seen [the workings of] government close up, I am able to perceive the crimes that are committed by it every day." Neither his colleagues nor anyone else made mention of this outburst, which gives some idea of the astonishment it must have provoked. Robespierre seems to have been on the verge of completing his apprenticeship in wielding power and his instruction in the instruments and methods of which he was to make such abundant use in the months to come. His colleagues on the Committee, sensing this, seem to have indulgently regarded his misgivings as the outward sign of a crisis of initiation that would soon pass. Subsequent events were to prove them right.

With Robespierre's appointment to the Committee of Public Safety came the stability that had so far eluded it, with the result that it promptly became the seat of a baroque system of power, crowned by a dictatorial executive that pretended not to be one. Officially, the Committee existed only to give impetus to executive power proper, which resided in the six ministries, and to supervise their operations. In fact, it took all the important decisions—a habit that ended up calling into question the status of the ministries. Nevertheless the Committee, which deliberated and voted in secret, was supposed to speak and act only in the name of the Convention, which in principle was to be reelected every month, a rule that soon ceased to be observed. In the person of Barère the Committee possessed a secretary who was effectively unremovable, renowned for his eloquence and endowed with an inimitable talent, bordering on ventriloquism, for presenting the Committee's decisions as if they were the decisions of the Convention itself. The surprising thing is that a regime constructed on false pretenses turned out to be workable, at least in the short term, but then with regard only to the normal functions of government, not to the extreme measures to which it was later to resort so regularly. Robespierre's initial scruples were rapidly overcome. On 29 August he rejected a proposal that a new body be created to oversee the Committee, in a manner that showed he had come to terms with the reality of the duties that he was charged with carrying out: "I perceive that a perfidious system exists to paralyze the Committee of Public Safety by seeming to assist it in its work, but which seeks to degrade executive power, in order to be able to say that no authority any longer exists in France capable of holding the reins of government." He went still further, on 25 September, at a moment when a part of the Convention balked at certain decisions taken by the Committee in respect of military matters, declaring that his aims were in no way different from those of his colleagues and calling for "unlimited confidence" in "the government."

So convinced was Robespierre by this point of the necessity of strong government, in fact, that he opposed implementing the provisions of the Montagnard Constitution, and therefore also disbanding the Convention and replacing it with a newly elected assembly, as some moderates and Exagérés demanded, though for rather different reasons. On 23 August, speaking at the Jacobin Club, he made himself unmistakably clear:

> It would be dangerous to change the Convention; the [assembly] that would succeed it would surely be composed of two parties. The men who have been expelled from [the Convention] with so much difficulty would now come back in greater force than ever, and perhaps another 31 May would not suffice to drive them out a second time: so great would be the people's suffering that perhaps they would prefer to keep the conspirators than to revive an insurrection.

Robespierre was plainly under no illusions with regard to the balance of power in the country. But he thought that by acting preemptively, imposing the government's will in order to preserve existing political institutions and, in this way, strengthening public spirit, it would become possible to tip the balance in favor of the constituted authorities.

In the end it was Saint-Just who was to carry the day, on 10 October, with one of those reports filled with dazzling summaries of events that he alone was able to compose. This one was particularly striking for its combination of hardheaded analysis and willfully unrealistic prognosis, relentless lucidity with regard to problems and almost dreamlike wishfulness with regard to solutions. At all events the guiding principle was succinctly stated: "The provisional government of France will be revolutionary until peace has been achieved." This program left no room for half-measures: "The Republic will be founded only when the will of the sovereign [people] has crushed the monarchist minority and reigns over it by right of conquest. All possible measures must be taken in combating the enemies of the new order of things; liberty must triumph, no matter what the price may be." Billaud-Varenne, speaking in the name of the Committee on 18 November, presented a "report on the mode of provisional and revolutionary government." After two weeks of vigorous and highly revealing debate, this regime was formally decreed on 4 December. A few days before, on 30 November, Merlin de Douai had demanded that "the Committee of

Public Safety be called the Committee of Government." To this Billaud-Varenne objected, "The center of government is in the Convention." Barère took the argument a step further: "The Convention governs alone and must govern alone. . . . We are the vanguard of the Convention, we are the arm that it causes to act, but we are not the government." The decree of 4 December consecrated the principle in these words: "The National Convention is the unique source of governmental impetus." Three weeks later Robespierre gave the doctrine a fuller statement. On 25 December, in his famous *Rapport sur les principes du gouvernement révolutionnaire*, he took it upon himself once again to explain to the actors of the Revolution where matters stood. "The theory of revolutionary government is as new as the Revolution that gave rise to it." At this stage he no longer had any hesitation about saying his role and that of the Committee of Public Safety were bound up with governing. He had openly acknowledged this state of affairs, on 28 November, in his reply to the Hébertist detractors of the Committee at the Jacobin Club:

> [C]ome take our places, come, we will cede them to you with plea-
> sure. We will see how well you handle the reins of government, how
> well you provide for the needs of the interior, how well you protect
> yourselves from the evils that threaten you within, how well you cast
> aside slanders on the one hand, and, on the other, impart to the nation
> a revolutionary impetus; you will direct the armies, ensure they have all
> the supplies they need, ensure obedience on the part of the soldiers and
> integrity on the part of the generals. You will govern.

This was the role, and the manner in which it was to be carried out, that he later sought to justify on 25 December.

The Turn to Terror

Before looking more closely at the grounds for his justification, it must be emphasized that his delay in saying more was not the result of chance. If it was only in late December that Robespierre was able to publicly defend this position, it is because until then the Committee of Public Safety had not managed to establish its authority—something that was by no means foreordained. From the outset he had had to compromise with the concurrent authority of the Commune, which, even though it could not do without the backing of the Convention and its various organs, was nonetheless determined to direct their course of action as far as possible. At the Hôtel de Ville, Pache, Chaumette, and Hébert were still under pressure from the

leaders of the Enragés, sustained in their opposition by the popular anger
aroused by the famine in the capital. The situation was aggravated by the
apparently grave, if not actually hopeless, military situation, against
the background of which sans-culottes and Enragés joined in denouncing
the irresoluteness of the Convention.

The crisis of early September illuminated the shifting play of forces
set in motion by this test of strength. News that Toulon had just fallen to
the English, on 2 September, alarmed the leaders of the Paris sections,
who saw their worst fears confirmed and seized the opportunity to take
advantage of the ongoing working-class protests against the rising cost
of living and chronic food shortages. The challenge was orchestrated by
the Commune, though it also enjoyed the support of a part of the Jacobin
membership and even of the most radical Montagnards, led by Billaud-
Varenne and Collot d'Herbois. On 5 September, with the newly elected
deputies of the Convention meeting in the Salle des Machines at the Tuileries, "an immense crowd of citizens" flooded into the hall, this time without violence. Robespierre, presiding over the session, recognized Pache
and Chaumette first, then delegations from the various sections, who
presented their demands. He sought to placate them with the usual fine
words about the Convention's devotion to the happiness of the people.
Apart from persistent grievances over food shortages, the petitioners'
chief demand concerned the immediate formation of a "Revolutionary
Army," already decreed but so far to no effect, for the purpose of combating "internal enemies," "traitors," and "starvers" (this last a reference to
famine profiteers). Billaud-Varenne added to the list of demands, calling
for "the promptest possible arrest of all suspect persons." It fell to a group
of Jacobins, later in the session, to utter the fateful words, "Legislators, let
us make terror the order of the day." The first consequence was to be the
trial of Brissot and "his accomplices." On this and every other point, the
Committee of Public Safety gave way. The Commune and the Hébertists
had won. At the end of the session, Barère proposed a series of decrees
in response to the demands of the sectionary representatives, beginning
with the creation of the Revolutionary Army, which "will finally act on
this splendid exhortation" (the phrase "Let us make terror the order of
the day" was originally due, he claimed, to the Commune of Paris). The
next day, on a motion of the Committee of Public Safety, the Convention
approved the appointment of Billaud-Varenne and Collot d'Herbois to
the Committee—a gesture of goodwill toward the most progressive wing
of the Assembly, but also a dependable way of neutralizing external dissent by absorbing it. Among the sans-culottes, the heirs to Marat's legacy

hastened to settle accounts. That same day, 6 September, Jacques Roux, the leader of the Enragés, was thrown in prison.

The Convention did not formally make terror the order of the day. The phrase figures in no statute. Barère was content to adopt it as his own, having plucked it out of the air, so to speak. The fact remains that this rhetorical appropriation was tantamount to unofficial validation. So commonly was it used as a watchword among the men of the Convention that one has the impression that terror had in fact been put on the agenda. At all events it quite neatly summarizes the repressive turn that government policy was to take over the course of the following weeks. The Revolutionary Army came into being at last. The Revolutionary Tribunal was reorganized. On 17 September, the Convention enacted the Law of Suspects; arrests soon multiplied. On the 29th, the Law of the General Maximum was decreed, setting a ceiling on prices and wages.

In spite of all this, pressure from the sans-culottes did not relax. On 27 September, Hébert demanded that the Jacobins make the trial of Marie Antoinette open to the public. On the 30th, he made the same demand with regard to the trial of the imprisoned Girondins. Both trials took place in October. Marie Antoinette was guillotined on the 16th. On the 31st, it was the Girondins' turn to be executed, following a most irregular proceeding. Robespierre had managed on 3 October, not without difficulty, to annul the indictment of sixty-three deputies who had signed a petition protesting against the arrests of 2 June, declaring them to be "misled" rather than culpable, unlike their leaders, who alone deserved to be brought to justice. This did not prevent him from elaborating a philosophy of revolutionary justice that deserves closer examination. He had doubts about the usefulness of pressing charges against the Girondins: "Citizens, the written evidence is exceedingly weak; it is the history of the Revolution that condemns them; it is public opinion that strikes down the conspirators whom we have just now arraigned." He was to say the same thing again on 24 October, speaking out against informing not only suspects of the grounds for their arrest but also the competent authorities. "When public notoriety accuses a citizen of crimes of which there are no written proofs, but whose proof is in the heart of every indignant citizen . . . , is not the prudence of revolutionary measures totally demolished?" Once again it was in the same spirit that, during the show trial of the Girondins, cut short when their delaying tactics threatened to prolong it indefinitely, he argued successfully on behalf of a decree permitting debate to be closed after three days if the jurors felt "their conscience has been sufficiently instructed." Earlier a deputation of Jacobins had come to urge that the

Convention "disencumber the Revolutionary Tribunal of procedures that stifle the conscience and prevent conviction," saying that "[t]hen, and only then, will traitors be disappointed and terror made the order of the day." Robespierre's draft bill incorporated this recommendation, which he justified on the ground that it is "equally absurd and contrary to the institution of the Revolutionary Tribunal to submit to endless proceedings in cases where the entire nation is prosecutor and the world is witness." It is the coherence of this idea, whose capacity for mischief was yet far from being exhausted, with Robespierre's thinking about the people, that we will need to consider more carefully.

The hardening line adopted in response to outside pressures did not fail to arouse strong resistance within the Convention. Opposition was condemned to manifest itself obliquely, for the most part, but occasionally it came into the open, as for example on 25 September. The pretext in this case was the simultaneous discharge of several generals whose reluctance to take the battle to the enemy suggested that they were potentially traitors, if not actually conspirators. But Thuriot, the Dantonist who led the charge, had a much broader purpose in mind. He had resigned his seat on the Committee of Public Safety a few days earlier, and one may guess, judging from his remarks to the Convention, the reasons for his departure. He made no secret of his low opinion of the Law of the General Maximum. The members of the Committee, he said, "are criminals who wish to make the nation believe that it cannot be happy unless it cuts off all the branches of commerce." He bluntly described the struggle for power hidden behind policy discussions, inveighing against those "ambitious [deputies] who seek to seize the reins of government." He had still harsher things to say about the embrace of terror: "An attempt is now being made to cause it to be believed throughout the Republic that it cannot continue unless everywhere are reared men of blood, men who, since the beginning of the Revolution, have distinguished themselves only by their love of carnage." In retrospect, his words seem prophetic: "This raging torrent that is carrying us away into barbarism must be stopped. The progress of tyranny must be stopped!" No one took any notice of this dramatic appeal, and debate reverted to the narrower military question, only now with a vehemence that suggests Thuriot had in fact touched a nerve.

The shock must have been quite profound. Robespierre made a lengthy and scathing speech in response, and that same evening returned to the subject at the Jacobin Club. His counterattack now had to be conducted on two fronts, since Hébert and the Cordeliers, for their part, pressed their advantage by calling for a "constitutional reorganization of the government," which is to say the elimination of the Committee of Public Safety. Robespierre rose to the defense of the Committee in terms that remain famous still today:

> Eleven armies to command, the weight of all Europe to be borne, everywhere traitors to be unmasked, envoys bribed by the gold of foreign powers to be frustrated, unfaithful administrators to be watched over, to be prosecuted, everywhere obstacles and hindrances to the execution of the most prudent measures to be overcome; all tyrants to be combatted, all conspirators to be intimidated.

Under these circumstances, calling into question the Committee's decisions, without knowing the reasons for them, necessarily secret, could only profit "the infamous Pitt." And while patriots were obligated to defend the freedom of opinion, "I do not understand those among the patriots who make only the pretense of it, and I shall expose the conduct of two or three traitors here who are the architects of discord and argument." The evil-minded had better watch out! As for Hébert and the members of clubs "who pretend to be more than patriots," their efforts to degrade the Committee were nothing other than an attempt to "ensure the triumph of intriguers at the expense of friends [who are] ardently devoted to the interests of the people and at the expense of the people themselves." With this he succeeded in completely restoring the Convention's confidence in the Committee, nullifying the initial successes, which he himself admitted, of its detractors—a temporary setback that had no immediate consequence. Nevertheless it was from this moment that the great cleavage that was to polarize debate in the coming months, between the moderate politics of the Dantonists ("moderantism") and the radical politics of the Hébertists ("exaggeration"), began to take shape. At the same time, the contours of Robespierre's search for a point of equilibrium between the two camps, which was to form the basis of his ultimate power, began to come into view as well.

In October, the Hébertists' energies came to be transferred to the campaign for de-Christianization, a phenomenon that to this day remains rather obscure. Insofar as it was part of a larger cultural revolution, the decisive element may have been the replacement of the Christian system of dating by a revolutionary calendar that projected contemporary experience onto a utopian temporality. I do not claim to be able to clear up the matter. As far as the leaders of this campaign were concerned, however, there could be no doubt of its political usefulness as a means of bringing pressure to bear on the Convention, and perhaps as a means of intimidating Robespierre specifically, whose convictions in this regard were well known. In early November, one delegation after another came before the Convention, each exhibiting the trophies of its victories over "fanaticism." On the 7th, the constitutional bishop, Gobel, mounted the podium and there solemnly resigned his episcopal functions. On the 10th, Chaumette, who directed the campaign at the Commune, organized a "Festival of Reason" at the former Cathedral of Notre-Dame, attended by all the members of the Convention. In rapid succession the sections renounced the Catholic faith. Robespierre quickly perceived the point of the campaign, all the more as Hébert, speaking at the Jacobin and Cordeliers Clubs and writing in his newspaper *Le Père Duchesne*, criticized the government's policy for its lack of vigor. With his consummate talent for the graduated response, Robespierre carefully constructed his argument in the course of a series of speeches to the Jacobins, and then in his *Rapport sur la situation politique de la République*, delivered on 17 November (27 Brumaire, Year II). The motivation for these attacks by the ultras was primarily ambition—"I would like to see them [come forward], these men who slander us and claim to be more patriotic than we are. They seek to take our place." Their aim was to divide the patriots and to "demean the authorities, who wish to save France." This design could only be the work of foreign courts, which had no other weapon at their disposal for the purpose of causing the Revolution to "destroy itself." In the face of maneuvers intended to "assassinate liberty with its own arms," true patriots must keep in mind that while "force can topple a throne, wisdom alone can found a republic." Thus he called upon his listeners to be "revolutionaries and political men . . . ; shun both the cruel moderantism and the routine exaggeration of the false patriots."

On 21 November (1 Frimaire), a day after a parade of sectionary complaints still more disrespectful of authority than the ones previously brought before the Convention, Robespierre met the challenge head-on. Addressing the Jacobins once more, this time eschewing generalities, he openly launched a counteroffensive: "Is it true that the principal cause of our woes is fanaticism? Fanaticism! It is dying; I might even say that it is dead. By directing our full attention to it, for some days now, do we not risk diverting our attention from the real dangers facing us?" As against the radicals' invocation of an imaginary peril, Robespierre vigorously reaffirmed the Convention's determination to maintain freedom of worship, with all due respect to those who, "on the pretext of destroying superstition, seek to make a sort of religion of atheism itself." What is more, "atheism is aristocratic" (the implication of a crime punishable by death could hardly have gone unnoticed), whereas "the idea of a great being who cares for the innocent downtrodden and who punishes crime triumphant is wholly popular." Robespierre then drove home the point: "The French people are attached neither to priests, nor to superstition, nor to religious ceremonies; they are attached only to worship in itself, that is, to the idea of an incomprehensible power, [because of their] dread of crime and love of virtue." Thus not only did those who promoted de-Christianization have nothing to do with the people; they were on the side of the people's enemies. They were in the pay of foreign courts, who devised this means of discrediting the Revolution and of undermining it from within. Robespierre did not restrict himself this time to speaking of a plot; he went on to suggest that he could identify the plotters. For the time being, he refrained from naming the principal figures—holding his audience in breathless suspense was, as I say, one of his favorite rhetorical techniques: "Soon this odious mystery will be entirely stripped away. For the moment, I shall limit myself to offering you some small measure of illumination." Spared of the need to take on either Hébert or the Commune directly, he could concentrate his attacks instead on a few minor figures whom he described as "aristocrats masquerading as sans-culottes." But no one could have been in the least doubt as to who his main targets were. The battle was joined. The next day, Chaumette, the president of the Commune, brazenly ignoring the warning delivered by Robespierre, ordered all the churches in Paris to be closed.

Robespierre was not content to leave matters there. He came back to the subject several times in the course of the following weeks, a sign both of the crucial importance he attached to it and of the trouble he had had in making his voice heard within his own camp. He needed to defend himself against the charge "of sustaining the priests, of supporting fanaticism." He needed also to make it clear that he took care to distinguish between "peaceable and patriotic citizens, who heap on the altar of the fatherland the useless monuments of superstition, and disguised aristocrats, who affect to insult the things that the people have revered." On 6 December (16 Frimaire), he managed with some difficulty to persuade the Convention to issue a decree guaranteeing freedom of worship and inviting "all good citizens, in the name of the fatherland, to abstain from all disputes of a theological nature or [that otherwise are] foreign to the main interests of the French people." Chaumette backpedaled. He concurred with the principle of the decree and, while insisting that churches remain closed, he left open the possibility that private spaces might be used for worship. But two days later, speaking before the Convention on 8 December, Barère stated in no uncertain terms that the measures taken by deputies sent on mission throughout the country to "help the citizens destroy superstition" would stand. De-Christianization continued for some time thereafter, both in the departments and in Paris itself, though unevenly and with diminished fervor.

The situation had grown more complicated in the interval with Danton's return to the scene. Having appeared to quit politics in October, he was persuaded to come back to the capital the following month and immediately involved himself in the controversies stirred up by Robespierre. On 22 November, at the Convention, he lent his support to the idea that "the Assembly abhors persecution" and urged that "the blood of men be shed sparingly." He spoke out still more forcefully four days later: "I demand that there be no more antireligious masquerades in the Convention. . . . Our mission is not to ceaselessly receive deputations that repeat the same words." He treated the official line with respect, while at the same time expressing reservations about the way in which it was commonly understood: "The people wish, and rightly so, that terror be made the order of the day, but they wish that terror be referred to its true end." At the same time he seconded Robespierre in demanding that a report be made on "what is called a foreign conspiracy." Addressing the Jacobin Club on 3 December (13 Frimaire), Danton warned that "those who wish to carry the people beyond the bounds of the Revolution and who propose ultra-revolutionary measures are to be mistrusted." This caused such an uproar that he felt bound to call for the appointment of a commission to examine the accusations that were brought against him. Robespierre came to his defense, associating Danton with his own cause: "I declare that Danton has been slandered, that I detect in this one of the most important strands of the plot hatched against the patriots."

The polemic spilled over beyond militant circles. Desmoulins, a veteran of revolutionary journalism, brought it to public attention with the appearance on 5 December (15 Frimaire) of his newspaper *Le Vieux Cordelier* (a reference to the Cordeliers Club of Danton's time, before Hébert and company became members). Desmoulins started off by instructing his readers to suspect that the machinations of foreign powers lay behind the current unrest. He developed this theme in the second issue, published 14 December, taking shelter behind Robespierre's claim that "Pitt has reconfigured his artillery: he undertakes now to accomplish by exaggeration what he could not accomplish by moderantism," by encouraging the schemes of "patriotic counterrevolutionaries." This caused a stir among the Jacobins, who called upon Desmoulins to justify himself. Robespierre hastened to defend him, testifying that Desmoulins' republican convictions were of long standing. At this juncture the affair took on the aspect of a "campaign for indulgence" (a reference to the old Cordeliers of the so-called indulgent faction, headed by Danton and publicized by Desmoulins), denounced at once by the new Cordeliers and the camp of "exaggeration wearing whiskers," as Desmoulins called it. The campaign was fueled by the repercussions of the terrorist agenda and the growing protest against the arbitrary arrests carried out by revolutionary committees under the aegis of the Law of Suspects. Complaints multiplied, until finally the subject came before the Convention on 7 December (17 Frimaire). Couthon, another member of the Committee of Public Safety, conceded their soundness: "We must not overlook the fact that, under the unsettled circumstances in which we find ourselves, injustices have been committed." On 12 December (22 Frimaire), and then on the 20th (30 Frimaire), a group of women appeared before the Assembly to demand freedom for their wrongfully detained husbands. Robespierre, who detected the hand of the aristocracy in this, clearly thought things had gone too far. Nevertheless he granted that "steps need to be taken so that the patriot will not be confused with the counterrevolutionary."

In the meantime Desmoulins had heightened tensions further by publishing, on 15 December, a third issue of *Le Vieux Cordelier*, still more provocative than the previous two. Not content to repeat the charge of Pitt's collusion in promoting "ultrarevolutionary measures" for the purpose of discrediting the cause of liberty and in calling for freedom of the press, he lashed out against the Committee of Public Safety for believing that "in order to establish the Republic it momentarily had need of the jurisprudence of despots." And that was not all. Two days later, on 17 December, Fabre d'Églantine, Danton's private secretary, mounted the podium at the Convention to denounce two of the leading figures among the Exagérés— Vincent, secretary general of the Ministry of War, and Ronsin, general of the Revolutionary Army—who were then arrested without the committees having been consulted beforehand. There ensued an immediate counteroffensive from the Hébertists, led by Hébert himself. Speaking at the Jacobin Club on 21 December (1 Nivôse), he charged the Dantonists with masterminding a neo-Brissotin plot, while putting pressure on the Convention to demand the trial of the seventy-three deputies who had been detained on suspicion of being Girondin accomplices. A stormy debate broke out two days later, again at the Jacobin Club, in connection with a report on the Vendée by another one of Danton's associates, Philippeaux, suggesting that responsibility for the severity of the repression there rested with the

Committee of Public Safety. "What!" cried Robespierre. "The Committee of Public Safety is accused of being composed of assassins!" Nevertheless he was obliged to admit that "Philippeaux has had no counterrevolutionary intentions whatever." The quarrel gave him the opportunity to polish his argument, assailing both moderantism and the "universal conflagration" deliberately fanned by "foreign powers." "The tactic of our enemies, make no mistake, is to divide us."

It was against the background of these disturbances, as Robespierre himself called them, and of the political struggle that had now come out into the open, that he read to the Convention his *Rapport sur les principes du gouvernement révolutionnaire* on 25 December (5 Nivôse). He suspected that the tense atmosphere might actually work to his advantage. It enabled him to place the Committee of Public Safety, on behalf of which he spoke, in a position of arbitrative (and therefore indispensable) authority, above the two camps into which the Montagnard Convention was split—this at a time when avoiding a direct confrontation with the Commune, the principal piece of the political puzzle, had become increasingly difficult. Also working in his favor was the fact that the military situation had in the meantime miraculously improved, thus confirming the wisdom of the Committee's war policy. The day before, Barère took the floor to celebrate the triumphs of the "genius of liberty": "The allied intriguers from abroad have been driven away; the allied intriguers from within [France] have been vanquished." Indeed, the armies of the foreign coalition had been repulsed on all frontiers: Toulon had been retaken from the English on 19 December; provincial revolts had been quelled in Lyon, Bordeaux, and Marseille; the "Catholic and royal army" of the Vendée had been crushed at Le Mans and Savenay. Robespierre began by speaking of "successes"— only then to immediately make it clear that if they "lull weak souls to sleep, they rouse strong souls to action."

The object of the *Rapport* was twofold. It sought at once to retroactively legitimize what in reality had been a series of improvisations and, on this basis, to announce what the future held in store. This legitimation was not limited to its institutional aspect; it also had a quite personal implication for Robespierre, who plainly needed to find a way to dispose of the apparent contradiction between the principles he had espoused while in opposition and the means he had been led to employ once he had joined the government. Hence the care he took in clarifying a distinction (which for many people, he admitted, was an "enigma") between two types of government: "The aim of constitutional government is to preserve the

Republic; that of revolutionary government is to found it." It was necessary first to establish liberty, so that its fruits could one day be enjoyed: "The revolution is the war of freedom against its enemies; the Constitution is the regime of victorious and peaceable freedom." From this there resulted a complete opposition between the terms and conditions under which the two regimes function: "Under a constitutional regime, it almost suffices to protect individuals against the abuses of the state; under a revolutionary regime, the state is obliged to defend itself against all the factions that attack it." This distinction permitted him to contradict the "stupid and perverse sophists" who declared revolutionary laws to be arbitrary and tyrannical. These people "confound contraries" inasmuch as "they wish to submit peace and war, health and sickness, to the same regime."

The main advantage of this way of characterizing revolutionary government, as a kind of preparatory exception to the normal state of affairs under constitutional government, was that it made it possible to look forward, beyond the bloody rage of the present, to a peaceful future. But this was not enough to satisfy Robespierre. He was determined to do his utmost to put law on the side of government in a state of exception, which he declared to be no less "just and legitimate" than ordinary government. "It is sanctioned by the most hallowed of all laws: the safety of the people; by the most irrefutable of warrants: necessity." Moreover, "it has nothing in common either with anarchy or disorder. . . . It has nothing in common with arbitrariness." It was, so to speak, a regular irregularity, essential for establishing the "rule of law." Accordingly, he was able to convince himself that there had been no deviation from fundamental principle.

Having now laid the theoretical foundation for his argument, Robespierre turned to the current political situation, which is to say to the divisions that were increasingly making themselves felt among the patriots. These divisions, he maintained, were in the very nature of revolutionary government. "One must navigate between two reefs, weakness and temerity, moderantism and excess. . . . The two extremes lead to the same thing. Whether one falls short of the end or goes beyond it, in either case the end is missed." He went on, by means of readily interpreted allusions, to catalogue the forms assumed by these two perversions, both of which he regretted. If forced to choose between them, however, he nonetheless indicated a preference for an "excess of patriotic fervor" over the "stagnation of moderantism"—evidently a way of distancing himself from the Indulgents. The significance of this remark surely was not lost on his listeners.

The most important point was saved for last. If too little and too much patriotic zeal were the usual dangers against which a revolutionary government had to protect itself, the greatest peril lay in the exploitation of internal disagreements by an external enemy, in this case the foreign powers leagued against the Republic. "They have had the time to establish in France a secret government, a rival to the French government," he declared—a government that was all the more formidable for possessing what the French government did not: "the unity we have so long been lacking, the policy we have too much believed we could do without, the agreement and the harmony whose necessity we have not always felt." The agents of this clandestine manipulation excited the passions of some and preyed on the weaknesses of others: "[T]heir principal object is to set us against one another." The urgent need to combat this foreign plot, whose ramifications were concealed by the pressures that the various parties were trying to exert upon the government, led Robespierre to conclude by announcing that "foreigners and generals accused of conspiring with the tyrants who are making war on us" would promptly be brought to trial, and that the Revolutionary Tribunal would be reorganized for the purpose of "making the action of justice still more favorable to innocence and at the same time inevitable for crime and intrigue."

The framework within which the tragedy of the next three months unfolded, culminating in the liquidation of the two rival factions, was now in place. The Committee of Public Safety could feel confident that it possessed the authority to strike out against anyone who opposed its policy and, considering the internal threat of a foreign-sponsored plot and the external threat of foreign armies, sufficient justification for the severe measures it was resolved to implement. This is not to say that Robespierre had a fully formed plan in mind that needed only to be put into effect. It is simply that, as the one whose self-appointed duty was to explain the course of the Revolution to its actors, he had been led to define and to rationalize the situation in ways that could be turned against him by his adversaries while restricting his own freedom of maneuver.

Exagérés and Indulgents

The facts are only too well known, having acquired a legendary significance; their disastrous consequences have not ceased to trouble historical imagination since. Hébert and the leading Cordeliers were arrested during the night of 13–14 March 1794 (23–24 Ventôse) and guillotined a few days later. Chaumette followed on 17 March. The sans-culotte Commune was decapitated. Two weeks later it was Danton's turn, along with Desmoulins and Philippeaux. They were arrested during the night of 30–31

March (10–11 Germinal) and executed on 5 April. It is tempting to connect
Robespierre's denunciation of a foreign plot with two faces directly with
the double blow delivered first against "exaggeration" and then against
"indulgence." The temptation must be resisted, however, for the intervening course of events cannot be summarized so simply. The dynamic of
the situation was governed by the veiled confrontation between the Committee of Public Safety and the Parisian sans-culotte movement in its
various expressions. The reasons for popular dissatisfaction with official
policy were many. Wage and price controls had had no effect. The problem of providing adequate food supplies, aggravated by a severe winter,
was more intractable than ever. The unrest it fueled only heightened the
appeal of calls for decisive measures to be taken. The Desmoulins affair
had provoked the radicals' indignation at the weakness, if not actually the
complacency, of the Committee, and of Robespierre in particular, in the
face of so obviously counterrevolutionary an offensive—and all the more as
Desmoulins had been allowed to carry on his campaign for moderation in
the pages of *Le Vieux Cordelier* for so long. Finally, and above all, the deten-
tion of Ronsin and Vincent represented a travesty of justice in the eyes of
the sectionary militants. Anger grew to such a point that on 31 January (12
Pluviôse), with the failure of attempts to obtain their release, the Declaration of the Rights of Man was covered with black crepe at the Cordeliers
Club—a sufficiently strong preinsurrectional signal that the Convention
released the two men two days later, on 2 February, on the recommendation of the Committee of General Security. This further encouraged the
radicals to persist in demanding a more vigorous policy of terrorism on all
fronts, whether in the interest of assuring food supplies or of prosecuting
Brissot's accomplices and other enemies of the people.

Here again the Committee of Public Safety made concessions, this time
in the form of the "Laws of Ventôse." On 26 February (8 Ventôse) the Convention decreed, on a motion by Saint-Just, the sequestration of the property of "persons acknowledged to be enemies of the revolution" with a view
to distributing it to the poor, a purpose that was approved on 3 March
(13 Ventôse). Saint-Just memorialized this legislation with the famous
words: "May Europe learn that you no longer will tolerate a wretched person nor an oppressor on French soil; may this example fructify on Earth;
may it everywhere promote a love of virtue and of happiness! Happiness
is a new idea in Europe." None of this was enough to lessen the impa-
tience of the sans-culottes, who increasingly came to believe that only a
new 31 May would do away once and for all with the traitors who gave
cover to the moderates and the monopolists. On 4 March, the Declaration

of the Rights of Man was once again shrouded in black at the Cordeliers Club. Hébert called for an uprising in order to crush a conspiracy that he claimed had paralyzed the government.

For the moment, the mood was ominously restive, though what the outcome would be no one could say. The hesitation of the leaders of the sans-culotte camp, divided over which course to follow, belied the vehemence of their rhetoric. In the event, the authorities of the Commune balked; Hanriot's National Guard, with its cannons and gunners, indispensable for any armed takeover, refused to march. It was this weakness that led the Committee of Public Safety, after much indecision, yet again, to take the calculated risk of arresting the Cordelier leaders on the charge of conspiring against the Republic.

Robespierre had little to say in the matter, publicly at least. For a month he was absent from the Convention on account of illness. He returned on 13 March, at the same time as Couthon, who had also been indisposed until the very day when it was decided to arrest the Hébertists, and surely not by chance. Saint-Just came forward to lead the attack, proceeding exactly along the lines laid out by Robespierre. The full title of Saint-Just's report succinctly sums up its point: *Rapport sur les factions de l'étranger et sur la conjuration ourdie par elles dans la République française pour détruire le gouvernement républicain par la corruption et affamer Paris* [Report on Foreign Factions and on the Plot Hatched by Them in the French Republic to Destroy Republican Government by Corruption and to Starve Paris]. Everything is there, not least the allusion to daily unrest over food shortages in the capital—a warning to anyone who might be tempted to exploit a volatile situation. Appearances to the contrary notwithstanding, the various factions were united in furthering a single purpose, and the warning in this instance, to the Indulgents, could not have been more clear. The factions did the bidding of the external enemy: "The first author of the conspiracy is the English government"; their aim was to "substitute royal government for [revolutionary government]." Aware of the skepticism such a claim was liable to run up against, Saint-Just met it head-on: "This problem, to all appearances inconceivable, is to be explained on the basis of the disagreement among the various factions." What passed for an explanation in this case, one will not be surprised to learn, depended on a series of highly inconclusive generalities.

Nevertheless it will be instructive to examine them more closely, for the insight they give into the real preoccupations of the Jacobin general staff. It was in any case only to be expected that the Hébertists would be associated with a Dutch banker, a Belgian financier, and the Prussian baron Cloots, whose rantings about a "universal republic" had long been an object of Robespierre's ire, in order to lend a measure of credibility to an otherwise implausible accusation. There is good reason to suppose that Robespierre had closely monitored events, from his bedroom in Duplay's house, two steps from the Convention and its committees, as the fate of the Hébertists was being decided. Once again, the decision was formulated in his language and in accordance with the interpretive framework that he had put in place. Thus he was content to signal his approval on his reappearance at the podium of the Convention on 15 March, the day after their arrest. "All the factions must perish together," he added, while emphasizing the urgency that had led the Committee of Public Safety to strike first against "the one that was nearest [to threatening] liberty, [the one] that encircled the entire National Convention." He had not ceased to stress the importance of this way of looking at the matter since the beginning of 1794, with an obstinacy equal to the difficulty of making himself heard, as when he sought to give his ideas fuller expression by urging, in a speech to the Jacobins on 7 January (18 Nivôse), that debate be opened on "the crimes of the English government and the vices of the British Constitution." The result did not live up to his expectations, as he explained with some exasperation on 28 January (9 Pluviôse). Further developments in the Desmoulins affair, together with a fresh controversy involving Fabre d'Églantine, were to provide him with more solid grounds for pressing his case.

Robespierre saw himself as Desmoulins's mentor. He plainly wished to protect him from the fury of the sans-culottes, advising him in a fatherly way to make amends. Alas, Desmoulins was of a mind to resist—and did he ever! To Robespierre's suggestion that the offending editions of his newspaper be publicly burned, and so never talked about again, he famously retorted, "Burning is not answering." With this, Robespierre's tone changed. While continuing to describe Desmoulins as an unwitting puppet, Robespierre caught him up in the wider conspiracy that he claimed to have unraveled. Desmoulins had become "the organ of a nefarious faction that borrowed his pen in order to distill its poison with greater audacity and fearlessness." He returned to this point the next day, having no doubt been informed in the meantime of the financial scandal involving forgeries committed by Fabre d'Églantine, which allowed ample room for innuendo. Behind the conflict between Desmoulins and Hébert, he told his audience, "the observant eye of an enlightened patriot" could detect the intrigue of foreign parties. The antagonism of the two was only apparent, meant to deceive the "watchfulness of patriotism": "Those who are of ardent temper and exaggerated character propose excessively revolutionary measures; those who are of a milder and more moderate spirit propose insufficiently revolutionary measures," but, in reality, "they conspire like bandits in a forest." Two plots that seemed to be at odds with each other were in fact only one, in the service of "Pitt and Coburg." Hence the necessity of calling attention to the true source of these seemingly uncoordinated schemes, which is to say the English government. Was this a way of making a doubtful scenario more believable by relating it to a very real war? A way of defusing the confrontation between Indulgents and Exagérés, while at the same time mobilizing the spirit of patriotic defense against both—without forgetting Robespierre's constant concern to plead the superior significance of the French Revolution by comparison with a prestigious competitor? "You are mistaken," he told the Jacobins on 28 January, "if you believe that the morality and the intellectual capacity of the English people are equal to yours; no, [the English] are two centuries behind you." The idea must have seemed incongruous to more than one of his listeners. Still, the club's members fell into line. There followed a series of labored and monotonous speeches embroidering on this theme. Disappointed with what he heard, Robespierre scolded the speakers as though they were so many dim pupils: "All the orators who have addressed this subject [here] have missed the true aim on behalf of which they ought to have spoken." It was not a matter of lecturing the English people, but of "impressing upon the soul of the French people a profound indignation against the English government"; the English people could not fail to draw the proper lessons themselves.

Two days later, on 30 January (11 Pluviôse), Robespierre ratcheted up the pressure another notch by protesting against the "Anglomania" and the remnants of "Brissotinism" that he discerned in the distinction made by certain speakers between the English people and their government. The implication seemed to be: "May they destroy their government; [in that case] perhaps we could still love them." But had not these people manifested their complicity with the crimes of their government? "As a Frenchman, and as a representative of the [French] people, I declare that I hate the English people." The widespread applause mentioned in newspaper accounts could not obscure the incomprehension with which these rebukes were bound to have met. Paris was not Rome, and Robespierre's call to "destroy Carthage" evidently did not produce the effect he intended. Despite their abiding goodwill, Robespierre's most faithful listeners were now beginning to find it difficult to follow their guide.

But alongside this indirect strategy for combating the factions via an attack on a foreign mastermind, there is good reason to believe that the Committee of Public Safety was already searching in January 1794 for more expeditious means of crushing them. Evidence may be found in a draft report on the Fabre d'Églantine faction, probably composed sometime in the middle of this month but left unfinished and never delivered, that was subsequently found among Robespierre's papers. Fabre d'Églantine's proven corruption furnished a golden pretext for opening hostilities. A leading figure of Danton's circle, his denunciation of Ronsin and Vincent in the Convention had led to their arrest. This providential connection made it possible to grasp the full extent of the problem by taking in both its aspects. "Two rival coalitions have struggled with scandal for some time now. The one tends to moderantism, the other to patriotically counterrevolutionary excesses." There is this interesting detail: "The one seeks to take advantage of its credit and its presence in the National Convention, the other of its influence in the popular societies." But both of them, inspired by the "agents of foreign courts," pursued the same end, namely, to "dissolve the National Convention" and to "topple republican government." Moreover, "the moderates and the false revolutionaries are complicit in pretending to quarrel, the more readily to carry out their crime." This argument was subsequently elaborated at some length, and there is no need to dwell on it here. The real value of the document is the inside view it gives, as vivid as it is partial, of the battles that the Committee of Public Safety had to fight in order to establish its authority, the last of which led to Robespierre's indictment of the rival factions. Remarkably, Danton went completely unmentioned. The unfortunate Fabre d'Églantine found himself elevated to the rank of grand master of conspiracies—"the man of the Republic who knows best which spring has to be touched in order to impart a particular movement to the various political machines that intrigue has at its disposal." For the moment, he was the ideal scapegoat for intimidating the Indulgents before turning to the faux-revolutionaries. The course of events decided matters otherwise, however, reversing the order of priorities. When Fabre d'Églantine mounted the scaffold, it was only as a minor player in a plot directed by figures of far greater stature.

This theme of a single foreign conspiracy with two faces, and a rotating cast of almost interchangeable characters, was the hallmark of a systematic way of thinking that seems to have been fixed in Robespierre's mind for several months. The protean plot facing the Committee of Public Safety, which it had to convince the Convention to join in combating in order to ensure its own survival, was the dark side of a luminous resolve to bring the Revolution to a successful conclusion, precisely as a result of destroying the conspirators. This was to mark a new beginning as well, the establishment of a truly authentic republican regime. Alongside the volatile struggle against the factions, and in concert with it, Robespierre pursued this foundational ambition with methodical and characteristic single-mindedness. It was the guiding thread of his activity during this last phase of his revolutionary career, extending from Frimaire to Thermidor in Year II, which is to say from November 1793 to July 1794. The stages of his journey may be briefly recapitulated. The first was occupied with defining the means required by the undertaking he had set for himself. This was the object of the *Rapport sur les principes du gouvernement revolutionnaire* of late December 1793. The second was devoted to clearly identifying the end needing to be attained. This was the object of the *Rapport sur les principes de morale politique qui doivent guider la Convention nationale dans l'administration intérieure de la République* that Robespierre submitted to the Assembly on 5 February 1794 (17 Pluviôse). The third stage involved determining under what conditions the regime of virtue embodied by the Republic could be established and its proper functioning assured. This was the object of his speech *Sur les rapports des idées religieuses et morales avec les principes républicains*, delivered on 7 May 1794 (18 Floréal). The factions having been crushed, it was now possible at last to formally affirm the existence of the Republic.

The *Rapport sur les principes de morale politique* was presented as the counterpart in respect of domestic policy to the argument Robespierre had expounded in respect of foreign policy in his *Rapport sur la situation politique de la République* of November 1793. It was part of an effort to legitimize the revolutionary government's rule inside France, by rationalizing it, for want of the external legitimacy that the coup d'état by a minority against the legally elected majority had deprived the Convention since 31 May of that year. In order to do this, it was necessary to provide some measure of reassurance by dispelling the impression that the country, carried away by the chaotic pressures of the moment, was haphazardly groping its way forward, at the mercy of the shifting fortunes of the warring parties—an impression to which, as Robespierre admitted, the intervening course of events may have seemed to lend credence. Nevertheless this apparently erratic trajectory had a clear direction, and the promised land was finally in view. "The time has come to clearly indicate the purpose of the Revolution and the end we wish to arrive at; the time has come to be honest with ourselves, about the obstacles that still stand in our way and the means that we must adopt in order to attain [the end]—a simple and important idea that seems never to have been noticed." That this "simple and important idea" should have gone unperceived was an indisputable sign of the mental confusion of the Revolution's actors, so distracted by political infighting that they had lost sight of the purposes for which power was being contested. Robespierre's claim to enjoy full powers, whose cathartic significance must be placed in its proper context, could only be temporary. To find a way out from this unavoidable state of exception, it would be necessary to consult the people. But there was no mystery about what they expected. They expected that the Revolution would soon be finished once and for all, that it would be possible at long last, as Robespierre himself said, to enjoy in peace the great promise of liberty and equality, still unfulfilled after the terrible ordeals of the past five years. By taking care not to use the same words in presenting it, he was able to adopt what had been the program of his unfortunate adversaries in the Constituent and Legislative Assemblies and in the Convention. His report prepared the way for a dramaturgy of the revolutionary process in its final phase. But this phase carried with it a cost, and the immediate objective was to justify this cost by the benefit that would result from it.

There was nothing fundamentally new in the definition of the end to be attained: the empire of virtue, achieved through democratic and republican government—one and the same thing, Robespierre assured his listeners. His liberal conception of democracy had not changed. It was, he said, "a regime in which the sovereign people, guided by the laws they have made, do by themselves everything that they can do and through delegates everything that they cannot do by themselves." Even so, one should not expect "wonders" from such a regime, even once morality, which is to say virtue, had been substituted for selfishness, and the public good preferred to individual interest—a preference that came naturally to the people: "[T]o love justice and equality, the people have no need of any great virtue; it is enough that they love themselves." None of these themes was surprising to anyone familiar with Robespierre's oratory; they were recycled once more, only now in a particularly polished form enlivened by splendid turns of phrase.

The novelty of his speech of 5 February resided in its analysis of means. Robespierre accepted responsibility for the use of terror and sought to justify it in its essential features. Indeed, he made it a key element of his doctrine of virtue. It is this aspect of the speech that is generally remembered, in the form of a number of striking passages that are nonetheless difficult to make sense of apart from their original context. Given the lofty goal of the Revolution, he argued, it would be fatal if along the way it were to run afoul of so many "depraved men," including those who embraced its cause only out of ambition or greed, regarding the Revolution "as a trade and the Republic as a spoil." In passing, he explained why executions on a large scale would soon be necessary: many of the Revolution's leading figures "had not begun the journey in order to arrive at the same end" as the one true patriots sought. Faced with political corruption of this kind, there was no other instrument than terror, which was only another facet of virtue in action. Hence these famous and deeply disturbing lines: "If the mainspring of popular government in a time of peace is virtue, in a time of revolution it is at once *virtue and terror*: virtue, without which terror is fatal; terror, without which virtue is powerless." By itself, terror is an abomination. But once it is coupled with virtue, it acquires another character. It becomes "justice—prompt, severe, inflexible"; without it, virtue has no chance of prevailing over vice. Robespierre then replied to Desmoulins without naming him: "It has been said that terror is the mainspring of despotic government." He granted the point, but insisted that a distinction must be made between despotism for its own sake and despotism as the temporary instrument of a higher cause, namely, its own abolition: "The government of the Revolution is the despotism of liberty against tyranny." What needed to be determined was whether the despotism of liberty actually leads to liberty without despotism, whether the instrument is in fact suited to the purpose; whether, in other words, the distinction between two kinds of despotism is something more than a merely rhetorical gesture, or whether in reality there is no difference between them. Robespierre made no attempt to do this. The logic in which he had imprisoned himself was inexorable. Once the definition of virtue as a sacrifice, as an "abasement of the private self" to the public interest, had been laid down as a fundamental principle and identified with the inner-most nature of the people whose rule needed to be established, any behavior that departed from it signaled the presence of an enemy of the people and had to be suppressed by whatever means necessary. In this sense there was no difference between war against an external enemy and civil war: "There are no citizens in the Republic but that are republicans. Royalists and conspirators it considers foreigners, or rather enemies." Saint-Just was to say the same thing three weeks later, on 26 February (8 Ventôse), with the inimitable and categorical concision for which he was famous: "A republic consists in the total destruction of whatever is opposed to it."

These preliminary remarks were not intended solely to furnish a theoretical justification a posteriori for an improvised policy. They also had a practical objective: to prepare public opinion for the offensive about to be launched by the Committee of Public Safety against the enemies lurking within. Indeed, the leading themes having been introduced, it was to this immediate purpose that Robespierre's speech was mainly devoted. The argument was developed from a familiar premise: "The internal enemies of the French people are divided into two factions, two army corps, as it were. They march under banners of different colors and by diverse routes; but they march toward the same goal." The leaders of these two factions, the one representing weakness and the other excess, "belong to the cause of kings and of the aristocracy and are forever united against the patriots." The only innovation in this statement of the argument concerned the usual characterization of the Exagérés, which Robespierre was at pains to correct. Rather than "ultrarevolutionaries," he said, one should speak instead of "false revolutionaries," easily identified by the variableness of their positions, whose only constant feature was the systematic obstruction of measures decreed by the government, this on the orders of their sponsors, "the Prussian, English, Austrian, even Muscovite committees." The political priority of the moment was self-evident, in light of this domestic conflict: "Such an internal situation must seem to you worthy of your full attention, above all if you keep in mind that you have at the same time to combat the tyrants of Europe, two hundred thousand men under arms to provision." If the perils of the hour were to be overcome, the power of France's foreign enemies could not be allowed to cause the treachery of its domestic enemies to be forgotten. Robespierre proceeded at once to indicate the rest of the plan: "What is the remedy for all these evils? We know of none other than to develop the Revolution's main source of impetus: virtue." Once the foreign plot had been eradicated and the "men who seek their own advantage," rather than the public good, permanently disarmed, it would be necessary to consider which "religious and moral ideas" were best suited to the task of implanting republican morality.

A few days after giving this speech, illness took Robespierre away from his duties for a little more than a month, until 13 March, just when the test of strength with the Hébertists was about to take a decisive turn. Does this mean that he took no part in the decisions of the Committee of Public Safety? No one can say. But the greatest mystery, destined forever to remain the most elusive aspect of his biography, is the nature of the recurrent malady that laid him low at crucial moments of his political career. After the arrest of the Dantonists, on 30–31 March, and their execution five days later, he was once more to vanish from public view, this time for almost three weeks, from 19 April (30 Germinal) until 7 May (18 Floréal), when he delivered his great speech on religious and moral ideas—no doubt a sign that he had nonetheless been able to work in the interval. Still more striking were his absence from the Committee of Public Safety during the last weeks of his life, in June and July 1794, and his silence at the Convention, which have long occupied the attention of historians and aroused much speculation, if only because they are difficult to reconcile with the received view of an omnipotent dictator.

Robespierre made no secret of his lack of vigor, of his tendency to exhaustion, of the fever that periodically sapped his strength. A favorite theme, as we have seen, was his imminent and inevitable sacrificial death; it was part of the public image he carefully cultivated, so much so that one does not know how seriously it should be taken. But in this final phase, when the achievement of his political purposes hung in the balance, things were different. His physical weakness and troubled state of mind came to play a role that cannot be ignored, even if no firm conclusions can be drawn from it. Any interpretation of his behavior is therefore irremediably marked by uncertainty. The Robespierre of the final days sinks into an impenetrable obscurity, which was to account for a great deal in the mythical image that came to be created later. The fact remains that when he returned on 13 March, the day of the arrest of the Hébertists, the major problem with which the Montagnard Convention was confronted— the rivalry of its authority with that of the Commune of Paris and of the sans-culotte movement backing it—was settled. The process of reasserting control that began once de-Christianization had been more or less brought to a halt and that led to a reorganization of the government was completed this time by the smothering of violence in Paris and the muzzling of the sections that fanned it. The Committee of Public Safety now had the upper hand for good. Methodically it went about installing the intermediate organs of its authority. In the aftermath of the execution of Hébert and the Cordelier leaders, on 24 March (4 Germinal), the Parisian Revolutionary Army, the paramilitary arm of the Hébertist movement whose ranks were populated largely by sans-culottes, was disbanded. The Commune was placed under the direction of a new group of officials loyal to Robespierre. The executive branch of the government was restructured, with the abolition of the ministries and their replacement by twelve committees reporting to the Committee of Public Safety. Envoys suspected of collusion with the Exagérés were recalled. But even though the battle against the ultrarevolutionaries had been won, it remained to decide the fate of the Dantonists, since the whole argument concerning the struggle against factional influence had been predicated on the symmetry of ultras and moderates and their mutual connivance. How could the one faction be attacked while leaving the other alone? It was impossible to stop at the liquidation of the Exagérés without giving the impression of excusing the Indulgents. Once this implication had been grasped, however, it was still necessary to determine how the operation was to be carried out and within what limits.

On this point it is plain that the fierce disagreements between the Committee of Public Safety and the Committee of General Security, each intent on protecting its own turf, concealed much wavering and indecision. Nevertheless it is hard for us at this distance to see the larger picture very clearly. The difficulty arises chiefly in connection with Danton, the emblematic figure of the Revolution in Paris, an orator of exceptional talent who still enjoyed great popularity, notwithstanding the controversies that since the summer of 1793 had caused his star to dim in relation to that of Robespierre. The difficulty also arises, though to a lesser degree, in connection with Desmoulins, the seventh (and last) issue of whose newspaper, *Le Vieux Cordelier*, had been seized at the printer's at the same time that the Hébertists were arrested. It would appear that Billaud-Varenne and Collot d'Herbois—both appointed to the Committee of Public Safety under pressure from the sans-culottes, it must be kept in mind—sought to offset the strike against the left by a no less forceful strike against the right with the elimination of the most prominent Indulgents. In this they had the support of a majority of the Committee of General Security. Robespierre, for his part, seems to have had second thoughts. While he had proclaimed on 15 March, as we saw earlier, that both factions must perish together, now he was reluctant, at least to begin with, to press the charge of conspiracy that far. It would be enough, he felt, so far as the search for scapegoats was concerned, to draw upon the evidence discovered in connection with the Fabre d'Églantine affair (now enlarged by the scandal surrounding the liquidation of the French East India Company), or so one is inclined to suppose in light of his subsequent remarks. On 16 March (26 Ventôse), Amar, speaking in the name of the two major committees jointly, presented to the Convention a report on this murky tale of bribery and fraud that concluded with the indictments of Chabot, Delaunay, Basire, Julien, and Fabre d'Églantine. Robespierre, coming after Billaud-Varenne, sharply criticized Amar's investigation for not having adequately brought out what was really at issue in the affair, namely, its links with a foreign plot. He made a draft of a speech on the subject that in the end was never delivered, but it seems to have described in considerable detail

THE RULE AND THE EXCEPTION [117]

the circumstances making it necessary to subdue the moderates, along the lines of his earlier report on the Fabre d'Églantine faction, likewise neglected. The opening lines ring out like a thunderbolt: "You citizens who represent the people, you expect from us the revelation of a great conspiracy; we are going to give it to you; above all, we are going to work our way back to its true leaders and seize the invisible hand that has woven its threads in dreadful darkness." But Robespierre's disclosures did not go beyond the already familiar circle of protagonists, with the sinister Baron de Batz once more furnishing dispositive evidence of the machinations of a foreign cabal. He made no mention of either Danton or Desmoulins, despite the transparent allusions to patriots exhibiting "a dangerous propensity for overconfidence, and perhaps a propensity for pleasure, more dangerous still." So long as they were not explicitly identified, the necessity of offsetting the elimination of the leading Hébertists could be postponed, at least for a time. Sooner rather than later he would have to make up his mind whether to enlarge the target.

Negotiations ensued, some with Danton directly, but to no satisfactory result. Finally, Robespierre allowed himself to be persuaded. Saint-Just was charged with writing the report. On 30 March (18 Germinal), six days after the execution of the Hébertists, the two committees, meeting in joint session, issued a writ for the arrest of Danton, Desmoulins, Lacroix, and Philippeaux. The eighteen signatures that appeared at the bottom of the document, an unusually high number, testified to the perceived gravity of the situation. There had nonetheless been disagreement about how to proceed, a further sign that the operation was thought to involve a considerable degree of risk. Following Saint-Just's speech to the Convention, he and Robespierre urged that the arrest be made in accordance with established procedure. But a majority of the two committees, fearing the Assembly's reaction, ordered that the four men be taken into custody immediately, that very night.

It must be admitted that this episode, destined to become legendary, not least for popularizing the image of the Revolution at its height as a duel to the death between two iconic figures, constitutes the least glorious chapter of Robespierre's career. Apart from still more fundamental considerations, the manner in which the trial was conducted and the role that Robespierre played in it are proof of an indefensible arbitrariness that even his most unconditional supporters have had, and will continue to have, a very hard time justifying. Evidently the Dantonists were no more guilty than the Hébertists of carrying out a foreign plot. At least the Hébertists, with the support of the nebulous sans-culotte movement, posed a real threat to the power of the committees. On the side of the Dantonists, by contrast, there was not even the semblance of a threat. The indictment drawn up by Saint-Just was made out of whole cloth, a sheer fabrication, the fantastic unlikelihood of which no amount of overbearing rhetoric could disguise. Nevertheless it succeeded, not unskillfully, in filling a vacuum. Saint-Just knew that Danton's reputation was his greatest asset. It was therefore on just this point that he concentrated his attack from the outset: "Citizens, the Revolution is in the people and not in the renown of a few persons." Moreover, for want of any evidence having even the slightest plausibility, he fudged the issue of a presumptive Indulgent conspiracy by insisting on the reality of a more general conspiracy going back to the earliest days of the Revolution, and in this way caused it to be subsumed under "a change of dynasty" that the Indulgents were on the verge of finally bringing about. This had the advantage of portraying them as the last faction needing to be eliminated. Once they had been gotten rid of, Saint-Just promised the deputies of the Convention, "[Y]ou will no longer have any examples to give; you will be at peace; intrigue will no longer enter this sacred chamber." This was, in other words, the proscription that announced the end of proscriptions—a way of reassuring and comforting an audience numbed by an apparently endless succession of revelations, each one more frightening than the last. The time when "only patriots will be left" was now finally at hand.

This is not the place to examine in greater detail what amounts to a catalogue of exercises in bad faith. Let us nonetheless recall, in order to have some idea of their tone, this remarkable charge hurled at Danton: "Hatred, you said, is unbearable to you. But are you in no way criminally responsible for not having hated the enemies of the fatherland?" From notes in Robespierre's papers, we know that he collaborated with Saint-Just on the report. Nothing could be more astonishing than this pathetic attempt at self-persuasion, having ransacked his memory for anything that could possibly convince him of the truth of an accusation he knew perfectly well to be absurd, falsely alleging duplicitous intent and dishonorable behavior—the "certain signs" by which one recognized "the party opposed to the Revolution, which always dissembles," as Saint-Just put it.

What follows in his report is no better than this pitiful prologue. News of the arrests had quickly spread. At its session the following day, the Convention was in a state of shock. Once again, a few members rose to speak in defense of the accused. Legendre, a Dantonist from the beginning, expressed a sentiment that no doubt was widely shared, declaring that he could not believe Danton to be guilty. He demanded that, at the very least,

Danton be granted a hearing by the Convention. Robespierre, called to the rescue from the Committee of Public Safety next door, swiftly reduced Legendre and like-minded deputies to silence by a speech that deserves a prominent place in an anthology of attempts at intimidation. His angle of attack was the same as that of Saint-Just, focusing on the "privilege" that was attached to Danton's name: "In no way do we require privilege; no, we have no need whatever for idols." And then he went a step further: "We will see today whether the Convention will be able to shatter a supposed idol who has long been corrupt." Next, he deployed the invincible weapon of suspicion. What could be the motives of those who cast doubt upon the authorities, whose duty is to defend the "interests of the fatherland" with the aid of "public trust"? "I say that whoever trembles at this moment is guilty." Robespierre nonetheless hastened to reassure the mass of deputies. "The guilty are not so very numerous; I bear witness to the unanimity, the near unanimity with which you have voted for the past several months in favor of principles." The implication was clear: continue to be quiet, and nothing bad will happen to you—a friendly way of keeping in line anyone who might be tempted to stray. The message had its intended effect. The unfortunate Legendre all but apologized for his doubts and withdrew his demand. No one dared to follow his lead. Opposition to Saint-Just's findings having been silenced, the indictment that came at the end of his report was "unanimously adopted in the midst of unrestrained applause."

But the trial itself was to pose problems, as the two major committees had rightly feared. In addition to the advantages presented by his prestige, Danton was not a man to give up without a fight. He defended himself fiercely, and his eloquence was convincing. It swayed the public, which had turned out in large numbers, and so deeply unsettled the members of the jury—though they had been instructed to do their duty (which is to say, to deliver a guilty verdict)—that the public prosecutor and the chief judge of the Revolutionary Tribunal called upon the two committees to intervene. Saint-Just at once took matters in hand and had a bill rushed through the Convention—once again "unanimously" approved—that cut off debate and denied the right of appeal to anyone "accused of conspiracy who resists or insults national justice." At this juncture a fresh plot, opportunely discovered in the prisons, accelerated the course of events. On 5 April (16 Germinal), Danton was guillotined, together with his codefendants, the victim of a hodgepodge of charges that associated him with the leaders of the "Fabre d'Églantine faction" and a few shady financiers, all of them indispensable in giving the plot a foreign coloring. That same evening, at the Jacobin Club, Robespierre angrily inveighed against Dufourny, a Dantonist of long standing, who had made the mistake of demanding proof of Danton's guilt, which is to say of suggesting, as Robespierre put it, that "the Convention sends men to the Revolutionary Tribunal without proof." The fury of his indignation gives some idea of how great the skepticism he had aroused was and how urgently he now needed somehow to dispel it.

CHAPTER FIVE

Governing the Revolution

THE UNDISCOVERABLE FOUNDATION

THE OPERATION HAD BEEN A SUCCESS. The two committees could claim to have triumphed over the forces of exaggeration and indulgence. But at what cost to their political credibility—the imponderable, though ultimately decisive, variable in the exercise of power? If this was less than ever the moment to raise the question publicly, doubt had insinuated itself in the minds of many deputies, perhaps even in the minds of the more lucid members of the committees. How otherwise are we to interpret this enigmatic note found in Saint-Just's papers, apparently written shortly afterward: "I have attacked men whom no one had dared to attack, everything conspired to make a criminal of anyone who did so dare, I alone had to carry out this dangerous mission. It falls to the youngest to die and to prove his courage and his virtue." There is something poignant about the tone of uncertainty that can be detected in this piece of self-justification. Power was now in the hands of the Committee of Public Safety and, to a lesser degree, the Committee of General Security, both free at last from the pressures exerted by the sans-culottes and no longer hampered by the uncooperativeness of a good part of the Convention, Montagnards included. But also, by the same token, the Committee of Public Safety no longer enjoyed what was left of the legitimacy, however weak it may have been, that it formerly derived from popular approval, having now only very limited support within the Convention itself, notwithstanding the superficial unanimity of its votes. It was a solitary body presiding over nothing more than a "frozen Revolution," as Saint-Just put it on the same occasion, an executive agency unsure of the purpose for which its power was to be used; and only by answering this question of fundamental intent can a government durably establish its reason for being. Abroad there was a war to be conducted, of course; and of course the "league of tyrants conspiring against France" had to be combated, as Robespierre never failed to insist. But at home? The elimination of the two factions could be defended only in relation to the promise of pacification that it held out. Now, in the early spring of 1794, the chapter of domestic struggle was finally closed. As Saint-Just emphasized, "[W]e have opposed sword to sword, and liberty is now secure."

The members of the two committees were well aware that bringing stability to the country was the only way that the liquidation of so many imaginary conspirators could be justified after the fact. The day before the arrest of the Dantonists, and surely not by chance, Barère announced to the Convention that the Committee of Public Safety was occupied with "a vast plan of regeneration, the result of which must be to banish from the Republic both immorality and prejudice, both superstition and atheism." For, he insisted, "it is necessary, at whatever cost, to found the Republic on principles and morals." This was the program that Robespierre laid out a month later, on 7 May (18 Floréal), in his major speech on religious and moral ideas. It may be that this statement—to which he attached such great importance, but for which he was sharply criticized by several colleagues—was the price of his agreeing to Danton's elimination, apparently more out of a concern for evenhandedness in the treatment of the two factions than because he favored it on other grounds. For the moment, however, it was Saint-Just who was to give more practical expression to the need to devise a stabilization policy, in his *Rapport sur la police générale, sur la justice, le commerce, la législation et les crimes des factions*, delivered on 15 April (26 Germinal).

The report's full title gives some idea of the extent of its ambition. It set forth a plan for restoring order in the country under the direction of a government that was finally in a position to respond fully to the wishes of the people. "Citizens, it is not enough to have destroyed the factions, it remains for us to repair the harm they have done to the fatherland. As they wished to bring back the monarchy, they needed to make the citizens hate the Republic and to make them very unhappy in order to prepare them for the change [to come]." The factions were to blame! Saint-Just's explanation, brief though it is, is worth examining for the insight it provides into how the main figures of the Revolution saw France during this period. In this regard, as we have already seen, what unmistakably set Saint-Just apart from the others was his firm grasp of what was happening—a realism that stands in bizarre contrast with the extreme vagueness of his language. This is not the place to examine in detail the account that Saint-Just gave of the situation of the country in these terrible first months of 1794 and of the harm done that the authorities had a duty to remedy. What matters for our purposes here is how one of the most lucid members of the Committee of Public Safety (and probably the only one who influenced Robespierre) perceived the task that lay ahead, in order to understand why he recommended the policy he did.

Saint-Just's analysis proceeded from what he called "civic federalism." While naturally bringing under this head the narrower "federalism" of the Brissotin faction, he was more interested in considering its unfortunate consequences for social relations in general. Its "crimes" were not limited to the political sphere; they had the effect of destroying "exchange, commerce, trust, social intercourse." Federalism, he went on, "does not consist only in a divided government, but also in a divided people." It led to the estrangement of one part of society from another, under the influence of mutual distrust, which had become so widespread as to affect family relations: "For some time now there have been few marriages outside the family; each house has been, so to speak, a society apart." The fundamental task of revolutionary government, under these circumstances, was to restore the unity that ought to obtain "between all the interests and all the relations of citizens." Accordingly, "you must make a polity, that is, [a society of] citizens who are friends, who are welcoming to one another and brothers; you must reestablish civic trust."

The program Saint-Just laid out assumed the paramount authority of the government and its agencies. This was not a new idea with him. It had been a central part of his *Rapport sur le gouvernement*, presented to the Convention in October 1793, which introduced this memorable maxim: "Laws are revolutionary; those who execute them are not." In the meantime anarchy and terror had intervened. The massive disruption that followed in their wake was due to the arbitrary behavior of an "obliging police," relaxation of ordinary justice in the face of crime, administrations populated by "creatures of intrigue," indifferent and unscrupulous officials. In short, "the moment has come to rouse from their sleep all the trustees of public authority." The speech concluded with a vigorous plea that deputies do their utmost to reassert control over the nation: "Make law with all the powers [available to you]," on the clear understanding that the object of law is to "subject men to the duties and other obligations of which liberty does not absolve them."

While appealing to a shared ideal of the "revolutionary man," of whom he sketched a striking portrait, Saint-Just did not try to lure the members of the Convention with entrancing prospects of the fate that awaited them. Even though the laws they enacted would make it possible to "save the fatherland," he told them, "you should expect no other reward than immortality. I know that those who have sought to do good have often perished." Allowance being made for the ambient rhetoric of heroism, which no one practiced more expertly than Saint-Just, we must take seriously the invocation of sacrificial death. This was the fate that, like Robespierre, he foresaw for himself, as we have already seen. There can be no doubt that it was constantly on the minds of the Revolution's main actors, nor that it influenced their behavior, sometimes in dramatic ways, at this convulsive moment in the history of the Revolution. Apart from the willingness to die for one's country, noblest of all deaths, it is difficult to understand why they acted as they did.

With regard to the decree approved on the strength of Saint-Just's report, we need to recall in particular the first article, which provided that "Those accused of conspiracy shall be transferred from all places in the Republic to the Revolutionary Tribunal in Paris." I will come back to this point, the centralization of the Terror, for it is one of the guiding threads that led directly to 27 July (9 Thermidor). But the purpose of the decree was much broader. It was concerned not only with speeding up administrative procedures, monitoring officials, procuring supplies, and drawing up a legal code, but also with establishing a "corps of civil institutions suited to safeguarding morals and preserving the spirit of liberty." It was meant, in other words, to allow the Committee of Public Safety to take control of the reins of government, and in this way to get back in touch with the people, whose mistrust was implicitly acknowledged. The centralization of repression was nonetheless very much a priority. The question of "oppressed patriots," which is to say of the arbitrary arrests made in conformity with the Law of Suspects, had not gone away since the Indulgents had first raised it in the fall of 1793. In the meantime this faction had been crushed, but still it was necessary to respond to protests that gave credence to its cause. Popular outrage was amplified by the use of terror by local officials to gain political advantage and by the selective ruthlessness of certain representatives sent on special assignment to the provinces by the Convention, making it a matter of considerable urgency that the grounds for judicial conviction be subjected to careful scrutiny. The Revolutionary Tribunal in Paris was supposed to offer the surest guarantees in this regard. At least it was more or less under the supervision of the Committee of Public Safety. Saint-Just was so convinced of the Tribunal's crucial importance that he personally oversaw the creation of a General Police

Bureau, in March 1794, placing himself in charge—evidence not only of his lack of confidence in the Committee of General Security (something its members were not to forget), but also of his belief that an administrative apparatus rotten from corruption had to be purged at once. During his mission to the Army of the North, from 3 May (14 Floréal) to 29 June (11 Messidor), Robespierre took over responsibility for the Bureau's affairs, the only administrative position to which he actively devoted himself in the course of his political career. It was therefore the only moment when he actually came to grips with the difficulties involved in implementing a policy that he himself had formulated.

Virtue as the Order of the Day

Robespierre's 7 May (18 Floréal) report on religious and moral ideas was conceived in the same spirit as Saint-Just's report; indeed, it was an extension of it. It fulfilled one of the objectives of the program set forth by Saint-Just, namely, the establishment of a corps of civil institutions concerned with protecting morality and liberty. This was a topic on which Saint-Just continued to develop his ideas, which have come down to us in the form of a tentative and unfinished section of his *Fragments sur les institutions républicaines*. One of his annotations to the draft version is revelatory: "Terror may rid us of the monarchy and the aristocracy; but who will deliver us from corruption? Institutions? One wonders: one believes everything has been done when one has a machine for governing." This "one" who cannot be sure and yet who thinks he can rely on the machinery of government may be one of the keys to explaining what happened on 9 Thermidor. It probably refers to his colleagues on the two committees, unconvinced by the course of action he advocated. It was this difference of opinion that was to isolate Robespierre, Saint-Just, and their ally Couthon (said to have formed between them a "triumvirate") from the rest of the leadership. The two reports should be read in parallel. They were the product of slightly different sensibilities—roughly speaking, Robespierre placed his trust in ideas, whereas Saint-Just, in some ways a sociologist before his time, placed his trust in morals, which is to say ideas incorporated in customary ways of life—but they were animated by a common conviction and they responded to the same questions. The Republic had been decreed, but it had not yet been established. For want of a mooring in the spontaneous behavior of citizens, without which no comparably demanding regime could long survive, it floated in a void. How could this void be filled? How could the citizen's identification with the good of the country, which will turn him away from selfishness and inaugurate the reign of virtue, be made immediate and intuitive?

The very title of Robespierre's report tells us the answer: republican principles by themselves are not enough; they require the assistance of religious ideas and morals. However natural virtue may be to the people, still it cannot do without the support of common beliefs sanctioned by public recognition and sustained by worship and ritual in order to be effectively exercised. One also detects in Robespierre's exposition an element of doubt with regard to the presumptively instinctive aptitude of the people for integrity and justice. The appeal to popular virtue, an essential part of his impassioned early pleadings as an opponent of the government, is seldom encountered in this last attempt by Robespierre, now as a member of the government, to provide solid foundations for the sovereignty of the people. Great attention is paid, by contrast, to the corruption of the public spirit, which made the revolutionary experience so violent and so intractable a struggle between vice and virtue. The battle against the factions, reviewed in terms that were now familiar, could not be reduced to an unrelenting and single-minded campaign against Danton (described as "the most dangerous of the fatherland's enemies, if not also the most despicable"), for this was only the last episode. It was necessary to go back to the intellectual origins of 1789, which Robespierre located in what he called the sect of the encyclopedists: "Anyone who is unaware of its influence and its politics will not have a complete idea of what led up to our Revolution." All evils sprang from this sect, because in politics it "always remained above the rights of the people," and in morals it "zealously propagated the opinion of materialism," another name for the "system of self-interest."

It therefore is no surprise that its heirs, considering the English Constitution to be "the masterpiece of political thought and the acme of social happiness," should have found themselves during the Revolution on the side of the Orleanist faction, the mother of all factions, and worked only to "debase republican principles and corrupt public opinion." Robespierre went on to say that "men of letters generally dishonored themselves in this Revolution"—a claim that only threw into sharper relief the exceptional example of Rousseau, the one man who, "by his high-mindedness and by the greatness of his character, showed himself worthy of the office of tutor of the human race," which could not fail to bring upon him "the hatred and the persecution of his rivals." He alone was able to paint "with luminous strokes the charms of virtue" and to defend the "consoling dogmas that reason gives the human heart for support." There could be no doubt that, "had he witnessed this Revolution of which he was the precursor ... ,

[he] would have rapturously embraced the cause of justice and equality." That "common sense without complication and genius without instruction," which characterize the "reason of the people," should have managed to triumph would have seemed a foregone conclusion to Rousseau. Even so, the influential legacy of the encyclopedists, these "intriguing sophists who usurped the name of philosophers," profoundly contaminated the revolutionary movement, as the plotting of the factions demonstrated, by encouraging "all that tends to justify selfishness, harden the heart, and efface the idea of [Rousseau's] noble ethic." Under these circumstances, the battle against the factions could now be brought to a successful conclusion only by solemnly adopting a contrary philosophy and instituting a new model of worship capable of counterbalancing and gradually eradicating the seeds of dissolution.

Uncertainty had begun to take root in the minds of many deputies, and not only with regard to popular morality. In an adjuratory appeal to those who were now unsure of the ultimate outcome of the Revolution, Robespierre vehemently took issue with the view that signs of the present state of corruption were in agreement with the lessons of history in confirming the impossibility of a reign of liberty and virtue on earth, apart from a few rare exceptions found only in remote antiquity. To the contrary, no impasse had been reached. Virtue was not a figment of the imagination: "Founders of the French Republic, take care not to lose faith in humanity, do not for a moment doubt the success of your great enterprise!" Even so, it was to history that Robespierre looked for arguments in support of this confidence—not history in the classical sense of a written record preserving the exemplary deeds of the past, but in the modern sense of a creative force driving the evolution of human society: "The world has changed, it must go on changing." The progress made so far justified the expectation of still greater and, above all, more far-reaching transformations in the future—for "if everything has changed in the physical realm," the situation was exactly opposite "in the moral and political sphere." Only "half of the revolution of the world" had been completed; the other half had yet to be accomplished. "The peoples of Europe have made wonderful progress in what are called the arts and sciences, but they seem ignorant of the rudiments of public morality. They know everything, except their rights and their duties." The future, Robespierre assured his listeners, portended a degree of advancement in social relations equivalent to that which had already occurred in the understanding and mastery of nature.

It was the narrowing of just this gap between the two spheres that the French Revolution had set in motion. "The French people," Robespierre mused, "seem to have overtaken the rest of the human race by two thousand years; indeed, it is tempting to look upon it, in the midst of [the Revolution], as a different race." As a consequence, everything needed to ensure the Revolution's success in France and beyond was within reach: "Yes, you can show to the world the novel spectacle of democracy established throughout a vast empire." It was now a matter only of strengthening its foundations in the country of its birth.

It is at this juncture that a contradiction emerges. To Robespierre's mind, the advance of reason he confidently anticipated in the political sphere was conceivable only by returning to a natural order of things that ruled out the very idea of progress. This contradiction was not at all peculiar to Robespierre; it was characteristic of the spirit of the Revolution as a whole, torn between the heritage of natural law and the new perspectives opened up by a history that led on inexorably to the future, divided between the desire to give political life a permanent foundation, timelessly anchored in reason, and the prospect of making society progressively more rational. The tension is simply clearer and more acute in Robespierre on account of his exacting vision of a republic that rests solely on virtue, which is to say a state of affairs where each citizen makes the public interest his own, identifies his fate with that of the fatherland, and "merges his happiness with the happiness of all"—an ideal that, in the poisonous atmosphere of the spring of 1794, was more urgently in need of being realized than ever. Because morality is an inner impulse that makes it possible to prefer the common good to one's own interest, the science of politics and legislation becomes a matter of "putting into laws and administration the moral truths that have [until now] been relegated to the books of philosophers." These moral truths find their surest guarantee in religious ideas:

> The masterpiece of society would be to create in [man] a swift-acting instinct that, without the belated assistance of reasoning, causes him [at once] to do good and to avoid evil. . . . Now, what produces and replaces this precious instinct, which compensates for the insufficiency of human authority, is the religious sentiment that impresses upon [men's] souls the idea of a sanction given to the precepts of morality by a power superior to man.

It was therefore indispensable to preserve the meaning of the "sacred bond" that unites men with the "author of their being," by purging ancient religion of its superstitious beliefs and casting aside the hypocrisy of the priests, keeping only the fundamental core of religious faith. It was no part of the legislator's duty to ponder questions of metaphysics and theology;

the only criterion he had to keep in mind was practical utility: "The idea of a Supreme Being and the immortality of the soul is a continual summons to justice; it is therefore social and republican." There was in any case no way of doing without a Supreme Being: "The man who could replace the deity in the system of social life would be, in my eyes, an impossible genius."

The problem was that the utilitarian reappropriation of the deity by a republic of virtue made it all the more difficult to bring such a regime into existence. It went hand in hand with the revival of the idea of a political body united by the inviolability of its agreement with its foundational law and, for this reason, capable of reconciling each of its members with himself and with his fellow citizens in their common devotion to the public interest. In Robespierre's vision one readily recognizes the modern metamorphosis of the ancient ideal of religious unity brought about by a new conception of nature that put the original and the eternal within the reach of the rational. But it is also a vision that was incompatible with the independence of political parties, the disruptive force of technological innovation, and the novel dynamic of labor relations implicit in the prospect of an indeterminate future—incompatible, in other words, with the nineteenth century.

All this is clearer still in Saint-Just. The web of "eternal and imperturbable" institutions in which he sought to embed social life in order to "promote concord within families and friendship among citizens, and substitute the public interest for all the other interests," is a typical example of this rereading of the ancient doctrine of holy unity in the light of free reason. But the sort of Arcadia he imagined, immutable in its stern harmony and frugal happiness, is hard to reconcile with the dynamism of an industrial economy, the advent of which he clearly foresaw. Saint-Just was both more of an ancient and more of a modern than Robespierre, more radical in his vision of a well-formed republican system of government, based on laws capable of "substituting the ascendancy of morals for the ascendancy of men," and more sensitive to the actual conditions under which an unprecedented social order had to be established. But both were similarly torn between a philosophy of the new—a faith in progress, an awareness of how societies develop over time—and an ideal having its roots in the religious past.

No doubt this is what caused them to look back to the republics of antiquity. The question of foundations was now uppermost in their minds; until then they had been chiefly concerned with the advancement of knowledge. But in the face of the adversity that had to be overcome, and the uncertainty of success, ancient models uniting political liberty and piety gave reason for optimism. As Robespierre put it, "liberty and virtue settled for a brief moment in a few parts of the world. Sparta shines like a flash of lightning in an immense darkness." Even so, neither he nor Saint-Just turned exclusively to the ancients for inspiration. Both sought to institute something new, a liberty of the moderns, the nature of which they understood very clearly. Yet the obstacles they faced in achieving this liberty at a moment of extreme tension irresistibly drew them back to the ancient conception of political community, based on a self-conscious identification of citizens with the polity.

How did Robespierre manage to win acceptance of his views by his colleagues on the Committee of Public Safety, most of whom are known to have been either uninterested in philosophical ideas or else frankly hostile to an official deism of the sort Robespierre had in mind? This is something we will never know. If we did, much of what remains obscure to us would become clear. But the basic fact of a profound temperamental difference between Robespierre and the other members of the Committee makes it tempting to infer a dictatorial preeminence that reduced potential adversaries to silence. While Robespierre's domination is incontestable, it nonetheless appears more probable that his colleagues were interested above all in the political aims his policy was meant to achieve and with which they could only be in agreement. The metaphysical foundations of the Republic may not have preoccupied them to the same degree, if at all, but as a practical matter its stabilization and reorganization certainly did. Even Billaud-Varenne, philosophically more opposed to Robespierre than any of the others, had submitted a *Rapport sur la théorie du gouvernement démocratique* to the Convention on 20 April (1 Floréal) whose purpose was not fundamentally different.

For Robespierre it was primarily, and rather prosaically, a question of finally filling the void created by the adoption of the revolutionary calendar in September 1792. What was to be done with the *décadi*—the tenth and last day of the new week and the day of rest that substituted for Sunday—if one did not wish to encourage people to frequent taverns, rather than places of worship, as they had quickly gotten into the habit of doing? In a speech to the Convention at the end of February, he proposed, not for the first time, that the *décadi* be devoted instead to "festivals instituted under the auspices of the Supreme Being." It was in executing this program during the weeks that followed that Robespierre saw an opportunity to transform it into one of far greater scope. But the main part of the Decree on Worship of the Supreme Being issued at once in response to his speech of 7 May, on religious and moral ideas, was concerned with a schedule of festivals to be held every ten days for the purpose of "making man mindful once more of the deity and of the dignity of his [own] being." The larger objective of the decree was to do away with wars of religion altogether. In this connection the text of the decree contained a section as brief as it was to be decisive, article 12, stipulating that "freedom of worship is maintained in conformity with the decree of 18 Frimaire [8 December 1793]." This amounted not only to confirming the end of the campaign for de-Christianization, but also of guaranteeing the right to practice the Catholic religion. What was chiefly at stake was winning over people in the countryside, in particular, who had been alienated by the depredations of revolutionary armies and various local authorities; in many parts of France, violence had escalated to the point that one could speak without exaggeration of a cultural war between urban and rural populations. Robespierre remained vague about the precise form that free expression of religious faith would be permitted to assume and how established religions would be allowed to coexist with the official civic religion. Saint-Just, in the draft manuscript of his *Institutions républicaines*, was clear at least on the main point: "All faiths are equally permitted and protected. Public temples are open to all faiths." The official religion was meant, in other words, to provide a comprehensive framework within which each of the various confessions would have its place.

But the ultimate purpose of the speech of 7 May was still more ambitious. It involved a dimension of social life that is difficult to define, because it cannot be reduced to what is properly called the legal sphere, and yet it is crucial because of the way in which it orients individual behavior and orders personal relationships. Someone obsessed with the paramount importance of virtue, as Robespierre was, and convinced moreover of the naturally virtuous character of the people was bound to be alert to the effects of demoralization, in every sense of the word, produced by the turmoil of recent years, even among the ranks of the most fervent supporters of revolutionary aims. He spoke of it only in veiled phrases, but the place occupied in his papers by the search for trustworthy servants of the Republic leaves no doubt about the intensity of this obsession. Once more it was Saint-Just who gave it its most candid expression. We have already noticed a few of his most famous phrases, one of which needs to be put back in its proper context: "The Revolution is frozen; all its principles are weakened; there remain only revolutionaries carried away by intrigue." Saint-Just's disillusionment bore primarily on people in positions of power, but his conclusions concerning the state of society in general were no more heartening. Faced with this bleak state of affairs, one last effort had to be made to restore the basis of common morality—hence the need for a civic religion. The opening articles of the Decree on Worship of the Supreme Being constituted a formal statement of the duties of man, the precise wording of which left no doubt about the gravity of the evil to be combated. Article 1, announcing that "the French people recognize the existence of the Supreme Being and the immortality of the soul," led on directly to the solemn avowal in article 2 that "the proper worship of the Supreme Being consists in fulfilling the duties of man." These duties, though they were certainly political in nature, were no less associated with the private, rather than the public, sphere. Article 3 laid down that the French people "place in the first rank of these duties [the obligation] to detest bad faith and tyranny, to punish tyrants and traitors, to rescue the unfortunate, to respect the weak, to defend the oppressed, to do to others all the good one can without being unjust toward anyone."

Robespierre's new line was all the more remarkable considering that he had been strenuously opposed from 1789 until quite recently, in connection with the Constitution of 1793, to the idea of a declaration of duties. Only the seriousness of the present situation could have brought about such an agonizing change of mind, which Robespierre was careful for the moment not to admit. Once again the deputies felt obliged to follow his lead, notwithstanding that many of them must have suspected the reservations of the other members of the Committee of Public Safety. Robespierre proceeded with caution. No doubt he was keenly aware of his colleagues' misgivings, and had set about allaying them in such a way that they would find his proposal acceptable. He sought compromise. I have already emphasized how skillfully he put forward the argument from political utility, in order to remove worries that unwanted philosophical disputes would interfere; indeed he went so far as to say that, in the eyes of the legislator, "the truth is all that is useful in the world and good in practice." The cynicism is rather astonishing, coming from him, but his main interest was to win the support of the most refractory minds, both on the Committee and in the Convention. Above all he sought to dispel fears of a revival of fanaticism and the return of priests to positions of power as a consequence of the protections officially extended to the Catholic faith. The opposite would be true, he assured his listeners: "Recalling men to the pure worship of the Supreme Being is to strike a mortal blow against fanaticism. . . . Without constraint, without persecution, all sects are bound by themselves to merge into a universal religion of nature." As for priests, they have "killed themselves" as a result of betraying their mission. "They are to morality what charlatans are to medicine. How different is the God of nature from the god of the priests! He knows nothing so like atheism as the religions they have made." There was nothing to be dreaded on this score, then, once worship of the Supreme Being had been established, a religion whose "true priest" was nature itself. Moreover, all possible dangers had been duly foreseen by the decree, two articles of which were devoted to the suppression of any "aristocratic gatherings" that might take as their pretext freedom of worship and the unrest that was likely to arise from "fanatic preaching." Plainly, as Payan, the new leader of the Paris Commune since March 1794 and a loyal Robespierrist, explained to his allies on 3 May (14 Floréal), navigating this hazardous moment in the nation's history meant steering "a middle course between superstition and atheism." In this way it would be possible to beat the Church at its own game, by satisfying the popular need for devotion while detaching it from the institutions of the ancien régime, with the result that Catholicism would gradually be absorbed into the peculiar deism that was now France's official cult.

These purposes and arrangements bore much less resemblance to the imposition of a republican religion presided over by a self-proclaimed pontiff than to a practical policy of political compromise, which Robespierre invested with his usual conviction and which even the independent-minded men of the two committees felt obliged to rally behind. All of them agreed that it was necessary to find a safe passage between two treacherous reefs: on the one side, the resistance of popular religiosity, and, on the other, the disintegration of social relations under the influence of atheistic belief. The objective announced by Robespierre, of "inspiring in man a religious respect for man, a profound sentiment of his duties, which is the sole guarantee of social happiness," could not have helped but hold a certain appeal for men willing to set aside their personal philosophical opinions in order to meet the daunting challenge of governing the country. The sense of "walking on a volcano," to recall the image attributed by Saint-Just to Billaud-Varenne in his last speech of 27 July (9 Thermidor), never delivered, must have been rather widely shared. Determining whether the remedy Robespierre proposed was a realistic response to the crisis was quite another matter, however.

In spite of the precautions he had taken, Robespierre's initiative encountered criticism, even opposition, from certain elements of his own party. An echo of this may be found in the record of a meeting of the Jacobin Club on 15 May (26 Floréal). Jullien, Robespierre's eyes and ears in the departments of the West, urged the society to publicly declare its support

for the Decree on the Supreme Being. "[T]he aristocracy in [these] departments," he reported, "is saying that the Jacobins are silent and that they
do not approve of what the Convention has done. It is necessary to put an
end to such calumnies." One of his listeners cautiously objected that the
Convention's intent could have been misunderstood, since the text of the
decree had been proposed in the first place by a member of the Committee
of Public Safety. At this Robespierre flew into a tantrum, lashing out not
so much against the unfortunate interlocutor as against the "miserable
conspirators" who "seek to slander . . . the noble principles professed by
the Convention," those who "rail against principles and against the Committee of Public Safety." He went on to enumerate their scheming attempts
to neutralize the "sublime and immortal decree in which the great truths
of nature are recognized," notably by preventing the address that Payan
delivered to the Convention on 13 April, congratulating it on behalf of
the Paris Commune, from being printed in the *Moniteur*. Most striking
of all, however, was how vigorously Robespierre tried to clear himself of
the charge that he sought to impose his own ideas—a sign that he saw this
as the main line of attack pressed by the "perfidious ranters." The decree
adopted by the Convention, like Payan's address, did no more than express
sentiments already present in the hearts of all good patriots. "It is you
[patriots] who have spoken in this address; its sentiments were suggested
to you by no one." His manifest exasperation nonetheless did not cause
him to lose sight of the need for circumspection. "It is [the] truths [of
nature] that must be carefully presented," he insisted, dismissing Jullien's
overly zealous and thoroughly Rousseauist call for "banishing from the
Republic all those who do not believe in the deity."

Events were to confirm suspicions that the threat of conspiracy had
not yet been eliminated. On 22 May (3 Prairial), Collot d'Herbois was shot
at twice by a neighbor, an unemployed man who was rumored to have
selected him as a target in desperation after failing to get within range
of Robespierre. Both bullets missed. The next day, a sixteen-year-old
girl named Charlotte Corday, acting and talking strangely, tried to gain
entrance to Duplay's house, where Robespierre was a lodger. Brought
before the Committee of General Security, she was discovered to be carrying two small knives, which led the authorities to conclude at once that
she was bent on assassination. Even before learning of this latest attempt,
Barère, speaking to the Convention on behalf of the Committee of Public Safety, set the tone. Behind these criminal plots, he said, "everywhere
you will find the fatal genius of the Englishman and of the internal factions he ceaselessly nourishes in our midst." Needless to say, the news of

a second attempt on Robespierre's life raised the temperature by a few more degrees. Barère's revival of the theme of foreign conspiracy was not without a certain irony: his speech of 26 May (7 Prairial), repudiating the image of Robespierre as a dictator propagated by English newspapers, gave currency to the very accusations that were to be turned back against Robespierre on 27 July (9 Thermidor). Robespierre was now understood to be the man who had to be brought down—a position that well suited him, as we have already seen.

This emotional moment furnished him with the opportunity to make a grand display of the sacrificial fate that was at the heart of his carefully cultivated public reputation. On 25 May, speaking at the Jacobin Club, he exhibited a haughty indifference. Patriots, he said, "have never believed they had to live to an old age." All the more, then, was he now resolved to deny himself the normal pleasures of life in order to devote himself fully to his mission. "Myself, I do not at all believe in the necessity of living, only in virtue and in Providence . . . ; more than ever do I feel myself to be free from the malice of men." But this inner sense of liberty did not lead him to renounce the world; to the contrary, it was a force that became magnified in the service of action: "My heart is prepared more than ever to identify the traitors and to tear off the masks with which they dare still to cover their faces!" And indeed, in the course of this same session at the Jacobin Club, it became clear that mistrust, and the determination to exact vengeance to which it gave rise, had been strengthened in him still further. He lost no time uncovering ulterior motives that lay behind the motion made by certain members of the society, who no doubt were guilty of nothing more than overzealousness, that "civic honors" be awarded at the Festival of the Supreme Being to a collateral victim of the failed attempt against Collot d'Herbois, the "brave locksmith Geffroy," and that "representatives be given bodyguards." In all this he discerned "a clever trap invented by the partisans of tyranny" for the purpose of discrediting the beneficiaries of these "superfluous honors." He went on to call attention to "another insidious motion," more ominous still, but fortunately nipped in the bud, "demanding that thanks be given to the Supreme Being, in the temple of reason, for having preserved the lives of the representatives [of the people]." The cunning calculation in this case was that by "reviv[ing] ancient religious ceremonies," it would be possible to discredit the cult of the Supreme Being.

Robespierre's hypervigilance, concentrated on a tangled web of relentless scheming, suggests that he was well aware of the weakness of his position and of his narrowing room for maneuver. No matter that he had won victory after victory, having managed most recently to gain approval for one of the ideas that was closest to his heart, and no longer had to deal with any avowed opponents, he nonetheless increasingly began to feel that hidden enemies were leagued against him. The widespread hostility and skepticism encountered by the cult of the Supreme Being, which he saw as his last line of defense, allowed him to gauge the distance that separated the nation from the reign of virtue this religion was meant to bring about. This is what led him to embark upon a new offensive—the final one.

The Last Battle

Robespierre addressed the Convention the day after the 25 May session at the Jacobin Club, again speaking in veiled terms, though surely his meaning was understood by almost everyone in the audience. His speech came after an interminable lecture by Barère on "the combination of crimes that agents in the pay of England [carried out] in our midst," which concluded with the adoption of a famous decree authorizing murderous reprisals: "No English or Hanoverian prisoner will be taken." Robespierre stood at the podium under the dual halo of martyr and survivor. He began by expanding upon the sacrificial theme he had introduced the day before, laying stress on the renewed vigor that enabled him to carry on. "I now cling to an ephemeral life only by love of country and by a thirst for justice; and freed more than ever from all personal consideration, I feel better prepared to energetically attack the scoundrels who conspire against my country and against the human race." He had long been aware, he suggested, of "the perfidious hands that direct the fury of assassins and who are not yet visible to everyone." He mentioned "dreadful secrets" that "perhaps" he would reveal. For—and this was the crucial point—"the destinies of the Republic are not yet entirely secure." Crushing the factions was not enough to ward off all danger, as an "improvident insouciance" might suppose. "What constitutes the Republic is neither the pomp of denominations, nor [military] victory, nor wealth, nor fleeting enthusiasms; it is the wisdom of laws and above all the goodness of morals." In this regard, everything remained to be done. The enterprise of regeneration had to be given fresh impetus.

Robespierre proceeded to reduce the subject to its essential aspect, once more employing his favorite couplet: the virtue of the people. Their singular excellence, he went on to say, was "attested by the whole of the Revolution." Nevertheless he recognized its limits. Popular virtue "will not by itself suffice to reassure us against the factions that work ceaselessly to corrupt and tear apart the Republic." This was because "there are two peoples in France: one is the mass of citizens, pure, simple, ardent in their love of justice and liberty. . . . The other is this band of ambitious and intriguing men, these garrulous, deceitful, artificial men who are everywhere visible, who persecute patriotism, who monopolize the tribunes and often public offices [as well]." In what followed it was difficult not to recognize a great many revolutionaries—the only ones, Robespierre emphasized, who were able to place themselves "between the French people and their representatives, in order to deceive the former and slander the latter, to frustrate their purposes, to turn the most useful laws and the most beneficial truths against the public good." The outlook was grim: "So long as this impure race exists, the Republic will be unhappy and [its stability] precarious." This only showed how far the task was from being accomplished. Robespierre called upon his fellow deputies to rise to the occasion: "It is up to you to deliver [the Republic from danger] through an overpowering energy and an inalterable unity of purpose." As for Robespierre himself, he passed the torch to them, anticipating his own departure from the scene: "In saying these things I sharpen daggers against me, and it is for this very reason that I say them. . . . I have lived enough." It was as though he sensed the futility of trying to eliminate the false people who had interposed themselves between the true people and their governors, and relieved himself of responsibility by handing it over to others.

It is possible, of course, to see Robespierre's embrace of the role of victim as merely a rhetorical ruse, the trickery of a man aspiring to supreme power who sought to strengthen the allegiance of his accomplices. So long as no additional evidence that might settle the question is forthcoming, agreement is unlikely ever to be reached. We are, and in all probability will remain, limited to conjectures based on nothing more than the presumptive coherence of a personality and of a career. The most plausible interpretation along these lines, as far as Robespierre's behavior is concerned, seems to be his unwavering determination in the pursuit to a single aim, come what may. The course of events had evidently contradicted his vision of popular virtue. He managed nonetheless to rescue this vision by turning the energy of his own despair against those who betrayed it—in spite of whom he thought the promised land of virtue had come into view. In the worst case, if for the moment the horizon was unattainable, it would at least survive as an example to be bequeathed to posterity. It was on this note that he concluded his invitation to the members of the Convention to carry on the work that he felt sure he would soon be deprived of the opportunity to bring to fruition himself: "With our blood we will trace the way for you to follow to immortality."[1] In the meantime, however, he was unflinchingly to go on fighting a battle that he had reason to suspect had already been lost. The most desperate battles are the fiercest.

Listeners who knew from long experience how to decipher Robespierre's coded messages would have realized that the signal had just been given for a new campaign of denunciation and purification. The targets remained vague—for the moment, there were no known factions—but the general thrust was clear enough. Anyone who could not work out what was meant had only to wait for Couthon's report on proconsuls— parliamentary deputies sent on mission for the purpose of personally administering affairs in various parts of the country—delivered three days later, on 29 May (10 Prairial), which concluded by announcing the intention of the Committee of Public Safety (tellingly, Couthon speaks of the "government") to assert its authority by prosecuting members of the Convention who had exceeded their authority. To be sure, Couthon proceeded cautiously, but his reference to the apparent contradictions between the "general views" of the Committee and the views of the representatives, "founded on local interests," was an ominous sign. It resulted from this, he said, "that the particular good has offset the general interest and often prevailed over it; that the action of the government, which must be unified in order to be strong and sure, has been divided and paralyzed." Hence the need for "severe" measures, as Couthon himself described them, to "bring everything back to a common seat of authority." The targets now became clear: proconsuls guilty of abusing their prerogatives had better beware. Battle lines drawn, troops were put in position on both sides and maneuvers shortly gotten underway.

It is quite plausible to suppose that the maneuvering commenced with Robespierre's "unanimous" election as president of the Convention for a two-week term beginning 4 June (16 Prairial), thus enabling him to officially preside over the Festival of the Supreme Being, scheduled to take place four days later. His supporters saw this as a way of honoring the preeminent role he had played in disavowing atheism and instituting the new religion. But for those who now counted themselves among his adversaries, it was an opportunity to expose the dictatorial isolation that prevented him from seeing the error of imposing his own personal beliefs, if not also to

---

1. The preamble to *Institutions républicaines* concludes on a similar note: "I also had the touching idea that the memory of a friend of humanity must one day be dear, for man, obliged to cut himself off from the world and from himself, now at last casts his anchor into the future and impresses upon his heart a posterity innocent of present evils."

ridicule him as the pontiff of an artificial cult. On this view of the matter, very different motivations converged to produce a superficial unanimity.

It must be said that the organizer of the festivities, the painter David, had shown great imagination in mobilizing the people of Paris and multiplying the symbols of the Revolution's triumph over "all the enemies of public happiness." This moment heralded an era of reconciliation that his plan described in lyrical terms: "All the French merge their sentiments in a fraternal embrace; from now on they have but one voice, whose general cry—Long Live the Republic!—rises up to the deity." Whether owing to deliberate calculation or not, the festival fell on a Sunday of the old Christian calendar, the Sunday of Pentecost, no less—a coincidence that raised tensions on both sides. The fact remains that the festival seems undeniably to have been a popular success. In all probability what the people in attendance noticed above all was the introduction of a new watchword. They were relieved to discover that "virtue is the order of the day," a phrase repeated over and over again by the authorities since Robespierre's most recent speech, had been substituted for "terror is the order of the day." What stuck in people's minds was the promise of the *Hymn to the Supreme Being*, composed for the occasion by Chénier, a member of the Convention: "May the French Hercules, standing on the wreckage of tyrants and crimes, bring down his rivals; may he profit at last from his works!" But the people's understanding of David's scenography mattered little to their representatives. Sacral symbolism is something that must be handled with the greatest care, for the pomp that inspires awe is never far from the masquerade that arouses derision. And derision, rather than awe, was the mood of at least some of the members of the Convention who took part in the celebration, whether they wanted to or not; indeed, the boldest of them made it abundantly clear how they felt. Beneath the brilliant sun that shone that day, the gaiety of the people, who thought that the end of their trials was finally at hand, must have been in striking contrast with the anxiety of their representatives, who looked forward to the coming confrontation with growing unease.

It was not long before the suspense was broken. Two days later, on 10 June (22 Prairial), Couthon's draft decree modifying the powers of the Revolutionary Tribunal was enacted by the Convention. In one sense, and this is how Couthon presented the matter, the Law of 22 Prairial was intended only to give effect to measures that had already been approved, with a view to limiting the arbitrary behavior of local authorities by centralizing the elimination of counterrevolutionary elements, while recognizing that the massive transfer it entailed of suspects to prisons in Paris

made it necessary both to simplify and accelerate the Tribunal's procedures. But at this tense moment the law took on another meaning for
some members of the Convention, who feared that it might be directed
against them. The atmosphere following Couthon's speech was electric.
The first deputy to take the floor, Ruamps, one of those who had openly
mocked Robespierre during his address at the Festival of the Supreme
Being, well expressed the intensity of feeling in the hall. He demanded
an adjournment, in view of the decree's importance, and insisted that in
the meantime the text be printed, so that its provisions could be carefully scrutinized, article by article; if the bill were to be passed without an
adjournment, he threatened, "I will blow my brains out." At this, the com-
motion on the benches was so great that Robespierre felt it necessary to
put his authority in the balance, assuring his colleagues that only "conspirators" had reason to fear the immediate examination of the proposed law.
He prevailed and the bill was adopted shortly afterward, almost without
discussion. This did not prevent debate from resuming the next day. From
one session to the next it grew more acrimonious, and what was at stake
became increasingly clear—so much so that the debate over the Law of 22
Prairial should probably be regarded as the starting point of the crisis that
was to culminate in 9 Thermidor.

Many members of the Convention detected in one of the articles of
Couthon's draft the possibility that either or both of the committees might
betray them to the Revolutionary Tribunal without submitting the charge
to a vote by the Assembly beforehand. Bourdon de l'Oise expounded this
view during the session of 11 June and his arguments met with enough
approval for an amendment to be added to the decree providing that no
representative of the people could be brought before the Revolutionary
Tribunal without the consent of the Convention. But beyond this immediately pressing concern, the philosophy of revolutionary justice gradually
came to be called into question. On 12 June a deputy wondered about the
vagueness of the accusation of "depraving morals." Another expressed perplexity about the meaning of the article stipulating that "the law appoints
sworn patriots as counsel for the defense of slandered patriots." What was
a sworn patriot? Objections and doubts of this kind, though they were
quickly dismissed by the true believers, nonetheless showed that the legitimacy of this summary manner of trying "enemies of the people" was not
universally admitted. Couthon and Robespierre, alert to any challenge
to their authority, at once denounced the "appalling calumnies hurled
against the Committee of Public Safety" and demanded that the original
text of the decree be restored. The Convention submitted to their will,

but by silencing their timid adversaries they succeeded only in making a volatile situation more dangerous. Robespierre, in particular, in lashing out so vehemently, inadvertently revealed the nature of the campaign of purification he had in mind, at least in part, intensifying still further the growing sense of alarm. If "virtue, morals, and uprightness" were the order of the day, as Couthon did not tire of saying, a new wave of terror was in store as well. For a moment it had looked as though one order was going to supplant the other. As it turned out, they were meant to coexist.

Robespierre's rhetoric left no doubt about the present danger. "Who does not see," he asked, "that [the] system [of Chabot, Hébert, Danton, and Lacroix] is still intact?" This served only to emphasize the gravity of the accusation brought against those who had dared to oppose him more recently. The evening before, at the Jacobin Club, he had quarreled with Fouché, declaring in a similar spirit: "There still exist two parties in the Republic: on the one side, patriotism and integrity; on the other, the counterrevolutionary spirit, roguery and dishonesty." Fouché, a deputy sent on mission to the department of Nièvre, had assisted Chaumette in launching the de-Christianization campaign in September 1793. Robespierre saw clearly that he continued to aid and abet the resistance to the cult of the Supreme Being that had grown up in the meantime, notably in Nevers, and that testified to the persistence of this second party. The following day, at the Convention, the need to reprimand Bourdon de l'Oise and Tallien led him to adopt an aggressive tone that clarified his intentions still further. To contest the decisions of the Committee of Public Safety, he thundered, was to seek to divide what normally was one, since "the Convention, the Mountain, the Committee are all the same thing"; it amounted to taking the side of the "counterrevolutionary hypocrites," who took cover among "patriots." Bourdon tried to defend himself, provoking this scathing retort: "I have not named Bourdon. Woe be to him who names himself." To another deputy who demanded that he identify the "intriguers" whom he accused of plotting within the Mountain, Robespierre resorted to a favorite dodge: "I will name them when it is necessary"—suggesting that a carefully considered plan was now being carried out.

He then proceeded at once to review surreptitious attempts to prejudice deputies recalled from their missions against the Committee, and in this way to turn them into "enemies of the government." He went so far as to present a quite recent piece of anecdotal evidence in support of his charges, involving an incident between Tallien, whom he did not name, and agents of the committees whom Tallien had recklessly accused of espionage. Tallien disputed his account, but Robespierre would have nothing of it.

"Tallien," he reminded his audience, "is one of those who ceaselessly speak of the guillotine with fright, and publicly, as though it were something that concerns them, in order to debase and disturb the National Convention."

This mixture of denials and denunciations was unconvincing. Asserting on the one hand that the committees had no intention of going after members of the Convention, and on the other that the mere suggestion of such a thing proved the existence of a conspiracy bent on working in the shadows to carry out the plan of the "foreign faction" to undermine the Republic, a crime that therefore called for punishments no less harsh than the ones meted out to other counterrevolutionaries, could only sow confusion and compound fears of what the next wave of endless repression would bring.

Moreover, the effects of the Law of 22 Prairial were not slow in making themselves felt. Prisoners poured into the prisons of the capital; convictions and executions sharply increased. Whereas 1,231 death sentences had been handed down by the Revolutionary Tribunal between 6 April 1793 and 10 June 1794, a period of more than a year, the number for the six weeks between 11 June and 27 July 1794 was 1,376—hence the name "The Great Terror" that came to be attached to this bloody month and a half. It is not impossible that Robespierre's best-placed opponents, particularly within the Committee of General Security, deliberately sought to turn this situation against him. On 14 June, Lacoste came before the Convention on behalf of the Committee of General Security to present a report on the conspiracy allegedly behind the assassination attempts against Collot d'Herbois and Robespierre, conjuring a scheme of fantastic proportions connected with the plotting of the elusive and diabolical Baron de Batz. The inquiry concluded three days later with the sentencing and execution of fifty-four persons, all of them led to the scaffold dressed in the red shirt symbolic of parricides, as Charlotte Corday had been. Was this an oblique way of conferring an office of exceptional distinction on Robespierre, as a sort of civil patriarch, while tacitly imputing to him full responsibility for a massive and spectacularly arbitrary abuse of police power? Comparing this episode with others of a similar nature, the suspicion seems not to be misplaced.

The day after Lacoste delivered his report, Vadier, speaking once more in the name of the Committee of General Security, opened another front. Pretending to bring to light new conspiracies that carried on old ones, he grossly exaggerated the importance of the "discovery" in Paris, in the Faubourg Saint-Marcel, of a small sect that had grown up around a sixty-nine-year-old prophetess named Catherine Théot, long well known to the authorities since, as Vadier put it, "she has spent half her life [in prison], at the Bastille and Salpêtrière." Théot claimed to be the "mother of God" and promised corporeal immortality to her followers. In the eyes of the Committee, which had conveniently arrested her on 17 May, shortly after the decree on the Supreme Being, she was of interest chiefly for providing two ways of implicating Robespierre. Her followers included a former member of the Constituent Assembly, Dom Gerle, with whom Robespierre had remained in touch and who had made certain predictions concerning him. At all events, if anyone was immediately convinced that the affair had been concocted to bring him down, it was Robespierre himself. I will come back to this, because it marked the true beginning of his feud with the committees. In his last speech, on 26 July (8 Thermidor), he was to accuse Vadier of having sought to bury the memory of the Festival of the Supreme Being beneath ridicule of a "farcical mystic." But the reasons for excavating a grotesque scandal went deeper than this. Robespierre's opponents took aim at his attempt to achieve conciliation on religious matters, asserting that the most menacing conspiracy of all issued from superstition and fanaticism, as in the case of the Vendée. In this regard Vadier gave voice to a sentiment that was widely shared by his fellow revolutionaries. His report benefited from the largest distribution network available to the members of the Convention, with "delivery to the armies and all the communes of the Republic." The Jacobins were to adopt Vadier's report and publicize it along the same lines two days later. If the objective of this maneuver was to further isolate Robespierre and his coterie, it succeeded. From now on he ran up against a muffled resistance that could not be ignored. It only confirmed his sense of being the object of a more extensive and still more insidious conspiracy than the ones that had come before.

Similarly, one cannot help but entertain similar suspicions about the so-called prison plots, one of the most obscure facets of the Great Terror. They involved police provocations, likewise no doubt sponsored by the Committee of General Security, in collaboration with the Revolutionary Tribunal, that made it possible to dispatch people to the guillotine in impressive numbers: sixty on 7 July, forty-eight the next day, and thirty-eight the day after that. It is hard to see these mass executions having any other purpose than to arouse disgust and revulsion at an increasingly murderous tide of repression whose motivations were more and more incomprehensible, but which were artfully associated with the will of the supposed master of the Convention, whose rhetoric had done nothing to dispel the most sinister insinuations.

It was in this climate of widespread fear, aggravated by clandestine intrigues and veiled attacks, that the dénouement of what had become a death struggle within the Convention was to unfold. Alongside those who had reason to feel threatened, directly or indirectly, by Robespierre's innuendo, there were many, even in the ranks of the most zealous Montagnards, who had been bewildered by his sudden abandonment of the assurance that the peaceable reign of virtue was now at hand for its opposite, the bloody obligation once more to combat conspiracy, and who no longer took their cues from him. Their number is impossible to estimate with any precision, but they were to be decisive when the time came. Among this group, Robespierre had until then enjoyed the authority of an infallible guide; until then, they had followed him unquestioningly. While they were not necessarily convinced of the necessity of appealing to a Supreme Being, the accompanying political gesture—of proclaiming an end to the cycle of violence that had ravaged the land—had come as a great relief. And yet now the infernal mechanism of denunciation abruptly started up again, more vigorously than ever, as though it had never stopped. Suddenly the principles of revolutionary justice, whose susceptibility to arbitrary application was only too clear to everyone by now, were codified and consecrated as instruments of government.

In this regard it is impossible to overstate the extent to which the trial of Danton and of the Indulgents, with its extravagant accusations and shamefully irregular proceedings, had undermined the credibility of all such criminal prosecutions. Danton's trial had a more or less identifiable political meaning. But what meaning could trials have in a Convention purged of its factions and officially dedicated to unanimity? Robespierre had plainly lost touch with his base; he no longer grasped how his instructions were received and understood by the majority of his colleagues. For him, it went without saying that "the conscience of jurors enlightened by love of country," as the Law of 22 Prairial put it, sufficed to recognize an "enemy of the people." An authentic patriot could not be mistaken when it was a matter of distinguishing between another "oppressed patriot" and a conspirator against the Republic. Nor did Robespierre have any doubt that if the native virtue of the people were not expressed more frankly, it was because it was prevented from manifesting itself by the corrupt interference of plotters aiming to perpetuate the vices of the aristocracy. These were so many articles of faith, intimately bound up in his vision of the reign of virtue through law.

The difficulty was that Robespierre's personal incorruptibility had lost its magic. In this spring of Year II, between the desire for peace to be restored and the "nausea of the guillotine," the inexorable succession of death sentences isolated him from all but a small group of unwavering loyalists. Now more than ever he was the prisoner of a way of thinking that transformed all resistance, all opposition into a sign of conspiracy and that held out no other prospect than an unbroken succession of purges. For a time his doctrinaire intransigence had rallied support by making people believe that it was indispensable if the Republic were one day to be securely established; now it had only the discouraging effect of pushing this moment unattainably far into the future.

Robespierre, though he sensed his growing isolation, was incapable of seeing it as the result of anything other than the work of indefatigable enemies. After the stormy session of 12 June (24 Prairial), he did not take part in the Convention's deliberations for six weeks, intervening again only during the fateful session of 26 July (8 Thermidor). Until 18 June (30 Prairial) he limited himself to presiding over debate in the Assembly while saying nothing on his own account. Did he continue to attend its meetings after that? We do not really know. At all events he seems to have made himself scarce, for his reappearance on 8 Thermidor attracted comment. What we do know is that his relations with his colleagues on the governing committees became strained, in some cases to the point of rupture, without our being able to precisely identify the reasons for this. The retrospective testimony of the protagonists is too much colored by a determination to distance themselves from the policies of a "tyrant," and in particular to clear themselves of responsibility for the Law of 22 Prairial, to be trustworthy. The Théot affair gave rise to additional disputes, Robespierre having at once persuaded Fouquier-Tintin, the public prosecutor, to hand the Revolutionary Tribunal's file over to him, thus preventing his colleagues from making any further inquiries. These repeated clashes, notably with Billaud-Varenne, culminated on 29 June (11 Messidor), in the course of a still more tempestuous session than the previous ones, when Robespierre found himself called a "dictator." He abruptly left the hall with Saint-Just and from that point ceased to participate in the daily business of the Committee of Public Safety. He did not reappear until 23 July (5 Thermidor), in response to a belated attempt at reconciliation. On 30 June, the day after he walked out, he was officially replaced on the General Police Bureau by Couthon, a staunch loyalist. There remained to him the forum of the Jacobin Club. It was from there that he carried on his campaign and made his grievances known. Nevertheless it is clear that he no longer enjoyed the aura of infallibility that he once did. His manner was still domineering, only now the grumbling was audible. Even in this bastion, the unanimous bloc of support he had managed to assemble over the years now showed signs of crumbling.

Are we therefore to suppose that, apart from a few public appearances, Robespierre was holed up alone in his room, nursing his resentments and cursing his loss of influence? This seems very doubtful. For the time being he still had the support of a genuine faction. In the first place there were his allies on the two committees, Couthon and Saint-Just, who went on performing their duties as before. It is reasonable to assume that they kept him informed. He could also count on a network of men loyal or otherwise indebted to him in the Convention, the Commune of Paris, the Revolutionary Tribunal, and in a variety of other key positions of the government, thanks to whom he was able to monitor events as they developed. Additionally, there were informants who voluntarily came forward as well as personal spies whose services he had no reason suddenly to dispense with. It seems much more probable that he spent the first weeks of July carefully planning an offensive that he knew would be decisive, assuring himself of his alliances, sizing up the forces arrayed against him, and waiting for the right moment to act. Those who knew they were his targets, or feared they might be, were surely no less busy, meeting in secret and negotiating alliances of their own.

As a consequence of this maneuvering, a forgotten group of moderate deputies once more assumed a prominent role: the Plain, as they were known, disdainfully looked down upon from the heights of the Mountain as the Marsh. Since the elimination of the Girondins these men had been marginalized, reduced to the status of mute bystanders. Robespierre's crucial insight, as we saw earlier, was that the continuing presence of the Plain was essential if the Convention were to retain any credibility as a representative assembly in the wake of the coup d'état of 31 May–2 June 1793. Silent though their presence may have been, it allowed him to claim that a "generally pure majority" did in fact survive, above and beyond the Montagnard core, following the purge of the Girondin "traitors." Thus he assured them of his protection, extending it to include seventy-three deputies who had been expelled from the Convention and jailed for their protest against the events of 31 May—this against the will of the most vindictive elements of his own camp and of the sans-culotte movement, who insisted on eradicating the last vestiges of moderantism. The deputies of the Plain, for their part, were only too happy to save their necks, even at the price of making themselves invisible, and therefore welcomed the tacit bargain Robespierre offered them. But with the cracks that had suddenly opened up in the façade of Montagnard unanimity, their existence was rediscovered. Insignificant phantoms until this point, the unaligned representatives now seized the opportunity to mold themselves into a cohesive force capable of tipping the majority from one side to another. The need to win their support was by no means the least aspect of the interlocking intrigues being conducted behind the scenes, which we are able to dimly make out through the fog of the various personal accounts that have come down to us.

Robespierre's addresses at the Jacobin Club on the eve of battle reveal a pathetic figure, the captive of all that was paradoxical about his intentions. On the one hand, he dismissed fears inspired in the Convention by false rumors of a new round of proscriptions, while describing these same rumors, on the other hand, as proof of a plot still more menacing than the earlier ones, whose authors therefore had to be ruthlessly hunted down— with the result that the more he tried to reassure, the more disturbing he seemed to be. Thus on 27 June (9 Messidor) he solemnly warned his listeners against the "dark calumnies" aimed at him and his fellow Committee members, from whom he had not yet dissociated himself. "Know . . . that there exists a league of corrupt men who endeavor to make people believe that the Committee of Public Safety seeks to attack the Convention in general and [its] estimable members in particular. We have this on the authority of some of our own colleagues, who [dare] not sleep in their own homes, stricken by terrors that these scoundrels have inspired in them." Vile rumors all, which he categorically denied: "No, the Committee of Public Safety has not drawn up a new bill of indictment against anyone." But when he went on to say that he was not in a position to "expose in its entirety a system of conspiracy too vast, and containing too many threads, for the voice of one man to be able to unveil it," one was left to wonder what fate was reserved for these "corrupt men," these representatives whom he declared unworthy of their office.

Four days later, on 1 July (13 Messidor), Robespierre adopted a still more dramatic attitude before the Jacobins, describing himself in no uncertain terms as a man faced with the gravest circumstances imaginable, where nothing less than the country's survival was at stake. This was two days after sitting with the members of the Committee of Public Safety for the last time, and just five days after the announcement of the French victory in the Battle of Fleurus, the turning point of the war on the northern front, which was received by the people of the capital as a signal of imminent peace and therefore, in its wake, of the end of revolutionary government. Hence the reappearance of the Indulgents in Robespierre's rhetoric. It was this faction, "today merged with the others," that dared to represent him "to the people as a redoubtable and dangerous man" and that went so far as to "put it about in the Convention that the

Revolutionary Tribunal had been set up only to slaughter the Convention itself." Even worse, it was working to spread the most unspeakable slanders manufactured by the English government: "In London, I am denounced to the French army as a dictator; the same calumnies have been repeated in Paris, you would tremble if I told you where." One may imagine that many listeners had already gotten wind of the session of the Committee of Public Safety at which the word was used and that they had no trouble interpreting the allusion. How could they have understood Robespierre's closing promise to give a fuller explanation "when circumstances permit" as anything other than a threat? Among these circumstances was one in which he would be made "to give up some of the duties with which I am entrusted." In that case, his absence from the meetings of the Committee of Public Safety in the coming weeks would be explained in advance as the result of his banishment from it. Did he consider this to be a temporary setback, or was he concerned mainly with preparing public opinion for the shock of his eventual downfall? However this may be, he assured his audience that nothing would prevent him from carrying on his "war to the death against tyrants and conspirators."

Tensions were ratcheted up another notch on 9 July (21 Messidor). Robespierre no longer limited himself to denunciation, but now openly contemplated a course of action. He appealed in the first place to the Decree on Worship of the Supreme Being, which made "uprightness and virtue the order of the day," to recall Couthon's familiar phrase. "If this decree were to be executed," Robespierre said, "liberty would be perfectly established," and "the Revolution would come to an end in a quite straightforward way." But the opportunity was willfully neglected. "The scoundrels have all abused [this] law that saved liberty and the French people." The example he gave was fraught with implications, for it involved the Committee of General Security itself. This body, instead of concerning itself with the fundamental task of "destroying the aristocracy," had found nothing better to do than arrest a few drunken craftsmen at the end of a holiday—an apparently deliberate dereliction of duty that must have angered him, since Saint-Just mentioned it in the speech of 9 Thermidor that circumstances were to prevent him from delivering. The Committee's act of sabotage culminated in a scheme to "vilify" and "destroy the Convention by a system of terror; every day there are gatherings aimed at spreading these deadly ideas; the attempt is made to persuade every member that the Committee of Public Safety has proscribed him." The purpose of all this was clear: to deprive revolutionary government of its foundation, to paralyze it. "So long as terror lasts among the representatives, they will be incapable of carrying out their glorious mission." They had to be liberated from it. But how could this be done without rendering the plotters incapable of doing harm—in other words, without having recourse to terror?

Let us recall in passing Robespierre's disconsolate mention of the "profound silence" that his words had met with "for some time" at the Jacobin Club. He saw it as a telling indication of the general mood, a product of the confusion that had been sown in the minds of the Revolution's main actors. Even within the circle of those who in principle were wholly in agreement with his views, Robespierre began to complain of his difficulty in "opening people's eyes to the dangers facing the country."

And for good reason. The previous month, the society had dared to make Fouché its president—the very man whom Robespierre attacked by name a few days later, on 14 July (26 Messidor), declaring that he regarded him "as the head of the conspiracy that we have unveiled." One can readily imagine the sense of disorientation that rank-and-file Jacobins must have felt, fearing that their camp was in imminent peril of being irreparably split apart. Given the seriousness of Robespierre's accusation, the outcome was bound to be violent, as the *Gazette de Leyde* foresaw. Commenting on Fouché's eviction from the Jacobin Club, pursuant to Robespierre's indictment, its editor concluded: "We regard this expulsion as a certain portent that Fouché will be among those representatives whom public opinion designates as having soon to be brought before the Revolutionary Tribunal."

The reason for this frontal attack, launched in concert with Couthon, went back to the brutal manner in which the rebellion in Lyon had been suppressed a few months before, and to its aftermath. Significantly, Robespierre and Couthon implicated both an Indulgent, Dubois-Crancé, whose offense had been a failure to act, and an Exagéré, Fouché (not by chance an accomplice of Chaumette, a promoter of de-Christianization), who was charged with crimes of senseless violence and oppression of authentic patriots. Once again the objective was to highlight the way in which these two "apparently opposed" factions "joined together for the purpose of sacrificing patriots"—and this at a moment when the sansculottes had begun to celebrate the imminent peace by "fraternal banquets," which moderates were sure to attend, and opportunists in the other camp were urging the death penalty for anyone found guilty even of taking God's name in vain.

To Robespierre's mind, this deliberate distortion of the decree on the Supreme Being plainly lay at the heart of the conspiracy, whether it aimed at rendering him odious or whether it feigned incomprehension with regard to the purpose of promoting virtue. The enemies of the Republic, he explained on 16 July (28 Messidor), understood "virtue" to mean only "faithfulness to certain private and domestic obligations, but never public virtues, never that generous devotion to the cause of the people which is the heroism of virtue and the sole support of the Republic." This amounted to vastly enlarging the number of the Republic's enemies, a most unsettling development for the narrow circle of representatives directly concerned, who could hardly regard this reactivation of the struggle against the factions as anything other than the sign of a return to a period that everyone wished to see come to an end, beginning with the old Dantonists and their Cordelier sympathizers. Many of these survivors were uncomfortable, to say the least, with the cult of the Supreme Being, and those who had resigned themselves to the policy of enforcing virtue quickly discovered to their dismay that it provided the authorities with a pretext for bringing fresh indictments. All this gives some idea of the immense, and immensely anxious, perplexity with which Robespierre's new line was received by the members of the Convention. When Robespierre declared that acting on his principles would "put an end to the spilling of human blood by crime," his listeners understood him to say that more blood would have to be spilled in order to achieve this result. No matter that Couthon sought to reassure them by stressing that the number of plotters was "small," that there were no more than "five or six scoundrels," veteran deputies could draw their own conclusions from the spiraling increase in executions. Robespierre had lost touch with events; his rhetoric pointed in the direction of a deadlock from which there was no way out, a state of chronic purge.

Nevertheless, in spite of the plain implication of his words, we may suppose that Robespierre put off acting for as long as possible, patiently waiting for the most favorable moment to launch his attack. The same must have been true in the case not only of his designated enemies, who surely were not inactive, but also of the committees, which had been driven into a corner by his intransigence. In the latter case, hesitation was understandable. The popularity and the authority that Robespierre still enjoyed was enough to give pause even to his fiercest critics. His identification in the public mind with revolutionary government, exasperating though it was, served them at the same time as a shield. It could be cast aside only at the risk of triggering a major upheaval—as events were soon to show. The reasons for wanting to arrive at some sort of accommodation were therefore compelling, however great the disagreement between the various parties may have been. Saint Just, a man of independent mind, notwithstanding his undoubted loyalty to Robespierre, and silent since his return from the northern armies during the night of 28–29 June (10–11 Messidor), offered to act as a mediator. The Committees of Public Safety and General Security met on 23 July (5 Thermidor) in an attempt to reconcile their differences, following preliminary consultations the day before. Robespierre obtained the concessions he sought regarding the implementation of the Law of 22 Prairial (and, in particular, the expedited judgment of suspects). Agreement appeared to have been reached. Barère informed the Convention of the relaxation of tensions in a long report on the political situation delivered on 25 July (7 Thermidor). Seeking to put minds at ease, he explained that the position of the Republic, both at home and abroad, had improved to the point that extraordinary measures were no longer called for. "Must one evoke the criminal shades of Hébert and Chaumette? The two committees, having deliberated on the current state of political matters, are not of this opinion: they do see a few storm clouds, but . . . these can easily be chased away." In short, all was well. France had passed from a "state of sorrow and heartbreak" to a "state of happiness and consolation" under the government's direction. It remained only to let it continue its work until peace was achieved.

But evidently not everyone had drawn the same conclusions from the apparent settlement. The session held on 25 July (7 Thermidor), at which Barère presented his report, was opened by a deputation of Jacobins whose address to the Convention expressed a very different view. They began by "denouncing the plots that the foreigner concocts in his desperation." Still more significantly, they called upon the Assembly to "preserve in all its purity this sublime cult of which every citizen is a minister, and whose sole practice is virtue"—language that unambiguously betrayed the hand of Robespierre's allies. As it happens, we know from the speech that Saint-Just was to be prevented from delivering on 27 July (9 Thermidor), one of the most revelatory testimonies of these fateful days, that Billaud-Varenne and Collot d'Herbois had asked Robespierre, during the meeting of 23 July (5 Thermidor), not to speak of the Supreme Being in the report on institutions that he was charged with drafting. The rest of the opening address was devoted to recalling the grievances regarding the committees that Robespierre had enumerated in his recent speeches at the Jacobin Club. It is difficult not to see this as a signal that hostilities were imminent.

It may be that Robespierre had interpreted the desire of his colleagues on the committees to come to an agreement as a sign that his assistance was indispensable to them, in which case there was a chance he would once more be able to impose his will. It may also be, however, that he had come away with the impression that he had gotten all he could expect from them and that the only option left to him was to stake everything, count-ing on their support and his prestige within the Convention. Reading the text of the two-hour speech he delivered on 26 July (8 Thermidor), it is impossible to disentangle the words of a man accustomed to giving orders and convinced of the justice of his case, to the point that nothing could tell against it, from those of a man deliberately courting political suicide, even death. At all events he had no choice but to give official expression to the very serious accusations that he had made unofficially from the rostrum at the Jacobin Club. If he was not to lose credibility altogether, he could not avoid explaining his decision to withdraw from the affairs of the Commit-tee of Public Safety, whether in order to announce his return or to justify his resignation. One way or the other, he had to make up his mind.

When Robespierre mounted the tribune on 8 Thermidor, having not addressed the Convention for more than a month and a half, everyone knew that the moment of truth had come at last—that "the veil was going to be lifted," to recall one of the favorite expressions of revolutionary rhe-toric. As it turned out, his listeners could only have felt a deep sense of frus-tration. The veil was not really lifted. The charges he had rehearsed before the Jacobins and now set out to expand upon were not demonstrated by anything resembling a proper argument. The allegation of a "conspiracy against the Republic," led by a "criminal coalition that intrigues within the Convention itself," was supported by nothing more than a train of vague allusions—with one bizarre exception—that left the masterminds lurking, as always, in the shadows.

The first object of the speech, and surely not the least important in the eyes of its author, was to justify himself once and for all against the defamatory accusation that he sought to exercise dictatorial powers. Here we find the Robespierre of old, with his deep-seated need to pour out his heart and his compulsion to cultivate the image of a just man unjustly persecuted. The self-pitying narcissism that we have encountered more than once before now reached its height. "Who am I, I who am accused? A slave of liberty, a living martyr of the Republic, as much the victim as the enemy of crime." Yet again he rejected the charge that he presided over a "system of terror." The manner in which he sought to reassure pro-spective targets of his vengeance shows that he knew perfectly well which members of the Convention were likeliest to abandon him: old friends of Danton, "sincere patriots" momentarily infected by the Hébertist fever; representatives on mission who had been recalled by the Committee of Public Safety; deputies of the Plain (to whom he showed an unusual warmth, even denying that he had referred to them pejoratively as "the Marsh"). Wounded feelings could not blur the cold gaze of the politician.

With regard to the fundamental question at issue, the threat posed by counterrevolutionary factions, this latest instance of *pro domo* pleading reminds us of another Robespierre, the one who owed his ascendancy over his colleagues in large part to his ability to explain to them the meaning of the Revolution that they were bringing about. He had already emphasized more than once that the Republic was not the original aim of the Revolution. The Revolution had initially been propelled by an internal dynamic of political struggle: "Between the people and their enemies, there was a continuous reaction whose increasing violence accomplished in a few years the work of several centuries." Now he restated the point in other terms: "The Republic, insensibly led on by the force of circumstances and by the struggle of the friends of liberty against conspiracies forever reborn, slipped through all the factions, as it were, though their forces were arrayed all around it and all the means of influence were in their hands." Factional opposition, in other words, was the price the Republic had to pay for the wonders it worked, its inevitable dark side. There was nothing surprising about this. But it also laid bare the precariousness of what had so far been achieved—hence the necessity, if the Republic were finally to be consolidated, of putting an end to this infernal cycle. This was the decisive role that Robespierre assigned to the cult of the Supreme Being, of which his speech that day—the final speech of his life, as it happened—was intended to be a defense and illustration. But what if his solution proved to be inadequate in the face of the irrepressible reviviscence of corruption? There was no further recourse to be had.

Robespierre no doubt conceived this defensive maneuver as a way of going on the offensive once more. The libelous attacks directed against him were both unremitting and perfectly deliberate, he claimed. Accusations of "tyranny" could only have been orchestrated by the tyrants themselves, who perversely applied this word to "the very ascendancy of the principles of truth"—principles that corresponded to "the moral influence of the old martyrs of the Revolution." The second part of his speech analyzed this enterprise in detail. The point of vilifying him was to destroy revolutionary government by using the methods pioneered by the original conspirators, the Indulgents and the Exagérés. "The system worked out by the likes of Hébert and Fabre d'Églantine" had been revived. "Revolutionary institutions are now openly slandered; excesses are used to make them seem odious." In this last respect Robespierre particularly blamed "subordinate agents" of the Committee of General Security, accusing them of carrying out orders to impute to him responsibility for all their own "iniquities" and for revolutionary violence as a whole. Who was behind this "plan"? Ultimately, the Duke of York and Pitt, that much went without saying. But the others? Their intermediaries in Paris, whose tentacles reached into the apparatus of government? At this point Robespierre stepped back, taking cover once more behind a familiar evasion: "Ah! I do not dare name them at this moment and in this place. I cannot bring myself to entirely unveil the profound mystery of such wickedness." In view of his position as the accused in this matter, however, he could hardly avoid naming names if he hoped to be able to sustain the pose of an accuser. His failure to speak plainly was to greatly weaken his case, as Saint-Just lucidly observed.

But his reluctance was also due to the fact that he preferred to argue from first principles, in order to come back to the subject that was dearest to his heart, public morality and the decree of 18 Floréal, from which the current discord issued. The conspirators at work today, he alleged, were recruited from "the impure apostles of atheism and of the immorality that is based upon it." Official recognition of the Supreme Being inflicted upon them a defeat whose damage they have been trying to repair ever since. Robespierre then went on to exalt the enactment by which the foundations of the Republic ought to have been laid once and for all. In order to magnify its glory still further, he modestly declined to take any credit for himself, giving the full share to the members of the Convention: "You saved the country. Your decree of [18 Floréal] was by itself a revolution; with a single blow you struck down atheism and sacerdotal despotism; you advanced the fatal hour of the tyrants by a half-century." Rhapsodically he celebrated the immense symbolic power of the "sublime gathering of the first people of the world" during the festival of 8 June (20 Prairial): "That day made a profound impression on France, of calm, happiness, wisdom, and goodness. . . . The cry escaped from every heart, that whoever had witnessed this grand spectacle could depart this life without regret." The promised land of the Republic, founded on virtue, had come into view at last. Alas, "when the people, in whose presence all private vices disappear, went back to their homes, the intriguers reappeared and the charlatans set to work once again." Before gaining the upper hand, intrigue had dared to show its face during the ceremony itself. Robespierre made a point of mentioning the "insults" that had been hurled at him by some of his colleagues. "This incident by itself," he said, "explains everything that has happened since"—the Théot affair being the outstanding example. There followed an account of the measures undertaken in order to make "revolutionary government hateful and so to prepare its destruction." This permitted him to skillfully introduce the subject of his recent retirement from public life: "[F]or more than six weeks, the nature and the force of the calumny [to which I am subject], the inability to do good and stand in the way of evil, have forced me to completely abandon my duties as a member of the Committee of Public Safety, and I swear that in this matter I have consulted only my reason and my country." This solemn vow permitted him by the same token to decorate his defense with an ironic flourish: "And so it has been at least six weeks since my dictatorship came to an end." Who noticed any change?

Robespierre proceeded at once to enlarge upon this theme. "In whose hands today," he asked, "are the armies and the finances of the Republic, and the administration of its internal affairs?" Who, in other words, now controlled the usual instruments of a dictatorship? "They are in the hands of the coalition that persecutes me." This amounted to a declaration of war against several of his colleagues on the Committee of Public Safety—the "technicians," as he called them: Carnot oversaw the armies, Prieur and Lindet administration; also the chairman of the Finance Committee, Cambon, whom he mentioned by name. The charge was a grave one, because Robespierre openly accused these confederates of plotting his murder. Not content with "having prevented an inconvenient watchman from doing good, out of desperation they made plans in the shadows, unbeknownst to their colleagues, to deprive him of the right to defend the people by taking his life."

What until then had gone unspoken was now finally spoken. There could no longer be any doubt that a fight to the death had begun, for he made no secret of putting his own life in the balance, setting against the "eternal sleep" of Chaumette and Fouché his own maxim: "Death is the beginning of immortality." The last part of Robespierre's speech was presented as a testament, a "fearsome testament" left to "the oppressors of the people": "I bequeath to them a terrible truth and death!"—no doubt his own death, but theirs as well, for while this was the fate usually reserved for "defenders of liberty," it would now be the fate that awaited their persecutors.

This last part consisted of two appeals, one addressed to the representatives of the people and the other to the people themselves. To the representatives, Robespierre presented a picture of the Republic's predicament at home and abroad that was diametrically opposed to the one that Barère had presented the day before. "You have been told that all is well in the Republic: I deny it. . . . Those who tell you that providing the Republic with a foundation is a simple matter are misleading you, or rather, they are incapable of misleading anyone." His appraisal was unsparingly bleak, beginning with what appeared to be the most auspicious aspect of the situation, the victories of the armies of the Republic (Barère's pompous rhetoric in this connection was harshly ridiculed). Even so, "our domestic situation is much more critical." Revolutionary government had to be restructured. This meant "reminding it of the principle [on which it is based], simplifying it, trimming the vast number of officials, and above all cleansing it [of corruption]." At the highest levels it was undermined by conspiracy, even if Robespierre was careful to make it clear to the people that he was "far from imputing abuses to the majority of those in whom you have placed your confidence." Nevertheless "the majority is itself paralyzed and betrayed; intrigue and the foreigner are triumphant. They skulk, they dissemble, they deceive; therefore they conspire." Of still graver concern was the fact that "the counterrevolution has [infiltrated] the administration of finances." Bizarrely, since he had never shown the slightest interest in this department of government, Robespierre suddenly used it to make his most pointed indictment yet, accusing individuals by name: "Who are the supreme administrators of our finances? Brissotins, Feuillants, aristocrats, and known scoundrels; men such as Cambon, Mallarmé, Ramel."

Let no one be deluded: "[F]ounding an immense Republic on the basis of reason and equality, reuniting all the parties of this vast empire by a sturdy bond is not an undertaking that fickleness can accomplish: it is the masterpiece of virtue and human reason." Everything remained to be done, or rather to be redone, for although the theoretical basis had been well formulated in terms of "the principles and . . . the universal morality you have proclaimed," a durable institutional foundation was nonetheless lacking because of the malfeasance of the factions, the enemies of virtue. Robespierre then made the puzzling claim that the destruction of the "rival factions" of Hébert and Danton, far from leaving the field open to virtue, had the paradoxical effect of "emancipating every vice." Those who came after "thought that all there was left for them to do was to share the country as though it were booty, instead of making it free and prosperous."

A return to the principles he advocated was therefore the Republic's last chance, he solemnly warned his colleagues, laying out before them a prospect that may justly be called alarming:

> Relax your grip for a moment on the reins of the Revolution: you will see military despotism seize hold of them, and the leader of the factions overturn a reviled [system of] national representation; a century of civil wars and calamities will ravage our country and we will perish for not having wished to seize an appointed moment in the history of men

in order to lay the foundations of liberty; we will deliver our country to a century of disasters and the curses of the people will fasten themselves to our memory, which ought to be dear to the human race.

Owing to his prophetic conviction that he alone possessed the secret of these foundations, Robespierre no doubt failed to grasp the question that must have occurred to his most attentive and most favorably disposed listeners: why should a supposedly sovereign remedy, which by his own admission had failed once, succeed a second time? He did not see that the new beginning he proposed would lead once again to an impasse.

The peroration of his speech, properly enough, was intended for the people themselves, and conveyed the same message. "People, bear in mind that if justice does not reign in the Republic with absolute authority, and if [it] does not signify love of equality and of country, then liberty is only an empty word." The counterpart to this exhortation followed at once: "Bear in mind that within your midst there lurks a league of scoundrels who struggle against public virtue and who have more influence over your own affairs than you do." The third and final thing always to be remembered was this: "[Y]our trust and your esteem will be the grounds for declaring all your friends outlaws." Here Robespierre spoke as a man who knew he was destined to mount the scaffold, who placed his life in the balance with no expectation that it would be spared. "What allegation can be brought against a man who has tried to speak the truth and who is willing to die for it?" The same phrase occurred again in a slightly different form: "What allegation can be brought against a man who is right and who knows how to die for his country?" At the close of the speech, Robespierre reverted to the imperious and scathing tone of the master of the Convention. The radical evil facing the Republic called for comparably radical measures: "killing the traitors," "reforming" and "purging" the Committee of General Security and the Committee of Public Safety, "constituting a unified government under the supreme authority of the National Convention, which is the seat [of legitimacy] and the [ultimate] judge." Whether this was to be done by means of a thorough restructuring of revolutionary government, or by engineering a new revolution within the Revolution, or by going a step further than the earlier liquidation of the factions (since this had left the committees intact and they were the ones who were now being called to account), he did not say.

Robespierre's last public words deserve closer examination, not least because here we find the enigma of the man in concentrated form. Indeed, the speech itself supports two completely opposite readings. It is possible, on the one hand, to see it as a small masterpiece of Machiavellianism, dramatizing the threats made against him—the indispensable figure of the Revolution—in order to seize power, ridding himself of colleagues who had gotten in the way and forming a government wholly subject to his will. For what would a government unified under the supreme authority of the Convention resemble if not a government utterly devoted to his supreme authority, itself identical to that of the Convention? On the other hand, one can also see his pathetically solitary determination to risk everything as the impassioned reaction of a wounded man, no more able to tolerate contradiction than to admit the failure of his dream, carried away by a lethal narcissism to the point that the idea of making one last senseless throw of the dice was irresistible. This interpretation, appealing to the force of emotions, is roughly the one Saint-Just intended to give in his speech the following day. He excused Robespierre's remarks as the result of a pardonable outburst of temper, refusing to ascribe to them a significance they did not have and calling upon his listeners to embrace prudence once more.

Still, even if we accept Saint-Just's view, the question of Robespierre's state of mind remains. Was he "worn out," as his detractors said at the time, "exhausted," as he himself often said, run down to such a degree that the political acumen and the tactical skill he had demonstrated until then were now beyond his reach? Or did he deliberately choose to die a hero's death, knowing that a glorious reputation would forever be his by turning his back once and for all on the "scoundrels" with whom until then he had had to compromise? After all, as he said in his speech, "seeing the multitude of vices that the torrent of the Revolution mixed together with civic virtues in a jumble, I sometimes fear, I swear it, being soiled in the eyes of posterity by the impure proximity of depraved men who insinuated themselves among the sincere friends of humanity." There is an element of truth in each of these interpretations, which have been formulated in a variety of slightly different ways, and so persuasively that it is futile to try to decide between them. Robespierre's motivations are inextricably entangled, making a clear view of the man impossible. We will never know what he really meant to do or hoped to be able to do; quite possibly he himself did not know any more than we do.

What he certainly did succeed in doing was to surprise almost everyone, even his closest associates. Saint-Just himself was plainly caught unawares. Only Couthon seems perhaps to have been taken into his confidence, at least in part. As for Robespierre's declared enemies, their confused reactions make it clear that they too were caught off-guard. Once again, one can interpret the absence of consultation and preparation either as the sign of the authoritarian temperament of a man sufficiently sure of his purpose and of the resources available to him personally to dispense with accomplices, or as the sign of a man who had made himself the prisoner of his own imagination? What tempted Robespierre was the chance that he might bring about another 31 May by the sheer force of his words, without having to rely on armed support from the sections or Hanriot's canons. Was this megalomania, fecklessness, or suicidal impulse? By the same token, how are we to explain why he bullied or openly showed disdain for some of his colleagues—Barère and Cambon most notably— whom it would have been prudent not to offend? Was this the arrogance of an aspiring dictator, already so confident of his power that he felt no need to behave tactfully toward anyone? Or a clumsy and ill-advised assertion of will by a man whose anger prevented him from realizing that it uselessly added to the number of his enemies?

We are told that the speech was "warmly applauded." But did this applause signify something more than the approval routinely expressed when one of the Assembly's leading figures had finished speaking? There followed a muddled discussion of the charges leveled by Robespierre against the two committees. Curiously, the motion to open debate was made by Lecointre, one of his fiercest enemies, probably with the ulterior motive of encouraging their self-destruction. Bourdon de l'Oise opposed it, citing the seriousness of the matter and calling for a prior examination of the committees' record. Couthon, for his part, thoroughly supported Bourdon's proposal, demanding moreover that a copy of Robespierre's speech be sent to "all the communes of the Republic." His request was granted—proof that Robespierre's magnetism continued to operate in spite of everything that had transpired in the interval. Finally his opponents (which is to say the men he had accused) roused themselves, timidly at first in the person of Vadier, then vehemently with Cambon, who turned the accusation against the accuser. "It is time to speak the whole truth: a single man paralyzes the will of the National Convention; this man is the one who has just addressed [the Convention], Robespierre; thus, pass judgement [on him]." Tongues wagged, tension mounted. Panis, a Dantonist, reproached Robespierre for "expelling whichever Jacobins he liked," and asked him straight out whether his name, Panis, was on the enemies list he had drawn up. Another deputy called upon him to identify the persons he accused. Robespierre refused, though he defended himself very badly, standing firm without explaining himself

any further—"I have done my duty; it is now up to others to do theirs."
Finally, the decree authorizing publication of Robespierre's speech was
revoked, after which Barère sought to calm emotions: "Had Robespierre
followed the deliberations of the Committee [of Public Safety] for [the six
weeks he was absent], he would not have delivered this speech. It is necessary above all that the word 'accused' be erased from all your thoughts."
The Assembly then turned to other matters. No firm decision was reached.
This time, however, it seems that Robespierre, though he had captivated
his listeners, had not persuaded them. It is worth noting that none of his
close associates, with the exception of Couthon, rose to speak on his behalf
in the course of this session, neither to develop his accusations in greater
detail nor to attach names and deeds to the "conspiracy against public
liberty" that he claimed to have uncovered.

One can understand why this should have been the case when one considers the plain implication of his speech, which was apparent even to those
who were the most prejudiced in Robespierre's favor. To begin with, there
was something outrageous about the pose he adopted, of a man standing
apart from everyone else, in order to appeal to the Convention against his
colleagues on the two committees in the name of the people and of virtue,
on whose behalf he alone was privileged to speak. In defending himself,
and rightly so, against the charge of being a dictator, as the term was then
understood, he nonetheless claimed for himself an exceptional status that
went beyond ordinary dictatorship, as a sort of moral guide, disdainful of
the actual exercise of power and of its ceremonial trappings, yet the source
of its inspiration. He himself wished only to see the impersonal truth of
his purpose, behind which he modestly concealed himself; his listeners
heard only the haughty pretension to being the sole voice of this truth,
crushing in its sovereign condescension: "I was born to combat crime, not
to govern it."

Next, and above all, the program he laid out was bound to create
doubts, to say the least, in the minds of even his most fervent supporters.
On the fundamental point, that revolutionary government must continue,
he was in agreement with the majority of his colleagues on the committees. Where he differed with them was in respect of ways and means. In
their eyes, "all is well," as Robespierre reproached Barère for having suggested in his reassuring report. To his mind, everything had to be done
all over again, through the resumption, this time on a grand scale, of the
struggle against the heirs to the Indulgents and Exagérés that would make
it possible at last to provide the Republic with the moral foundations it
cruelly lacked. This program was completely out of step not only with

what the majority of the members of the Convention plainly wanted, but also with public opinion. The sans-culotte movement had reared its head, as I say, organizing civic banquets with a view to strengthening fraternal bonds and calling for the implementation of the Constitution of 1793—in a word, for the end of revolutionary government. The low profile adopted by Barère, hoping for the best, was clearly an attempt to reach a compromise. The time of purges in which Robespierre was stuck had now passed, and the regeneration they were supposed to bring about no longer seemed a plausible ambition. The combat against crime, as Robespierre defined it, had led only to the conclusion that it was unending. Yesterday's oracle now had nothing more to offer than unreasoning obstinacy in searching for a way to give the Republic a secure foundation that could never be found. The success of his speech depended on identifying the enemies of the Republic by name. His failure to do this is what unnerved a great many of his remaining supporters.

To be sure, he could still count on the enduring support of a small core of diehards when he gave the same speech again at the Jacobin Club that evening. But even there opinions were divided and the session was stormy. One member of the Convention told Robespierre: "We wish for no dominator among the Jacobins." Billaud-Varenne and Collot d'Herbois tried to remonstrate with him, but before they could speak, a fight broke out and they were driven from the hall to cries of "To the guillotine!" The society then expelled from its ranks all those deputies who had voted in the Convention against sending Robespierre's speech to the communes.

Did Robespierre really believe that this support was enough to permit him to impose his program? Or was he content to play the role he seems to have chosen for himself, by preparing to "drink the hemlock," as he had declared to the Jacobins? After 8 Thermidor, a day when he had nonetheless been able to estimate the difficulty of the struggle facing him, his behavior was astonishing. He knew who his enemies were. He had depicted them often enough as "scoundrels" not to imagine that they would idly stand by, twiddling their thumbs—and all the more as the choice he had left them was perfectly clear: resist or die. Just so, they spent the night conferring, planning, dividing up assignments, making contact with the deputies of the Plain in the hope of gaining their support. Robespierre did nothing of the sort. A man who was obsessed with imaginary plots seemed not to suspect the very real plot that was being hatched against him. His long experience of political infighting ought to have put him on his guard. How could he not have realized that he was in mortal danger? Yet he called upon none of his many intermediaries. Whether out of a false sense of security or because he was resigned, consciously or unconsciously, to defeat, he went to the Convention on 27 July (9 Thermidor) as if it were business as usual, without doing anything more, it would appear, than prepare a new speech, of which no good could possibly come. He was walking straight into a trap.

The members of the public who filled the galleries, and whose noisy adulation had played such a prominent role in his career up until then, would undoubtedly have been screened; at all events his usual supporters were not there, and no one in his camp thought to mobilize them. The coalition of his enemies had decided on a simple but reliable tactic: preventing him from speaking, and preventing his friends and allies from speaking. The fact that Collot d'Herbois occupied the president's chair made things considerably easier in this regard. In the meantime it would appear that there had been a sharp altercation between Saint-Just and Billaud-Varenne, following which Saint-Just decided not to share the report he had been charged with drafting at the conciliatory session of 23 July (5 Thermidor) with his colleagues on the Committee of Public Safety beforehand, as he had agreed to do. This was a powerful reason for his opponents to fear the contents of the speech he was scheduled to deliver late that morning, considering his close links to Robespierre, and to bar him from delivering it. In the event, his report testified to an admirable independence of mind. While he cast the deliberations of the Committee of Public Safety in a harsh light, taking a particularly hard line with regard to Billaud-Varenne and Collot d'Herbois, his treatment of Robespierre was both thorough and evenhanded. Here again it is clear that the two men had not conferred, and there is every reason to believe that Saint-Just was very displeased with Robespierre, not least on account of the policy of religious conciliation he sought to implement. In their panic, however, the conspirators paid no attention. No sooner had Saint-Just begun to speak than, according to plan, he was interrupted by Tallien, the leader of the cabal, who demanded the floor to raise a point of order. Saint-Just had just time enough to utter these prophetic words: "The course of things has wished that this rostrum may perhaps be the Tarpeian Rock for one who comes to tell you that some members of the government have strayed from the path of wisdom." These were to be his last public words, for the interruption left him dumbfounded. He offered no resistance, unlike Robespierre, who protested mightily, but to no avail.

Tallien's demand that "the veil be torn to shreds" was met with applause. In this connection Billaud-Varenne made reference to the meeting of the Jacobin Club the evening before, where, he alleged, "the intention of slaughtering the National Convention was exposed."

The Assembly's reaction to this, according to published reports, was one of horror. There followed a formal indictment of the authoritarian behavior of Robespierre and his network of accomplices, punctuated by "murmurs of indignation" and wild applause. Robespierre tried to respond. He was shouted down by cries of "Down with the tyrant!" The die was cast.

The decisive factor that brought about the reversal within the Convention, a body that until then had been notable mainly for its docility, was the Plain's switch of allegiance, which Robespierre seems not to have anticipated. In the past these deputies regarded him as a rampart against the more vindictive Montagnards; now they went over to the side of his enemies. The leaders of the Plain perceived that dissension within the Mountain presented an opportunity to kill two birds with one stone: by ridding themselves of Robespierre, they would have a good chance also of ridding themselves of the former Hébertists and their allies, who until then had represented the principal threat to their interests. And indeed this is what came to pass. With the disintegration of the popular movement, whose members no longer enjoyed the protection that Robespierre's authority once gave them, despite their excesses, the surviving sans-culottes soon found themselves isolated under the pressure of public opinion.

The formerly despised members of the Plain now held their heads high once more and willingly took part in the scramble for spoils, amid a crescendo of charges and curses skillfully orchestrated by Tallien. He began by persuading the Convention to order the arrest of "Robespierre's creatures," including Hanriot and Dumas. One thing led to another, and before long, in an outpouring of resentment that Robespierre tried in vain to mollify, the so-called triumvirate that he was supposed to form with Couthon and Saint-Just was placed under arrest as well. Once again it is important to note that apart from these two men, and Le Bas and Robespierre's brother Augustin, who were included in the indictment, no one seems to have attempted to defend him. In the meantime Barère, speaking on behalf of the Committee of Public Safety, encapsulated the meaning of the event: "Unjust rulers and free peoples are two antipodes, absolute opposites; enormous reputations and men who are equal cannot long exist together." His controlled manner of expression was very much the exception among the orators that day, whose dominant emotion was one of unreasoning hatred. In the end it was the language of conspiracy, so favored by Robespierre, that prevailed by being turned against him. Once the five accused men had been led outside the hall, Collot d'Herbois, speaking in the name of the Committees of Public Safety and General Security, promised "a detailed report" on the conspiracy. "It will not be difficult to convince you that something favorable to the cause of the routed despots was being prepared here." The great enemy of conspiracies wound up himself being arraigned as a conspirator.

The events that followed have been recounted a thousand times: Robespierre's arrival at the Hôtel de Ville after officers at the Luxembourg Prison refused to incarcerate him; the liberation of his associates, who then rejoined him, and their equivocations; the tactical indecisiveness of the Commander of the National Guard, Hanriot, which gave the Convention the time it needed to coordinate a response; the assault on the Hôtel de Ville; Robespierre's attempt to commit suicide (if that is what it was), which left him half dead; and finally the guillotine, in the afternoon of 28 July (10 Thermidor). The leaders of the Commune ought to have expected the counteroffensive that was bound to follow, and known that once launched it would gather strength. How are we to explain that, by and large, the veterans of the revolutionary movement remained on the sidelines? Even in the confusion of a belatedly improvised and very uneven mobilization (barely a quarter of the sections sent battalions to defend the Hôtel de Ville against the Convention), the troops of the Commune, had they been well led and deployed in a timely fashion, would no doubt have been capable of prevailing. What might have happened once the Convention had been subdued is another question.

No less astonishing is the wavering of the small group of Robespierrists, held back by legalistic scruples at a moment when they had nothing more to lose. Their indecision is a sign of the disabling uncertainty that took hold of them in the absence of any guidance from Robespierre himself, who plainly had no idea how to move forward. It is perhaps unsurprising that deputies accustomed to making speeches, more comfortable with rhetoric than the use of force, should have vacillated. But what are we to make of Saint-Just, tested in the heat of battle and an expert on military leadership? His sluggishness, bordering on paralysis, during the day and night of 27 July is not the least of these perplexities.

The unexplained circumstances surrounding Robespierre's injury only add to the obscurity of the events leading to his death. The hypothesis of a failed suicide attempt is appealing because it fits with the desperate atmosphere of these final days, but the possibility that his wounding was the heroic deed of a gendarme who had come to arrest the "tyrant" will never be able to be ruled out. How this altogether extraordinary career actually came to an end remains a profound and abiding mystery.

CHAPTER SIX

The Two Faces of the Revolution and Its Legacy

WOE TO THE VANQUISHED! Robespierre's downfall was accompanied by the creation of a legend whose darkness was equal to the shock that had to be explained and the popularity that had to be exorcised. Its repercussions still make themselves felt today. The session of 27 July 1794 (9 Thermidor) marked the beginning, the moment when Robespierre's indictment as a "dictator" and a "tyrant" was supplemented by anecdotal evidence meant to illustrate the perverse thirst for power that animated him. The plotters had no need to make any effort of imagination: his own conspiratorial rhetoric supplied them with an abundance of material. All the denunciations Robespierre had lavished on others were now turned against him. The "system of terror" he imputed to his enemies now became his own. Nothing was forgotten, not even the suspicion that he had wished to restore the monarchy—to his own advantage. He joined Hébert and Danton on the list of "scoundrels" who pretended to serve the Revolution, the better to lead it astray and profit from its confusion. The difference between them was that he was the last and the worst, the supreme scoundrel, making the tyrants of antiquity pale by comparison. He now officially acceded to the rank of "monster," charged with all manner of crimes, in Courtois's famous inventory of Robespierre's papers, the *Rapport présenté à la Convention le 5 janvier 1795 (16 Nivôse an III) au nom de la commission chargée de l'examen des papiers trouvés chez Robespierre et ses complices*. And since the palace revolution (for this is what 9 Thermidor was), which unfolded within the restricted circle of those who held power, rather rapidly turned into a change of regime, despite the wishes of its authors, the legend of

Robespierre was able to draw from it what it needed in order to be definitively accepted.

There can be no doubt that Billaud-Varenne and Collot d'Herbois intended to carry on the aims of revolutionary government without Robespierre. The problem was that they did not appreciate the extent to which Robespierre gave the existing regime legitimacy, something they were unable to supply themselves. One of the key elements of the argument made by a majority of the Committees of Public Safety and General Security on 27 July had been the repudiation of the Law of 22 Prairial, now represented as the tyrannical work of Robespierre and his henchmen alone, which he was accused of pushing through the Convention against the committees' advice. This charge was promptly recycled five days later, on 1 August, but to no long-lasting effect. In reality it signaled the gradual and irresistible dismantling of revolutionary government, notwithstanding the attempts of diehard Montagnards to slow its pace. The transfer of Marat's remains to the Panthéon on 21 September 1794 was to be the swan song of Jacobinism—with the consequence that the retrospective identification of Robespierre with the regime gained in strength in proportion to its increasing disablement in the wake of his demise. If the government stumbled and fell when Robespierre was no longer there, plainly he had to have been its soul and its master, the one who decided everything, the evil genius. In the public mind, then, the course of events served to corroborate the version promoted by the authors of his execution, who were all the more careful to distance themselves from their former colleague as their own power began to crumble and they found themselves accused in their turn of complicity with the tyrant whom they had long served before finally overthrowing him. Robespierre's memorialization as the embodiment of evil was due in large part to the unshackling of the press that accompanied the Thermidorian relaxation of censorship, which allowed counterrevolutionary opinion to put the Revolution as a whole on trial by prosecuting the misdeeds of its most emblematic figure; hack journalists bent on exploiting a bonanza of monstrosity only amplified the impression of wickedness. In death, the Incorruptible swiftly assumed a demoniacal aspect.

Before long, however, this situation changed. The rebirth of republicanism in France during the nineteenth century and the emergence of the socialist movement, together with the appearance of history as a scholarly discipline, combined to discredit legendary fabrications by refocusing critical attention on the Revolution itself. Little by little, accounts of events and actors were given a factual basis, though study of the documentary evidence did not manage to settle differences of interpretation;

to the contrary, it sharpened and nourished them. The year 1848 was a pivotal date in this regard, with the nearly simultaneous publication of the great histories by Lamartine, Michelet, and Blanc. These works inaugurated a new cycle of research and analysis, marked by an intrinsic ambiguity, never dispelled, that set the French Revolution apart from everything that came before or after. The reason for this is that it was not quite like any other revolution. For democracies throughout the world it came to have something of a mythical and sacral origin, so that every nation defined itself by the way in which it interpreted this origin and the way in which it related this interpretation to its own political traditions. Lamartine, Michelet, and Blanc, each in his own way, set this process of self-definition in motion. The search for critical exactitude, more or less rigorous depending on the case, but insisted on by each of these authors, harnessed a reconstruction of the events of the Revolution to a theory of its political meaning with the aim of providing future generations with a compass. The dual character of this enterprise, linking scholarly inquiry with ideological investment, became massively enlarged in the twentieth century with the annexation of the bourgeois revolutions of the past by the proletarian revolutions to come, following the example of the Bolshevik Revolution in Russia. This annexation went hand in hand with the rhetorical imposition of a social model of history conforming more or less strictly to Marxist principles. Prodigious archival investigations thus came to be fitted into the Procrustean bed of a dogmatic style of historiography that left hardly any doubt about their results.

The hegemony of the paradigm of class struggle by no means put an end to controversy. The Russian Revolution, which seemed to some to consecrate the interpretation of the dynamic of history in terms of antagonistic social forces, furnished others with a countermodel that likened the terrorist phase of the French Revolution to the totalitarianisms of the twentieth century, so that Robespierre became a sort of precursor of Lenin, and the Jacobin Club an anticipation of the avant-garde revolutionary party. Historical knowledge continued to accumulate, and all the more rapidly as disagreement about the conclusions to be drawn from it deepened.

All of this gives some idea of the thickness of the sedimentary layer that must be drilled through in order to approach the underlying truth of how the course of events appeared to the actors of the French Revolution themselves. The conviction that has guided my inquiry is that most of the studies available to us, however admirable they may be in establishing a factual record, neglect a crucial aspect of it: ideas put into action. It is true that we are seldom able to grasp this dimension of history. Generally we do not know exactly what actors were thinking, with the result that historians are unaccustomed to pay attention to it. But the French Revolution is exceptional in this regard. It was, to begin with, an experiment in making a political idea incarnate, an attempt to reimagine the conditions under which people can live together in obedience to a body of principles. What is more, the men of the Revolution continually reflected upon and talked about what was happening—and no one said more and reflected more deeply than Robespierre himself. He was the very embodiment of this revolution of principles. Not content to make himself its spokesman through his speeches, he sought as far as possible to epitomize in his person the austerity it required. It was to this dual quality of mind and example that he owed the moral authority that was acknowledged to be uniquely his—until finally it led him to practice an extraordinary type of dictatorship. Insofar as the words Robespierre left behind allow, we must attempt to penetrate the mystery of this period of five years, between his rise and fall, which contains in concentrated form the political problem that France was to spend the next two centuries trying to resolve. Otherwise we will be unable to free ourselves from the peculiar fascination, whether tinged with awe or horror, that Robespierre's career has exerted these many years and whose hold over the nation's imagination is scarcely diminished still today.

In Pursuit of a Mirage

Seen in the context of what he said and what he did, as I trust these pages have made clear, Robespierre ceases to be either the saint or the demon that he has so comprehensively and so complacently been made out to be. The roles of heroic martyr or bloodstained monster in which most historians have tried to confine him are of little use in discovering who he was and what his life meant. The categories through which Marxist historians have sought to account for what they take to be the objective meaning of his positions and his behavior, in the light of his class background and the grand struggle between the aristocracy, bourgeoisie, and emerging proletariat, are no more helpful. Nor are the groupings in which traditional accounts have enshrined the memory of the Convention (Girondins and Montagnards, federalists and Jacobins, to say nothing of Thermidorians), whose weakness—if not actually inadequacy—is plain on closer inspection, of any greater value.

Robespierre was neither a vulgar demagogue nor a prophetic theoretician. From the first he identified himself with what proved to be the guiding spirit of the Revolution, namely, the rights of man, the logic of which he persisted in expounding even when its ultimately pernicious consequences were manifest, to the point of making them the rule of his existence and the basis of his public image. No more than his colleagues in the Estates General did he anticipate the course that events were to take. Indeed, he had not been one of the group of eminences and nobodies who drafted the Declaration of the Rights of Man, and in the debate that followed he made only a brief and timid appearance. But whereas his fellow deputies appealed to this document, at the start, only in order to strengthen a tenuous legitimacy, without any thought to estimating the true power of the instrument they had created, Robespierre made this instrument completely his own. So great was its power that it soon took on a life of its own, until finally it succeeded in toppling a throne that had been secure for centuries. Robespierre gradually rose to prominence by establishing himself as the most adamant defender of these first principles of political order. He knew no better than anyone else where such remarkable intransigence would lead. Even so, he placed his faith in it, to the point of entrusting his fate to it, unreservedly relying on its inspiration, so that finally, and however improbably, he became the oracle of the Revolution.

More than this, Robespierre made himself the man of the Rights of Man and of the Citizen, modeling his personal life and his official conduct on their requirements. Sacrificing privacy and all selfish interest, he resolved to devote himself entirely to the public interest. In this way he embodied his own conception of the ideal citizen, a person who knows only the discipline of principle and has in mind only the higher good of his country. The title of "the Incorruptible," bestowed by his enthusiastic admirers at the close of the Constituent Assembly in September 1791, was not limited to praising his exceptional qualities of disinterestedness and constancy. It was above all a political title that qualified him for the exercise of an authority incommensurate with what anyone had enjoyed until then.

Here is the beginning of what fatally led Robespierre astray. For the situation in which he now found himself had the effect of blinding him to the innermost reasons that led him to enter public service in the first place— powerful reasons, to judge from the insistence with which he harped on the essential importance of virtue, of which he presented himself as a foremost example. There is no point trying to probe a psychology that will forever remain impenetrable to us. Even so, we cannot follow his career as a parliamentarian without taking notice of his compulsion to "talk about himself," as the most benevolent of his biographers put it, to portray himself in a manner bordering on obsessive self-celebration. Indeed the tendency is so pronounced that one can scarcely fail to detect, behind the moral exhibitionism, a profound identification with the "divine man" of Rousseau's *Confessions*—a self-idolizing impulse, supported by the argument from self-sacrifice, that soon was attacked by his adversaries. It was just this that was to trigger the cruel outpouring of resentment on 27 July 1794. Still, its interest would be merely anecdotal had it not been coupled with a political vision whose ramifications went well beyond the behavior of one man.

The idea of virtue that Robespierre claimed to embody was rooted in the conviction that this same virtue was naturally and spontaneously incarnated in the people. It was native to them, and waited only for the opportunity to manifest itself, once the enemies and the obstacles that diverted the people from their vocation had been swept away. Thus the blindness with regard to himself was inseparable from a blindness with regard to social reality. The myth of popular virtue is at the heart of Robespierre's politics. It remained nothing more than an inoffensive incantation—demagogic in the eyes of some, a proof of vanity in the eyes of others—so long as Robespierre was only the most vigorous opponent of royal government, which he held to be corrupt, by definition, in all of its forms. But the situation completely changed from the moment that the people overthrew the monarchy and found themselves called upon to exercise power. From 10 August 1792 onward, the myth of the people, propagated by one of the most compelling figures of the popular movement, along with Marat and Danton, was a political force to be reckoned with. Gaining impetus from the course of events, it quickly became the focus of an irrepressible dynamic that was to catapult its creator and exemplar to the pinnacle of power, before hurling him down into the abyss.

This vision of a people instinctively united in its devotion to country, which is to say united in the defense of its own interests, had dangerous consequences after the fall of the monarchy, above all for making it impossible to admit the truth of the political situation, namely, that the country was deeply divided; instead, it disguised the situation as a struggle of the people against their enemies. The reality is that the 10 August 1792 uprising in Paris was the work of an activist minority, relying no doubt on considerable popular support; but this support was very far from being unanimous, even in the capital itself. As a result, the divide between the Parisian movement and a majority of the provincial population—the peasantry in particular, among whom royalist loyalties remained strong—grew wider still. In the wake of the dissension caused by the Civil Constitution of the Clergy in the religious sphere, the institution of a republic could not fail to bring about one of those upheavals that touch the very depths of collective identity and to influence the way in which the actors of the Revolution conceived of community as a political ideal. But these profound differences of opinion should not have existed if the idea of a people necessarily united in the full and complete sovereignty that it had just claimed for itself had any basis in fact; the only possible opposition would have assumed the form of resistance from the remnants of the ancien régime, which, having been deprived of all legitimacy, now needed to be destroyed. Instead the manifest discrepancy between an avant-garde whose belief in its superior legitimacy rested squarely on the Robespierrist myth of the people and the reality of a deeply divided nation was to constitute the combustible material of fiery debates in the Convention in the weeks and months ahead.

Echoes of conflict reverberated from the very outset in the division of parties within the Assembly. This body did not faithfully reflect the state of popular opinion, of course. Owing to massive abstention among eligible voters and partisan manipulation of the electoral process, the selection of representatives was restricted to a rather small circle of politically active persons. But even within this circle, there were those who thought it necessary nonetheless to consult popular opinion, moderate on the whole and largely provincial, and those who felt that leadership of the revolutionary movement should reside in its avant-garde, which had just shown what "wonders" it was capable of. This was the real source of the infighting that beset the Convention from the moment of its inception in September 1792 and that later accounts were to romanticize as it pleased their authors, who did everything in their power to discover beneath the discord undiscoverable political doctrines and social forces.

Tensions crystallized at once around two issues—the September massacres (and by implication, the prerogatives of the Commune, which had covered them up) and the fate to be reserved for Louis XVI—that clearly mark out the dividing line between moderation and radicalism. On the one hand, there were those who were anxious not only to show the country that a republican regime was capable of limiting and punishing atrocities that nothing could justify, but also to use the same occasion to affirm the government's authority in the face of the encroachments of the Commune; and, on the other, those who preferred to say nothing about excesses that, while no doubt culpable, were nonetheless, everything considered, understandable. On the one hand, those who thought that a magnanimous attitude toward the dethroned king would be proof of the Republic's strength and greatness, and at the same time, in respect of public opinion, a sign of

wisdom and prudence; and, on the other, those who thought it indispensable to complete the break with the ancien régime by an act that would
render it irremediable, while at the same time consecrating the victory of
the sovereign people over tyranny. Between these camps, it must be kept in
mind, there were a great many undecided deputies who earnestly sought
compromise. On both sides, the virtuous people of Robespierre's imagin-
ing occupied a privileged place: in the one case, they served to minimize
regrettable acts of lawlessness, typically reduced to the death of a single
innocent person; in the other, they were used to justify the impulse that
provoked them—after all, as Robespierre put it in response to Louvet's
accusation on 5 November 1792, "it was a popular movement." More
importantly still, to his way of thinking, the idea of popular rectitude
dictated an unequivocable stance in the matter of the king's fate. A people
that was now finally its own master could give full expression to its virtuous nature only by giving the most striking possible demonstration
of the incompatibility of republican institutions with the pervasive corruption spawned by despotism. To consummate the conquest of liberty
required the annihilation of its contrary. This was a question not of
administering justice, but of founding a new political order by a judgment that gave its essence tangible form: "Louis must die in order that
the fatherland may live." Although Robespierre's line of reasoning was
not endorsed by his colleagues, he had nonetheless provided the decision that eventually carried the day, after much hesitation, with its most
radical and best known expression.

The events of the year 1793 lent support to Robespierre's philosophy by
making virtue—as he understood the term, which is to say unconditional
devotion to the common interest—an instrument of public safety. Gradually it came to be merged with what was called the "soul of Jacobinism," a
notion that was forged in the crucible of war and domestic unrest as part
of the improvised construction of revolutionary government. It furnished
him with the central theme of his combat against the Girondins, carried
out with the support of the Paris sections and of the working class of the
Commune. The Girondins suffered from the fatal misfortune of holding a
majority of the seats in the Convention and controlling the levers of government under immensely difficult circumstances that they were unequipped
to cope with, neither with regard to domestic or foreign affairs nor to the
formulation of policy or its practical implementation. It was their incom-
petence, much more than their principles, that invited criticism. They
too were Jacobins, and their intellectual assumptions were no different
than those of the Robespierrists. But they were overtaken by events. The
exercise of power made them vulnerable to charges of corruption, and all

the more as they were unable, for want of public confidence, to wield the authority that circumstances required. The unfavorable turn taken by the war against the European coalition made Brissot's optimistic assurances look ridiculous; the fact that the government was unable to mobilize the resources needed to support the gigantic effort that was called for in all areas, beginning with the military command, only made matters worse. Dumouriez's treason was to be the coup de grâce in this regard. At home, the government's legalistic concern with taking the real country into account, which is to say the web of local authorities that came into being as a result of the vast decentralization of administration between 1789 and 1791, had a paralyzing effect in the face of provincial secession, dramatized most vividly by the Vendée rebellion.

Robespierre's conception of the people, by contrast, was remarkably well suited to legitimize a government in a state of exception that could remedy the Girondins' unpardonable weakness by marshaling the forces needed to successfully meet the demands of a grave situation. A people that by its very nature could wish for nothing other than that the Republic be indivisible, undivided by federalist arrangements of any kind; by the same token, it could only approve a unanimous commitment to ensuring the Republic's survival, by purging itself of everything in it that posed an obstacle to patriotic devotion. Its sovereignty therefore had to be translated into a form of authority that was at once concentrated and unlimited—an absolute authority that, paradoxically, put the people in a position to govern directly by standing united behind their representatives. Accordingly, it could only be in such a moment of national mobilization, no matter how exceptional, that the nature of the people stands fully revealed. One imagines that Robespierre found this conclusion irresistible, even if it forced him to renounce the very liberties that until then he had defended more resolutely than anyone else.

Here we come to the heart of the matter. How was it that momentary political differences came to be hardened into permanent and bitter animosity? The Girondins upheld the same liberal philosophy of rights as the one in whose name Robespierre had earned his reputation for incorruptibility in the Constituent Assembly. The problem was that they could not bring themselves to go so far as to advocate revolutionary government, whereas Robespierre's fantastical conception of a virtuous people made it natural for him to do this. At the very most, the Girondins may be said to have been more sensitive than the Robespierrists to economic constraints—though one does find, it is true, a comparable awareness in Saint-Just. Jacobinism itself, whose active element brought forth its passive counterpart, was a by-product of the combining of contraries.

Between these opposing forces, to a certain extent at least, communication was possible. It was Robespierre who decided where and how this communication took place.

Jacobinism did not acquire a clear and settled identity until the Montagnard faction in the Convention, in collaboration with the Parisian sansculotte movement, prevailed over the Girondins. After the coup d'état of 31 May–2 June 1793, the people assumed power. But what in fact did the people want to obtain from power and political mastery? It was on this point that disagreement emerged between the sans-culottes and the Mountain, whose alliance proved to be fragile. Sans-culottism represented a variant of the culture of rights, its radical variant, something much more than the political expression of a particular social milieu; it was hardly incidental that the Cordeliers Club was formally known as the Society of the Rights of Man and of the Citizen. No doubt in this connection it is necessary to reverse the order of causation that a long tradition of social history has worked unceasingly (though unsuccessfully) to establish: it was the content of this culture that made it attractive to the working class and not the other way around. Its logic held particular appeal for the sans-culottes and gave them lasting influence even though they constituted a minority. On the basis of equal liberty, recognized as belonging to every person, it made a powerful argument for direct democracy, so far as this was possible in political affairs, and, in economic affairs, egalitarian authoritarianism. Additionally, in the context of 1793, one must take into account an uncompromising anticlericalism among many of the revolutionaries with regard to all denominations, not just the Catholic religion. So long as the Girondin majority remained their common adversary, an appeal to the overriding need to see the Revolution through to the end was enough to reconcile Montagnards and sans-culottes without too much difficulty. From the safe distance of the Convention, Robespierre may well have thought that he had found the people of his imagination among the most militant citizens of the Commune and the membership of the Cordeliers Club. From the moment that he had to govern, however, it was a different matter altogether. It was in the muted confrontation between sans-culottes and Montagnards, between the leaders of the Commune and the Committee of Public Safety, that the aims of Jacobinism were finally to become clear and Robespierre's politics finally to be made explicit.

The exercise of his duties on the Committee of Public Safety, as we have seen, changed Robespierre in one crucial respect. It forced him to reconsider his most basic views, with the result that after long and painful deliberation he was converted to the idea of government. A revolutionary government, to be sure, and therefore impermanent, but a government all the same—a distinct seat of authority that to his mind, until then, embodied an unacceptable separation between the sovereign people and the representative assembly speaking and acting in their name; a seat of authority that was the home of all political vices, which prospered there owing to the "pride" and "selfishness" that it could only encourage. The Girondin government, by amply confirming this analysis, presented Robespierre with a splendid opportunity to denounce its corrupting effect. At the same time, the Jacobin alliance with the sans-culottes, entered into with the aim of promoting the ideal of a fusion of the people and power, made it necessary to remain vague to some extent about how power was to be organized and how it should be exercised. Direct democracy offered only one possible version among others. As late as 10 August 1793, Robespierre's friend David could still use the identity between representatives and the represented as the theme for his celebration of the anniversary of the overthrow of the monarchy, eloquently expressed in these words: "There is no longer any division between [private] persons and officials. . . . Everything is intermingled in the presence of the people, unique source of all the powers that, in emanating from them, remain forever subject to them."

The exercise of power totally modified Robespierre's perspective. It caused him to adopt the principle of a separate authority that until then he had refused to entertain, and just as clearly to reject the sans-culotte conception of direct democracy. In each case he was at pains to emphasize, as against the pressures brought to bear by the sections and the clubs, that legitimacy resided with the representatives meeting in the Convention. The absolute authority that was reinvented in the course of these tragic months, in the name of the rights of the people, could legitimately be entrusted only to a special apparatus. That did not do away with the need for it to be identified with the people, but it did make this identification depend on the virtue of the governors, which as a consequence was invested with additional significance, since it guaranteed that their decisions would be taken out of a concern exclusively with the public good. With this clarification of the proper exercise of power, which firmly dissociated revolutionary government from spontaneous popular will, the essential elements of Jacobinism fell into place. The power of the people, in order to be effective, had to be concentrated in a government acting in the name of national unity, without becoming lost in a welter of "partial" deliberations, as it was said at the time, that raised the dreaded specter of federalism.

The divorce of Jacobinism from sans-culottism carried over into the economic sphere. The large-scale controls instituted in this connection by the Committee of Public Safety, the most far-reaching of which was the ceiling on wages and prices, must not be allowed to conceal the very clear inconsistency on which they were based. Early utopian socialists such as Babeuf were later to suggest that these measures somehow prefigured the collectivization of economic life that they hoped to bring about. A more substantial analysis, subsequently developed by Marx, laid stress— and rightly so—on the limits of what he considered to be a "bourgeois" conception of authority. The seemingly radical policies of the Committee proceeded from a compromise that can be summarized as follows: the greatest possible degree of public intervention was to be desired in order to assure the livelihood of all, and particularly of the poorest members of society, while at the same time respecting the basic principles of private property and free trade, or, as we would say today, the liberal organization of economic life. Jacobinism, as it was then conceived, in the context of what is now called social policy, was an opportunistic form of antiliberalism that nonetheless moved from liberal premises. It was this tension that prompted a group of sans-culottes to try to imagine what a genuinely collectivist society might look like. Their deliberations led eventually to the so-called Conspiracy of the Equals, the failed coup d'état against the Directory in May 1796 led by Babeuf, who sought to dress up communism in the rights of man.

But the most clear-cut divergence, and the one most fraught with consequence for Robespierre himself, was to make itself felt in the religious sphere. As in the case of political and economic affairs, where he became the most prominent Jacobin voice, the faithful spokesman at least of majority opinion within the Montagnard camp and of the Committees of Public Safety and Public Security, so with regard to the question of religious freedom he stood out for his views on a matter in which he took a very personal interest—so much so that in the end he found himself isolated. It is not hard to understand why most of his colleagues, whatever their true convictions may have been, had no qualms about following his lead in putting a halt to the de-Christianization campaign launched by the sans-culotte leaders in Paris. Even though many deputies probably had very little sympathy for Christian belief, and indeed deep down may have sympathized with the attack on organized religion, they could not help but consider the campaign to have been highly ill-advised at a moment when what was needed was to assert the authority of the Convention over the country as a whole, to begin with by winning over the rural masses.

The solemn proclamation recognizing the Supreme Being was a very different matter, however. It was one thing was to put an end to a needlessly provocative movement that promised only to make a difficult situation all the more intractable, but quite another to authorize the institution of what strongly resembled a state religion, no matter how often Robespierre denied that this is what it was. It was this complementary initiative that furnished the most convincing argument in support of the view of Robespierre as a dictator, namely, that his power over the Committees and the Convention was so great that he was able to get them to adopt, without a moment's hesitation, a measure that was bound to arouse widespread controversy. The evidence on which this argument relies is by no means dispositive, however. There is reason to believe that many deputies, even some of those least convinced on theological grounds, were nonetheless easily won over to the decree, considering it to be a sensible step that was likely to have a calming effect in the wake of the frenzy surrounding the trial and execution of the Hébertists and Dantonists. The fact that the people themselves seem to have responded enthusiastically to the festival held on Pentecost Sunday, 8 June 1794, suggests that the underlying political calculation was not misguided.

At all events it is clear that the cult of the Supreme Being was never a central element of Jacobin doctrine. It attracted little support among his closest allies and had no enduring influence. It marked the point when Robespierre's career began to branch off in a new direction, for now he found himself cut off from his usual audience. Combined with the Law of 22 Prairial—for which he probably was not solely responsible (contrary to what his fellow members of the Committee of Public Safety were subsequently to maintain), but which fit too well with his familiar techniques of parliamentary maneuvering for it not to be plausibly attributed to him—it alienated a public whose loyalty he had long been able to count on, and whose expectations until then he had known so well how to express and to place in the service of a larger purpose. It was decisive in helping to irrevocably identify him with the image of a solitary and authoritarian ruler that his enemies were to have an easy time exploiting on 9 Thermidor.

How are we to explain this loss of contact with his most devoted followers? Was it due to mental and physical exhaustion, to sickness, or to some psychological disturbance that deprived him of his abilities, however these are to be understood—proof of incomparable tactical skill, as those who admire him as a masterful politician would have it, or of a consummate talent for flattering his listeners, as those who denigrate him as a demagogue drunk with power insist? There is one other hypothesis that deserves to be considered. While it does not rule out the others, it allows us to go further by connecting the somewhat aristocratic obstinacy we have noted in Robespierre with the coherence of his character and his thinking. Much more clearly than his fellow revolutionaries, Robespierre grasped the fundamentally religious nature of the idea of the Republic that they espoused—an idea to which the superstitions and prejudices sustained by "sacerdotal despotism" were utterly foreign. He felt sure that the ideal of a nation united in its capacity to rule itself through the total devotion of each one of its members, representatives and represented alike, to the general welfare was the direct heir to the collective unity created since time immemorial by communities of faith and the longing for union with the divine. He felt sure, too, that a republic of the sort he had in mind constituted a new and improved version of the ancient model, cleansed of dogmatic error by reason and enlightened by an awareness of individual rights, while likewise requiring the sacrifice of each person's individuality to the common interest. Ultimately, self-abnegation, the surrender to something greater than oneself, could be motivated only by the conviction that by acting in this way one could once more act in accordance with the design of the supreme arbiter of all things. In the absence of a shared recognition of some higher authority than man, there could be no justice among men.

Robespierre did not act out of religious belief, under the influence of an authoritarian demon; he acted as a man of politics, persuaded that the Republic could be founded only at the price of authoritarianism, at least temporarily. It may also be that the perceived urgency of the situation did as much to diminish his lucidity as the decline of his physical health. If what mattered above all was seeing revolutionary government through to the end, in order to durably establish a regime of constitutional government, then it was necessary to make sure that solid foundations had been laid beforehand. As far as Robespierre was concerned, this had not yet been done. Probably this is why he felt that he had to obtain the consent of his colleagues at once for the formal recognition of a Supreme Being—and why Saint-Just set out at the same time to develop a theory of republican institutions. In Saint-Just's notebooks one finds this despairing entry: "The day when I am convinced that it is impossible to give the French people gentle, energetic, sensible, and inexorable habits for [combating] tyranny and injustice, I will stab myself." The popular success of the Festival of the Supreme Being seems momentarily to have confirmed Robespierre in the belief that a spirit of virtuous unanimity was soon to assert itself throughout the land—only then to see rampant corruption and intrigue spring up again on all sides. Hence the desperate and enigmatic final offensive, leaving future generations to wonder whether the order for it had been given by blind pride or by an unshakable resolve to commit suicide.

At this point a counterfactual thought experiment may be illuminating. Let us imagine that Robespierre's last gamble had paid off, that the forces of the Commune once more had the Convention at their mercy, that the purge Robespierre called for had been carried out; in short, that 9 Thermidor marked instead the moment when the Revolution was once again reinvigorated, as it had been on 31 May 1793. In that case its expiration date would have only been postponed. The Republic that Robespierre dreamed of would still have been lacking a solid foundation, for it could not be given one along the lines he contemplated. The supply of conspirators, factionists, and scoundrels needing to be gotten rid of would only have proved more clearly than ever to be a bottomless pit. The virtuous unanimity of the people, fleetingly perceived in the bright light of a fine day, would have been no more firmly anchored than before in a permanent order, the community of citizens of Robespierre's fevered imagination. For the mystical union of souls supposed to be brought about by subordination to the divine could not be transposed to the realm of human liberty in the form of the sacrificial identification with the common good to which he gave the name of virtue. The real world—a world of separateness rather than of union—has no choice but to construct a workable system of governance by other means. Robespierre had run up against the futility of his own vision. This is what brought about his downfall. The ninth day of Thermidor did not mark the interruption of a program that otherwise might have been carried through to a successful conclusion. It signaled the failure of a plan that could not possibly have succeeded. The man of the Revolution of the Rights of Man died because he fundamentally misunderstood what a republic that had any chance of winning the approval of a majority of the French people might look like.

The Impossible Has Its Reasons

But this powerlessness went far beyond Robespierre himself. Indeed he proved to be far more insightful, even in his pursuit of a chimerical republic, than the faux-realists who thought that his downfall delivered them from the delusion he had nurtured and kept alive. Because Robespierre perceived the essentially religious character of the society he was resolved to bring into existence, he sought to cultivate the spirit of piety on which it depended—without seeing the incompatibility of such a society with the foundation on which he intended to establish it. The faux-realists, unaware of the debt the Revolution owed to religion, sought to counteract the lingering effects of a despised mysticism by rooting the Republic in a more solid ground, the actual state of society. They were nonetheless captives of the same set of assumptions and hostage to the same conception of society, only seen in a different light. A republic of property owners, which the Thermidorean reaction thought would dispose of revolutionary fantasies, proved to be no more viable than Robespierre's republic of the people had any chance of being.

Property rights, by their tangible character, gave the reassuring impression of having a firm basis in enduring social interests, insulated against the demagogic harangues that promises based on abstract principles were liable to encourage. Nevertheless it did not become any easier to extract from this prosaic version of the rights of man the formula for an efficient and trustworthy form of government. The Directory, appointed in accordance with the provisions of the new Constitution of 22 August 1795, whose drafters were convinced that they had drawn the right lessons from past mistakes, turned out to be remarkably dysfunctional and in any case altogether incapable of closing what was called "the chasm of the Revolution." Political stabilization was to come from an extraparliamentary source, in the form of "military despotism," as Robespierre had prophesied on 26 July 1794. Bonaparte made no attempt to establish his power by grounding it in the legitimacy conferred by the rights of the sovereign people, even if the people in this case were the ones who owned property. He established it instead by cynically persuading the people to legitimize the abandonment of their own sovereignty.

The Napoleonic interlude left a profound mark on French political history in the form of an alternation between two types of regime: on the one hand—to grossly oversimplify—legitimacy without authority, and, on the other, authority without legitimacy. More precisely and more correctly, we may distinguish between, on the one hand, a popular legitimacy that, despite the failure to give it institutional form, was so well established that it was able, at least in the long run, to successfully resist attempts to restore traditional monarchical legitimacy, and, on the other, rulers with no claim to legitimacy other than the fact that they actually held power—a not insignificant advantage, everything considered. The history of republican democracy in France has consisted in gradually (though not yet completely, and not without great turmoil) breaking free of this cycle. England worked out a more peaceful alternative, which the rest of Europe found more attractive, within the framework of a constitutional monarchy (though there was no constitution in the English case). There the progressive rehabilitation of governmental authority served to strengthen popular sovereignty through a neutralization of royal prerogatives that nonetheless allowed the people to identify with the monarchy, now deprived of any real power.

A comparison of these two situations is instructive for bringing out the difficulty, in the French case, of devising a government based on principles that for the first time in history could give it a foundation in reason. Contrary to what had been promised, the rights of man did not supply the formula for creating a set of political arrangements capable of expressing them. Politics and law, because they are distinct domains, need to be properly aligned; but they can only be put into correspondence with each other once their independence has been admitted. This is why there is nothing more difficult to constitute than a republic that does not enjoy the support of a preexisting authority, which serves as a point of reference so long as the work of assimilating its powers in order to place the new regime in the service of a community of citizens remains unfinished. It was this Herculean task that the French Revolution tragically failed to carry out, leaving its heirs to scale a mountain of obstacles. And if they have now succeeded in this at long last for the most part, it is because they were able to lodge the Republic in the state built by the authoritarian governments they managed finally to overcome and by appropriating their administrative machinery.

Because the marriage of republic and state was never formally acknowledged, the two rival memories bequeathed by the events of the Revolution and its wreck on the implacable rock of politics were able to be perpetuated until the present day. On the one hand, we have the celebrants of a republic of principles, who wish to hear nothing about the impossibility of its ever becoming a reality and for whom it goes without saying that just ideas deserve to prevail, regardless of circumstances; and, on the other, the horrified abominators of the Terror, who are determined to recall only the transgressions and the atrocities to which republican principles gave rise, refusing to inquire into either what made it impossible to ignore these principles or what made acting on them so fraught with danger. The images of Robespierre that survived in collective memory raised this antagonism to its highest point, altogether logically, since he joined in his person an inflexible defense of principles with their bloody and sterile dictatorship. Naturally this made him a hero in the eyes of some, all the more incontestably as he ended his days a martyr, and a villain in the eyes of others, all the more indisputably in view of his ignominious downfall.

In both cases one fails to seriously ask what it was that connected the two phases and the two faces of the man. One is content, in the first case, to ascribe the drift into terrorism to the passions of the moment and, in the second case, to attribute it to the very nature of the principles invoked in defense of it. But Robespierre's exceptional importance from the historical point of view emerges only at the intersection of these two phases of his career. For it is in the leap from the absolutism of principles to the absolutism of power in the name of principles (the latter an absolutism powerless to provide a foundation for a rights-based government) that the essential elements of the five years between 1789 and 1794 are condensed. Robespierre's career sums up everything the Revolution represented, from its dazzling beginnings until its fateful miscarriage. For this reason he stands out as the only one of the Revolution's actors in whom its course as a whole can be grasped.

What fitted him for this emblematic role was a remarkable combination of public virtues and private failings that reflected an exemplary but at the same time flawed character. One thinks in the first place of Robespierre's reputation for incorruptibility. The perfect disinterestedness with which he made himself the unyielding champion of the rights of the people is beyond doubt. It seems probable that he sought to personify the republican passion for impersonality, for selfless devotion to the public good and subordination of one's own interest to the higher truth of principles. What he failed to see is that virtue in this sense is corrupted the moment it declares itself. It becomes an excuse for self-advertisement, if not actually for smug and garrulous exhibitionism—a tendency that Robespierre's adversaries seized upon at once and ridiculed from the time of the Constituent Assembly onward; it was to be mercilessly exploited by his former friends, now implacable enemies, on 9 Thermidor. Thus it was that his narcissistic infatuation with virtue, inoffensive on the whole so long as he remained in opposition, assumed quite a different aspect when he came into government. It was swiftly transformed into an intolerance of contradiction so that anyone who dared to disagree with him was answered with vituperation and defamation, and became the mainspring of an authoritarian impulse that escaped his notice by taking cover behind the uncompromising rigor of principles.

Things took a still more ominous turn when Robespierre's obsession with virtue was extended to include a mythologizing identification with the people, who were supposed to constitute its natural vehicle. As long as this celebration of the moral excellence of the people was useful only for demanding that their sovereignty be formally recognized, it posed no great problem; at worst, it stimulated a taste for demagogic rhetoric whose chief effect was to inflate the popularity of their spokesman, a matter of no immediate concern. But the situation completely changed when the overthrow of the monarchy made popular sovereignty a reality and elevated the people's staunchest champions, Robespierre foremost among them, to the highest positions of government. Not realizing that this was a trap from which there was no escape, he threw himself into it. Personal identification with an ideally virtuous citizenry led him to exchange a power exercised in the name of the people for one in which he substituted himself for the people, in the extravagant belief that he was speaking for them, without there being any reason to ask their opinion—a power that amounted to unconscious dictatorship. Closer examination of Robespierre's compulsive need to see himself as the agent of historical destiny will cast new light on the circumstances under which this potentially devastating power was exercised.

Let us briefly recall in its broad outlines the political and military context as Robespierre understood it. There was the war against "tyrants," creatures of the English, the enemy par excellence, on all the country's frontiers; within France, the war against the "fanatics" of the Vendée and various provincial irredentisms; and, in Paris itself, a struggle waged on two fronts, on the right against the governing Brissotin faction, whose refusal or inability to take the necessary measures had placed the nation in dire peril, and on the left against the sans-culottes, whose pretension to tell the Convention what to do and how to do it threatened to undermine the principle of popular representation—all this against the background of famine and misery caused by a complete breakdown of food supply chains. In short, the people found themselves besieged on all sides by the very persons who denied their sovereignty, some of them declared enemies, others hidden; in the last analysis, however, these enemies were but one. For the people it was now or never: the time had come for them to display their virtue not only by wholly devoting themselves to their own salvation, but also by eradicating all traces of their ancient subjection. Under these circumstances, where there could be no doubt about what was at stake, all those who resisted making the unconditional commitment that the popular cause required were at the very least suspect of an abiding attachment to the old corrupt order, and in the worst case of taking part in clandestine conspiracies aimed at widening the war being waged openly against the people by their avowed enemies. What could account for the failure of the Girondin government to combat this threat if not secret collusion with foreign powers? What could explain the escalating provocations of the sans-culottes if not a plot directed from abroad with the purpose of weakening from within the vital impetus imparted by revolutionary government? What was the purpose of so many appeals for clemency if not to prevent the French people from justly punishing their adversaries? All contradiction, all opposition, every obstacle to what Robespierre imagined to be the fusion of his own sacrifice with the cause of the people and their vital interests was invariably interpreted as evidence of a multiform and omnipresent foreign plot. Thus the struggle needing to be carried on against the quite real enemies of the Republic became enlarged into a campaign of terror directed against a fantastic enemy—an enemy that was none other than the discrepancy between the real people and the ideal people.

Robespierre's conspiratorialism might have been faintly plausible up until the trial of the Hébertists in March 1794, to the extent that this was connected with the undeclared, yet undeniable, political struggle between the Committee of Public Safety and the sans-culotte Commune. With the trial and execution of the Dantonists the following month, however, it tipped over into the improbable, if not also the delusional. Genuine threats to the country were always present, of course, but now the indefensibly arbitrary identification of conspirators was plain for all to see. Hence the sense of relief with which the decree establishing the cult of the Supreme Being in May was received. Even among freethinkers, who were prepared to make whatever concessions were necessary in order to reach some sort of understanding, it seemed to offer a way out from the abyss of proscriptions. Robespierre could not help but see the matter differently. To his mind it was not a question of tactics; he was destined to plunge into the abyss. No doubt the fact that he had managed to obtain official authorization from the Convention, while at the same time clarifying the implications of the measure for established denominations, must have seemed to him a kind of culmination—except that the solemn vow of allegiance to a sacred unity, calling upon the Republic to encourage citizens and representatives to join together in discharging their common obligation to France and to the "author of their being," appears to have had the effect of making him aware of the unbridgeable chasm separating the reign of patriotism, in principle now within reach, and the brute fact of its widespread absence. This chasm could only be explained by a conspiracy of the corrupt still more cunning than its predecessors, having now succeeded in infiltrating the government itself. Hence the final attempt at purification on which he now embarked, only this time no longer accompanied by a large circle of supportive followers. But what else was left for him to do than to leave an unrivaled example of virtue to posterity by seeing his sacrifice through to the end?

Thus a dictatorship the like of which is unknown to history was doomed to collapse from within before it could be brought down from without. It was an anonymous dictatorship in one sense, but in any case an informal one, since it presented itself as a dictatorship of principles—principles whose requirements came to be embodied by a man who imposed himself as their sole designated interpreter. To be sure, this dictatorship had a formidable coercive apparatus at its service, but Robespierre did not command it directly, and then only marginally. It was available to him only inasmuch as he dominated the Convention in the first place, and then the Committee of Public Safety, by the force of his words and the weight of his popularity—whence also the vulnerability of his position, illustrated by the circumstances of his downfall. It was not even a question of charisma in his case, only of an ascendancy due to the conjunction of intellectual rigor and the authority of his personal example. Robespierre did not enchant his listeners, perhaps did not even convince them; instead he impressed them. He spoke in the name of something greater than himself, and because he was taken to be its personification he was able to impose his will. As a result, this singular dictator was completely unaware of being one; the merest suggestion that he could be regarded as a dictator drove him into a rage.

This peculiarity did not escape the notice of at least one observer of the period, an obscure journalist from Lausanne known as Cassat the Elder, who, in an exceptionally insightful article published shortly after Robespierre's death, on 16 August 1794, called attention to the remarkable paradox of a despotism that was unaware of itself: "The fact remains that Robespierre exercised a very real tyranny and that he himself did not suspect that he was a tyrant."[1] Indeed, this seems to have been the driving force of his astonishing destiny. His blindness about himself was compounded by another profound blindness, collectively shared and so deeply rooted in French history that getting rid of Robespierre was not enough to escape its hold. It took many years to break free from the spell he cast, and then only after undergoing the trial of other tyrannies of several kinds. The nation's arduous apprenticeship in the art of taming power began with Robespierre.

---

1. Quoted in Gérard Walter, *Robespierre* [3 vols., 1936–1939], abridged version, 2 vols. (Paris: Gallimard, 1961), 2:26–28.

Robespierre has remained a figure of fascination for the French people ever since, notwithstanding the horror that came to be attached to his name. It is not hard to see why. He occupies a special place in the gallery of tyrants. He did not wish to have power for himself. As Cassat had rightly seen from a distance, Robespierre was not motivated by ambition. He sought, by radical means, to bring into existence the power that the rights of man demanded—rights of which he had made himself the champion and which the overthrow of the monarchy had suddenly made possible. Just so, it was a power that belonged to no one person; it was an indivisible power that expressed the will of citizens united in obedience to the law and respect for the public interest. The problem was twofold. On the one hand, no such power could possibly exist; on the other, Robespierre's total sincerity enabled him to personify the ideal of impersonality. In combination, these things made him a tyrant unlike any other: the embodiment of the impossible unity of an unfindable people. "In this way," Cassat wrote, "the most implacable enemy of every kind of despotism was himself invested with the most dangerous [one] of all. He came to it unawares, as it were, carried along by the irresistible torrent of circumstances." Robespierre "did not mistrust himself enough, and that is what ruined him." Thus virtue came to be converted into terror.

Robespierre had named, theorized, and defended the alliance of virtue and terror in his speeches, and it was in relation to this idea that his memory was to be indelibly etched in the minds of future generations. Formulation readily gave way to conception, expression to invention: the enunciator was now credited with authorship. His unshakable firmness of purpose echoed down the centuries, projecting the image of an omnipotent dictator. The reality was rather different, as a careful reconstruction of his checkered career makes clear.

It is not a question of trying to exonerate Robespierre, only of placing his responsibility in the proper perspective. He concealed everything, tolerated everything, justified everything, from the most appalling excesses of revolutionary violence to the most aberrant ad hoc proceedings. From the absolution of the September Massacres of 1792 to the recourse to the "conscience of patriots," disguised as judicial guarantees, there is no shortage of examples. It suffices to let Robespierre speak for himself.

But none of this makes him a sort of deus ex machina of the terrorist episode of the Revolution. For most of the first five years Robespierre was not its driving force, and when he did finally become its dominant figure the effect was to isolate him from the majority of his colleagues. The task he set himself had always been to clarify the nature of the revolutionary movement, to make the chaotic unfolding of events comprehensible, to point the way forward amidst the fog of circumstances, to illuminate the purposes of the Revolution, obscured by the messy uncertainties of everyday life in a time of famine, strife, and war. Fatally misled by his own sermonizing, he ended up making himself the prophet of a religion in which even the faithful no longer believed.

Nothing is more revealing in this regard than the theory of revolutionary government, an ex post facto exercise in justification that was meant to give some measure of logical coherence to what had initially been a series of risky improvisations. It is not hard to see how it could have made Robespierre appear to be the master of something he had done no more than magnify by his oratorical skill, two aspects of which combined to give it a baleful aura. To begin with, his determination to occupy the high ground of principles made him staggeringly indifferent to the fate of actual human beings. The Rousseauist invocation of moral sensibility was accompanied by a total insensitivity to the suffering and death it entailed. To put it another way, the lack of self-awareness of a tyrant who did not know he was a tyrant engendered an unconscious cruelty toward the sacrificial victims his theory required. They were no concern of his. What could be more frightening than such murderous innocence?

Then there was an aggravating factor, that the appeal to the rigorous logic of principles was inextricably bound up with Robespierre's rhetorical talents. Fine phrases were frequently placed in the service of minor causes. Purely tactical motives were often acted on under cover of the most noble ideas, as in the case of the attempt to undermine the Girondins during the first months of the Convention, a striking illustration. This tendency understandably encouraged suspicions of an underlying duplicity, in which oratorical brilliance masked a Machiavellian will to power. But it is more plausibly seen as the consequence of Robespierre's chronic misreading of political rivalries, aided and abetted by the certainty of his own virtue, which placed vice entirely on the side of anyone who dared to oppose him.

Cruel indifference and willful misunderstanding converged to produce the chilling words of 5 February 1794: "[T]he mainspring of popular government in a time of . . . revolution is at once *virtue and terror*." They were intended only to acknowledge a somber reality, while at the same time elevating it to the level of heroic majesty. But their dramatic quality made Robespierre appear in retrospect to have been not only the inventor of this motive force but also the leader of a government that he dominated—though to a much smaller degree than is commonly supposed—by the power of his oratory, which inevitably aroused distrust. His words that day gave rise to the image of a monstrous despot that was to sully, perhaps forever, the memory of a man whose legendary incorruptibility made the happiness of the human race depend on the execution of a good many of its members.

This haunting image became all the more firmly fixed in people's minds, it must be added, as some scholars who sympathized with the aims of the Revolution subsequently interpreted it in a positive light. Far from regarding the Terror as a product of Robepierre's lack of self-awareness, they argued on behalf of the proposition that violence is the midwife of history.

We must nonetheless try to break the spell of this image and free ourselves from its fantastical toils. By looking beyond its train of human tragedies, we may be able at last to make sense of the political tragedy that the French Revolution represented and that it was Robespierre's true destiny to embody.

Revolution Ended, Revolution Unending

Robespierre's vision of a marriage between virtue and terror was hardly the stuff of dreams, at least not outside the comfortable irreality of academia. For a time it appealed to people for whom the end he pursued had not lost its power of attraction, for whom the mystical unity of the people in and through their power seemed to be, in one form or another, the necessary expression of their rights. The sublimity of this end justified, concealed, or caused to be forgotten, depending on the case, the nature of the means employed and the reality of the results. But eventually this situation gave way to its opposite: now the means and the results commanded attention, to the point actually of monopolizing it, because the end was no longer meaningful. The charm of sacral unity, to which the end owed its magnetism, had worn off, while at the same time other ways were discovered of giving substance to the idea of popular sovereignty, and even to civic virtue.

Little by little, it became apparent that the right way to give the people a sense of their special power was to place it in a different context. Doing this made it possible to establish a new relationship with government, based on mutual respect and recognition, and to devise procedures for adjusting this relationship as necessary. In the meantime the ambition of expressing the identity of government and the people, stubbornly pursued by the revolutionaries, from Robespierre to Sieyès, and their innumerable posterity, no longer held any appeal. The conclusion to which experience had led in all its forms, from the first to the last, was finally grasped, namely, that insistence on this imaginary identity created a situation in which the people lost both the idea and the reality of their power. Locating the source of this power in popular virtue, as Robespierre had done, or in the rationality of property owners, as Sieyès had done, led to the same impasse; the advocates of the proletariat who came after them were no more successful. With the collapse of all these attempts to concentrate the power of all into a single body, however this body was conceived, so that will could instantaneously be converted into reality, the protean specter of Jacobinism faded away. The mirage of a virtuous people vanished as well. Taking its place was a people comprised of individuals, neither good nor bad, neither captives of their selfishness nor spontaneously civic-minded, but divided and undecided in their various ways; a people that could be induced to overcome individual doubts and hesitations only by throwing into relief its own contradictions.

In 1978, François Furet famously announced that "the French Revolution is over." Three years later Mitterrand came to power, inaugurating a period that bore out Furet's claim and gave it a solid basis in practice. The French Revolution was over because it had turned out to be a success, or, more precisely, because the ideals it sensationally brought into the world had turned out to have practical application after all, notwithstanding the political failure on which it had initially been impaled and of which Robespierre's fate offered the most spectacular illustration. This failure had been perpetuated so long as it was denied by a revolutionary tradition determined to go on recreating the original impasse. The time of blind obstinacy was now over and done with. The Revolution had come to an end, having rid itself of the illusions in which its principles had taken refuge and which prevented it from succeeding.

We would nonetheless succumb to a new illusion if we were to believe that the Revolution has now been put behind us once and for all and that it has spoken its last word. For within the political framework that finally managed to establish itself as the only one capable of accommodating revolutionary ideals, the source of these ideals has regained its initial luster. The very solidity of the institutional order in which they have been relocated has had the effect of reanimating their inspirational vigor. The Revolution of the Rights of Man has begun again in a certain sense, albeit in a different manner, no longer with a view to instituting a new political and social order, but with a view to perfecting the workings of the existing order. The problem is that, despite the impression of innocent tinkering, this apparently conciliatory intent has a destabilizing potential whose consequences are liable to be every bit as grave as those of the first eruption—with the difference that the force of the first one gradually dissipated. Having reached its end, the Revolution led on to an unending revolution that no longer so much as whispered the word "revolution"—a word that had galvanized the popular imagination for two centuries. Resolute enemies no longer stand in the way of this new revolution, for it has no need of insurrection or guillotine or terror in order to advance its purposes. Its potential for destabilization is nonetheless alarming enough to reawaken the antagonisms of the past, though they will have assumed a new form. The year 1793 has unmistakably receded into the realm of the unspeakable, but 1789 has enjoyed a magnificent resurgence, the purity of its promise undimmed. This shines a light once more on our subject. If the Robespierre of the Committee of Public Safety no longer excites fervent loyalty, the Robespierre of the Constituent Assembly resumes his place as a striking and compelling figure. His reputation as the inflexible defender of principles and as the unconditional champion of the rights of the people has acquired a new relevance, while at the same time reviving the unanswered question of an earlier age: was he a farsighted guide or a narrow-minded demagogue? Robespierre's exemplarity, whether as a man to be admired or despised, hero or villain, has been given new life. He has not finished speaking to future generations. Nor has he finished dividing them.

Under these circumstances, there is reason to fear that a dialogue of the deaf between two ways of forgetting the past may be prolonged. On the one hand, there is the principled forgetfulness, so to speak, of a majority of the French people, for whom the nation's revolutionary heritage no longer matters very much, if at all, because the contradiction it nourished for two centuries has been resolved—in favor of a democratic consensus that repudiates the extreme methods to which Robespierre's name remains attached. On the other hand, there is the selective forgetfulness of an activist minority that seeks to cultivate the radical inspiration of a foundational moment and of its emblematic figure, but that in order to do this tends to undervalue, or to gloss over, or actually to avoid dealing with the policy of terror in which the cult of principles and the dogma of the infallibility of the people were submerged.

It is against this habit of forgetfulness, in both of its aspects, whose alienating and deforming effects have already made themselves strongly felt, that I set out to write the present book, in order to restore what has been lost to memory. In this I have been guided by the conviction that a democratic consciousness worthy of the name, which is to say one that is fully alert to the difficulty of the task it faces, owes it to itself to reflect upon the tragedy of our republican origins by contemplating the example of the figure in whom its destructive tensions are summed up. The French Revolution introduced an idea that was to change the world—notwithstanding that the circumstances that first invested it with prophetic promise made its realization impossible in its native land. Robespierre is the man in whom this regenerative radicalism found its most eloquent spokesman, but also the one who embodied the bloody failure to bring it to fruition.

We have come a long ways from this foundational moment. The Revolution's promise has at long last been fulfilled. The means by which it was translated into reality turned out to be exactly the opposite of what Robespierre and his followers had imagined them to be. But the lesson of how these means came to be devised, and how they were employed, has only acquired greater significance in the interval. For their very soundness has had the effect of reinvigorating the impulse from which they sprang. If the original experiment is behind us as tragedy, more than ever it looms in front of us as a problem. The importance of having a clear idea of what the original experiment involved is therefore plain. It will illuminate both the road traveled so far and the road that lies ahead.

In view of the vast bibliography that has grown up around the French Revolution, any brief guide to further reading cannot help but be arbitrary to some degree. I have restricted mine to a few works that seem to me likely to be most useful to the interested reader.

As for the life of Robespierre, in addition to the recent biographies by Hervé Leuwers and Jean-Clément Martin mentioned in the Introduction, which are to be recommended in the first instance, the abridged two-volume edition of Gérard Walter's massive study, *Robespierre* (Paris: Gallimard, 1961), remains, despite the passage of time, a mine of information and suggestive insights.

To these works may be added the able and evenhanded biography by Peter McPhee, *Robespierre: A Revolutionary Life* (New Haven: Yale University Press, 2012).

John Hardman's study, *Robespierre* (London: Longman, 1999), is valuable for its detailed analysis of the system of power Robespierre inaugurated.

On Jacobinism, see Lucien Jaume, *Le discours jacobin et la démocratie* (Paris: Fayard, 1989).

On the Terror, see Patrice Gueniffey, *La politique de la Terreur: Essai sur la violence révolutionnaire, 1789–1794* (Paris: Fayard, 2000).

On the crucial episode of de-Christianization, see two works by Michel Vovelle, *Religion et Révolution: La déchristianisation de l'an II* (Paris: Hachette, 1976) and *La Révolution contre l'Église: De la raison à l'Être suprême* (Brussels: Complexe, 1988), the latter available in English translation.

On 9 Thermidor, see Françoise Brunel, *Thermidor: La chute de Robespierre* (Brussels: Complexe, 1989).

On the cultural climate in which the men of the Revolution acted, see Jean Starobinski, *L'invention de la liberté, 1700–1789* (Geneva: Skira, 1987) and the revised one-volume edition of his 1973 work, *1789, Les emblèmes de la raison* (Paris: Gallimard, 2006), both available in English translation. On the social and political climate of revolutionary Paris, see Haim Burstin, *Une révolution à l'œuvre: Le faubourg Saint-Marcel (1789–1794)* (Seyssel, France: Champ Vallon, 2005). On the memory and legend of Robespierre, see Marc Belissa and Yannick Bosc, *Robespierre: La fabrication d'un mythe* (Paris: Ellipses, 2013).